IN PASTURES GREEN

The inside stories of Albion's amazing 21st century odyssey

by Chris Lepkowski

Shareholders for Albion

First published in Great Britain in October, 2012
by Shareholders for Albion

Reprinted in December, 2012

ISBN 978-0-9574229-0-2

Shareholders for Albion

Printed and bound by TJ International, Padstow, Cornwall

Contents

A View From S4A

THE first decade of the 21st century was one of the most eventful in the entire history of West Bromwich Albion. Indeed, there is probably no-one alive who could have lived through another that started so inauspiciously yet delivered so many successes, promotions, memorable games, incidents and goals.

Off the field, too, there have been changes to both the operating infrastructure of the club and their share structure and ownership. Some, particularly the concept of a sporting and technical director responsible for player recruitment and development and a head coach instead of a conventional manager (as is the case in much of Europe), struggled to gain acceptance initially, not only from Albion supporters but also from the wider English football world. The moves have since proved their worth though, particularly to a club the size of Albion, who have to compete with clubs bearing much more financial clout. It has been a bumpy ride at times with disappointments along the way but, with hindsight, it has been a great time to be a Baggie.

I've been one for over 55 years now and enjoyed the high points of the mid-to-late 1960s, when I expected a cup final appearance every year, and of course the flowing football of the superb Ron Atkinson 1978-79 side. I chose to play Cowboys and Indians with my friends rather than go with my Dad, Charlie (the first Albion supporter in a family which now extends to four generations of season ticket holders), to The Hawthorns on Saturday, September 21, 1957; the day Albion beat Manchester City 9-2. That wasn't a bad City side either. We finished fourth in the old First Division and they were a point behind us in fifth. That is why I never miss a match now. I've seen Albion score six and seven numerous times and eight on a couple of occasions but never nine. I want to be there when they do.

Missing that game isn't the lowest point in my Albion-supporting life, however, nor are the many semi-final defeats or the FA Cup humiliations. No, the lowest ebb has to be December 14, 1999, on a bitterly cold, snowy night at Grimsby when I learned that our prize asset Kevin Kilbane had been sold. I thought then that Albion had no ambition, no direction and no money, and would never play in the top division of English football again. Probably the best single moment came less than three years later: the 96th minute of the game on April 13, 2002, when Igor Balis scored the penalty at Bradford that went a long way to sealing promotion back to the top flight after 16 long and largely forgettable years. That astonishing transition – and the many other unforgettable events that followed – are superbly detailed in these pages by Chris Lepkowski, who is not only a brilliant writer but also has unrivalled access to Albion players and officials to enable him to get the inside stories.

Shareholders for Albion (S4A) were formed in 2000 as a consequence of the turbulence at West Bromwich Albion at that time and the dismal – perhaps even non-existent – future prospects. Since then, we have seen two changes of chairman, changes to the share structure and a reduction in the number of shareholders from about 2,500 to 600, with a great many having to give up their shareholding with the utmost reluctance. These changes have occurred more frequently in the last few years than in any previous decade and are also worthy of documentation. I am proud to have been chairman of S4A since November, 2004 and it seems that much of my time since has been spent trying to understand changes to the shares and the impact upon our members, and relaying that information to them.

One of S4A's committee members, Dave Bassett, suggested that we write a book to record these turbulent times and all those dramatic events. The proposal was warmly received but, although the S4A Committee has many different skills between us, they don't include writing or publishing books! So we approached Chris Lepkowski who, it transpired, had quite independently also been thinking that Albion's renaissance deserved to be chronicled in book form. David Instone has produced and written many football publications, including several on Albion, and so was able to offer invaluable advice and guidance in bringing our ideas into fruition.

S4A commissioned this book so that Albion's odyssey this century – it is indeed an odyssey (definition: 'a long series of wanderings or adventures, especially when filled with notable experiences, hardships, etc') – could be recorded for posterity and enjoyment. S4A committee members have underwritten the project financially, to ensure that the organisation is not put at risk by this diversification into publishing, and of course have supported it fully in terms of their valuable time. The end result is a view of an amazing, unforgettable period through the eyes of those who made it happen, with an insight to what was going on behind the scenes during each absorbing season. Chris has done a wonderful job and reading the drafts has brought back many memories (mostly good, but not always!) and the occasional tear to my eye.

I am indebted to him and to the S4A committee for the help they have given, especially Dave Bassett, whose initial idea it was and who has done most of the research into the events off the field to provide Chris with the necessary background data. My thanks to all.

There have been many books written about West Bromwich Albion. As an avid collector of all things Albion, I have most of them. None is like this one. I have a vested interest, of course, but I honestly believe that every Albion fan who has stuck with the club from the thinnest of thins in the 1980s and 1990s to the great times we've been experiencing recently will want to read this book. Hopefully, so, too, will another generation, who will fondly reflect in years to come on what has been a new beginning for West Bromwich Albion.

Neil Reynolds
Chairman, Shareholders for Albion
July 2012

I had enjoyed watching the Albion in the 1960s and 1970s. My son, Daniel, and I endured the 1990s. Daniel loved going to the matches but, in truth, the Albion were a pale shadow of their former selves.

The new century brought about a change. Every season had many twists and turns with an exciting finish each time. We were back in the top flight and playing the big boys again. There were some disappointments along the way but, overall, the Baggies were back in business. I thought a book to cover these exciting times would be a good idea. Chris Lepkowski had been thinking along similar lines, the difference being that he could actually write it!

As a result of many discussions, emails and meetings between Chris, David Instone, Neil Reynolds and the S4A committee, the idea became a reality. The end result is an absorbing insight into what went on behind the scenes during those years. A lot of great memories, Igor's penalty, the Battle of Bramall Lane, the Great Escape and regular victories over the Wolves!

An Odyssey indeed!

Dave Bassett
Chairman, S4A book sub-committee

Forewords

DARREN MOORE

I sometimes get asked what West Bromwich Albion means to me. The best way to sum it up would be to look back at my experience of the Championship play-off final in 2007.

I was at Derby at the time and we faced Southampton in one semi-final while West Brom were playing Wolves in the other. I remember thinking: 'Oh no, it's going to be Albion in the final if we get there ourselves.' I was thinking: 'Anybody else but West Brom...ANYBODY else.'

When we got to Wembley, I felt like I should have been across the corridor in the other dressing room with the likes of Neil Clement, Jonathan Greening and Paul Robinson. Those were my mates - the people I still considered as my team-mates. If you look at me that day, I am warming up as far away from the West Brom fans as I could. It wasn't something I enjoyed. Nor was it much fun afterwards. When we won the game, everyone was celebrating. But I couldn't do it. I couldn't feel it. I still have pictures from that day. As happy as I should have been, while my team-mates are celebrating, I'm looking at the West Brom fans.

Being local and growing up in Handsworth, I found playing for West Brom special. I remember when I joined in 2001. I met Gary Megson in the Tom Silk Building and went to meet Frank Burrows, who was assistant manager. He said: 'Blimey, Gary, he's bigger than I thought.' Gary just said: 'Darren, we want you to add your mentality to this squad.' I was there on the Thursday night, signed on the Friday, travelled with the team on the Friday night to Watford and was on the bench. Then Tony Butler got sent off and I ended up going on and being told: 'Darren, win us this game.' We won 2-1.

The first time I heard myself being refered to as 'Big Dave' was against Burnley when people thought I'd scored in our 1-0 victory. I hadn't. It was Scott Dobie. The rest of that season, as they say, was history. And what history it was....great memories, happy times and plenty to celebrate.

Life at West Brom was never dull. While I was there, we won promotion twice, we did the Great Escape and the club went on to achieve so much during a memorable decade.

It was an incredible period for West Brom. They were special times for the players, the staff and, most importantly, the fans. It remains one of the happiest times of my career. I joined West Bromwich Albion to play in the Premier League and, within a few months, I was a Premier League footballer. I'll always be grateful that I was given such an opportunity with this football club.

I'm now back at the club in a coaching capacity. It's wonderful to be here again at MY club. That is exactly how it feels.

ADRIAN CHILES

IT is said that a Chinese curse goes as follows: "May you live in interesting times." Over the last decade or so, my team's interesting times have driven me to distraction. At the turn of the millennium, I was 32 years old; a relatively young man. Now, I'm past my middle forties and my hair is unrelentingly grey. It's not fatherhood, a stressful career or any of the other challenges this time of life presents that have brought about this change of colour. It's the Albion.

My first game was in April 1974; a 1-1 home draw against Luton Town. I was hooked. We soon got promoted to the top division and went from strength to strength before dropping into the Second a decade later. Then, apart from a harrowing two-year descent into the Third Division, nothing really happened or threatened to happen. We were stuck fast and that looked very much as if it would never change. My hair was flecked with grey but only a little.

Then came the new millennium. In successive seasons, we nearly went down, nearly went up, went up, went down, went back up, nearly went down, went down, nearly went up, went up, went down, went up, nearly went down but stayed up and, finally, stayed up again, having barely even flirted with going down. Thanks for the ride, boys, but I'm now as grey as a January morning on a black and white film.

What do the Albion mean to me? Everything. Too much really. I'm just reading a novel by the American writer Don DeLillo. It's called Underworld and, in it, a character talks of his love for his baseball team: "They were my team. I was the only Dodger fan in the neighborhood. I died inside when they lost. And it was important to die alone."

That's pretty much how I feel when we lose. Except, obviously, I'm not alone, Many others feel the same way. But, in the early hours of a Sunday morning after a Saturday defeat, when I wake up needing a wee, as men in their forties tend to, and I remember that we've lost and that I won't be able to read the paper or watch any football that day, I feel very alone indeed.

Sorry, this is all sounding a bit downbeat, isn't it? What I mainly feel for the Albion is unconditional love. Sheer joy when they do well; the opposite when they don't. It's like fatherhood.

And the pull for me remains gravitationally strong. By way of an example, I am writing this on a dawn flight from Nice to London, having worked in Monaco on the Super Cup last night. My colleagues are taking the opportunity to stay in Monte Carlo for a nice relaxed day. Not me, though. I was up at 4.30 to catch this flight to drive up to the Albion and see us play Everton. Monte Carlo or The Hawthorns? It's really no contest.

Introduction

"I must express my absolute disgust at the latest fiasco at West Bromwich Albion. I have followed the club all my life and, at 62 years of age, have never seen them at such a low ebb. Where on earth has the spirit gone from this once great club? We need leaders both on and off the field of play and directors that care. We also need financial backing to put us back where we belong among the elite. Where, oh where, has Albion's ambition gone? Come on Albion, if you are to remain part of our Midland sporting heritage, get your act together once and for all. The ball is firmly in your court."

An extract from a letter in the Birmingham Evening Mail during the first week of 2000.

And this is where West Bromwich Albion were back then.

January 3, 2000. West Bromwich Albion have been beaten 2-0 by Barnsley at The Hawthorns. It was the first match of a new year. A new century. But defeat was not unusual. This was same old Albion. Just 13,411 bothered to attend their first game of the new Millennium.

The Baggies were managed by Brian Little. Chris Adamson was the goalkeeper. His back four were Australian Andy McDermott, Daryl Burgess, Welshman Danny Gabbidon and Graham Potter. The midfield consisted of Northern Irishman James Quinn, Dutchman Richard Sneekes, future Juventus midfielder Enzo Maresca and Andy Townsend, whose Albion stay was blighted by a series of injuries. Micky Evans and Fabian De Freitas formed a less than potent forward line. Unused substitutes were Elliot Morris, Mark Angel, Adam Oliver, Adam Chambers and James Chambers.

The Birmingham Mail match report wasn't kind. "Relegation may not have been on the agenda less than a fortnight ago but Second Division football is now a distinct possibility," said the post-match review. "There doesn't seem a quick-fix solution to Albion's ills. Little wants some new players but players cost money. Yesterday's team are not strong enough to avoid the drop, of that there is no doubt. Some of the home side's play was comical at times. Team-mates bumped into each other while too many passes either went astray or were miscontrolled."

Who knew the 2000s were about to become the most exciting decade in the club's history? Some 138 players were used during the first ten years of the Millennium. By the time this tale ends, at the end of 2011-12, Albion have finished in the top half of the Premier League, as the highest West Midlands club for the first time since 1979. They are forced to search for a new boss due to Roy Hodgson leaving to take over the England vacancy. Rewind to January, 2000, and the climate was different.

A few weeks earlier, a few hundred Albion fans arrived at Grimsby to hear that star winger Kevin Kilbane would not be involved. He was sold to Sunderland for £2.5m because, according to chairman Tony Hale, the club were 'haemorrhaging money.' They were losing £30,000 a week. In the opening months of 2000, Maresca was offloaded to Juventus for just under £4.5m to ease further financial losses. Paul Thompson ousted Hale as chairman and swiftly replaced Little with Gary Megson.

Off the field, Albion were a mess; no training ground, outdated or inept corporate facilities at The Hawthorns and a non-existent scouting system. Their troubles were summed up by a 'sell us your stars' letter they sent to every club in the Second and Third Divisions and Nationwide Conference. It went out soon after Albion had lost 6-0 at Sheffield United and invited clubs to let them know if they had players with potential they would be prepared to sell. A scout from a rival club said in an interview with local media: "I have never known such a move in my life. It's an amazing thing to do but it may work. My other reaction is that Albion have almost no scouting system except for Richie Barker, their chief scout. They ought to know about all the up-and-coming players but don't appear to."

As I now write, in July 2012, Albion are regarded as having one of the best scouting networks in England. No other English club have experienced a decade quite like theirs. Between 2000 and 2010, Albion won four promotions, suffered two play-off failures and three relegations, and won two tense survival battles. There haven't been many games in which the outcome has been virtually irrelevant, apart from the relegation seasons, in which they were demoted before the final matches.

Twelve players spoke for this book. Some were success stories, others less so. One didn't even kick a competitive ball for the club. Managers were ruled out as potential interviewees. Most, during the period, were dismissed and are bound by confidentiality agreements. The players' version of events is not gospel or definitive. They are merely their personal accounts of their spells at the club.

They were chosen for various reasons. It would have been remiss to not involve the heroic duo of Bob Taylor and Kevin Phillips. Andy Johnson was part of a squad who almost went on strike; unthinkable but true. Des Lyttle tells us more about the transition from relegation candidates to Premier League during those early years and we find out how Geoff Horsfield prepared for his Great Escape contribution.

But there was also a need to include players who perhaps didn't make the most of their Albion careers or had unfinished business. Why didn't it work out for John Hartson? Or Darren Carter? What went wrong for Robert Koren in the final year? They reveal all. Simon Miotto is included due to his close relationship with Gary Megson. If any player knew Megson, he did.

The erudite Richard Sneekes opens the proceedings. Paul Scharner gives closure to the book in his own unique way. Jonathan Greening, the only captain to lift a trophy during the period, played for four different gaffers before signing for Roy Hodgson at a different club. He was a must for me to include. This is an anecdotal story as experienced by a dozen people who helped shape Albion during the first 12 years of the new century. The 'thank-you' bits? They're at the end. I hope I haven't forgotten anyone.

There are no rights or wrongs. You can agree or shake your head at the players' memories. Their references are not statistical; merely personal recollections and interpretations of their own mini eras of a bigger period. It's about individuals who wanted to do their best for the club. Some managed it. Some didn't.

This was a compelling era for the club. It's a story that needed telling....

Richard Sneekes

"I can honestly say that as soon as we played on a Saturday, I'd hate coming in on a Monday and I dreaded the following Saturday. I lost my love for football."

IT takes some doing for a footballer to claim he has reached the highs and lows of his career in the space of a few minutes. But then, Richard Sneekes was never one for convention. Born in Amsterdam, the scorer of ten goals in his first 13 West Bromwich Albion games in 1996 was to be unceremoniously dumped five years later. The double-figure return was not the pinnacle. Nor was his sudden release the nadir. Try May 7, 2000; a day which was to start a seminal period in the club's history.

Sneekes' own appearance has also changed. Once, he had to decide between pony tails and flowing locks with his long hair. These days, he has had the scissors out. When I meet up with him at his Sutton Coldfield home, he tucks his hair underneath a baseball cap. Some of it still juts out. Fidgeting around, he shakes his head and recalls the Sunday lunchtime which was to define a ten-year period of last-day escapes, highs, lows, traumas, celebrations, commiserations.

Gary Megson's Albion side are playing Charlton Athletic. The Londoners are led by ex-Baggies striker Andy Hunt and have a supporting cast of future Hawthorns goalkeeper Dean Kiely, eventual England international Scott Parker and Paul Konchesky. They are Premier League-bound. Champions of the division. An impressive line-up – and they're in town.

Almost 160 miles separate The Hawthorns from Portman Road. In real terms, zero points split Albion and Walsall. The Saddlers are visiting Ipswich. They need to better the Baggies' result as both start the final day on 46 points. A fortnight before, Walsall had beaten Albion in an Easter Saturday fixture at Bescot Stadium. Psychology gave Walsall the upper hand. Reality can snap back. Football merely added twists.

Albion win 2-0 at The Hawthorns. Walsall lose 2-0. Sneekes, scorer of Albion's first with a powerful 65th minute strike, recalls the victory – sealed by Bob Taylor's goal. The end product was satisfying. The process was uneasy. In the days before mass texting, mobile phones being glued to ears and 3G connections being clogged by airwave traffic, Albion players were having to rely on hearsay, rumour and any other snippets they could come by. Fans were listening to radios, hoping they could hear the commentary amid the din at The Hawthorns. Not all of the information passed on was correct.

"It was a tough afternoon," Sneekes recalls. "Charlton were the champions and it was absolutely roasting that day. The hottest day of the season. We were coming off the pitch at half-time and I heard that Walsall were leading 1-0. I tell you what: I have never felt so deflated walking into a dressing room. All the energy sapped out of me...only for me to find out they were drawing. Some fans gave us the wrong information.

"When we found out Walsall weren't winning, we got a lift and blew Charlton away in the second half. People ask if they were on the beach but they weren't. Had that been the case, they would have given fringe players a go. It wasn't a walkover but we dominated and it sticks with me. People ask: 'What is your most memorable game?' That will be it. I scored ten goals in 13 games at the start of my Albion career, played in play-offs, played at Ajax and Bolton. But it was that game. There was so much emotion.

"When it's staying up or being relegated, it's worse. We had the Player of the Year do the following night – back in the time when you could drink. A few had quite a bit that night. It was a good end to a strange season. To think Walsall were leading was the lowest point for me. But, because Gary Megson was there, I couldn't show it. Had he spotted the fear, he would have replaced me. He'd have dropped anyone showing those signs. If you blew it, that was it. You'd be on the bench. We got through. It wasn't pretty but we did it."

The Birmingham Mail was to sum up the mood 24 hours later......"Albion, so dull for most of the season, were transformed into a team full of passion, bright ideas and flair as champions Charlton were sent spinning to defeat," wrote their correspondent Phil Gordos. "The change was hard to comprehend. Was this really a team facing relegation to Division Two? Perhaps there had been a mix-up in the dressing rooms. Maybe the Charlton players had been handed Albion shirts by mistake."

In the same edition, Sneekes praised Megson. "He has made us work hard and be tough to beat," he said. "He has made a big impact. Everyone must have seen the difference since he took over." Sneekes was to note the difference, in more ways than one.

Sneekes stretches out on his leather settee and tucks into what looks like some form of dessert. He has just come home after taking a juniors' coaching session. It's early 2011. Any hopes he has of a quiet, relaxing night disappear when I roll up with a dictaphone. His dog seems more excited to see me than he does. But he's as courteous as ever, and, happily from my point of view, ready to talk.

I hold fire. He's still eating. The contents of the bowl disappear quickly. His appetite for football is also returning. For the first time in a while, he seems to be enjoying himself. The early days were different. Sneekes began his football education at Ajax. Think of a Dutch sporting version of Harvard. It's an institution, a university of football. Sneekes was one its undergraduates. Ajax were the seventh most successful club of the 20th century. He was a member of a youth finishing school which was to produce Johan Cruyff, Edwin van der Sar, Dennis Bergkamp, Patrick Kluivert, Marco van Basten, Wesley Sneijder and many more. A Who's Who of football.

Fast forward to 1996....Amsterdam is a world away. West Bromwich Albion are struggling. Badly. Manager Alan Buckley says all the right things; how it will take a while for the £400,000 signing from Bolton to settle and explaining why supporters mustn't expect miracles. The flamboyant, attacking midfielder opts against convention. His goals help Albion up to an unusually high finishing position of 12th. Frank Skinner lauds him on national TV. "Richard Sneekes...what a player! Of course we used to call him Richard Marathon," says the Black Country comedian with a gag which perhaps wasn't his finest. Nevertheless, the impact has been noted.

Four years on and Albion find themselves in similar territory. Struggling. More so. In March, 2000, some 61 days before Charlton visit, they are in decline. On the pitch, results are bad. Off it, Tony Hale is no longer chairman. Paul Thompson wants improvement. The club are losing money and at risk of relegation. Brian Little's time is coming to an end. Albion are 3-0 down to Birmingham at The Hawthorns. Larus Sigurdsson has been sent off, just two weeks after Sneekes himself has run an earlier-than-expected bath in a 6-0 loss at Sheffield United. Things are bad.

The Hawthorns is, at least, starting to take shape. The club have plans to redevelop the Rainbow Stand sometime during 2001. Away from B71, Albion have the small problem of having no training ground. Planning permission is being sought for a site but it will be a while yet. The facility being used by the club in 2000 rests on the Birmingham Road, next to the current state-of-the-art training ground which houses gyms, media suites, hydro-pools and facilities you would expect from a Premier League club. Back at the start of the Millennium, Albion used the rugby club next door.

It's very much CBeeBies territory, as Sneekes explains. "Training was Monday, Tuesday, Thursday and Friday," he added. "We trained at Tubbyland, named after the Teletubbies, because the pitches rolled up and down hills. When it rained, it would be heavy. English football was different then to how it is now.

"Bruce Rioch brought me to this country in 1994. I was playing in Switzerland for Locarno near the Italian border and scored 13 in 26 games for them. I was going to move elsewhere but nothing came of it, so I went home. The agent rang and said two Swiss clubs wanted to sign me. Then he came back and said a Spanish and English club. I said: 'Ok, the Spanish club sound good.' He replied: 'No, sorry, you're going to England.' And here I am.

"I played some games in Scotland for Bolton during pre-season. The ball was flying around at 100 mph and I was wondering what I'd got myself into. But I stuck around and it proved a good move. Yet, when I came to West Brom, we struggled for somewhere to train at times. It was a world away from what they use now."

The opening few months of 2000 were not good. Little's Baggies were defeated by a Birmingham side managed by his friend Trevor Francis. It was the Albion manager's final game. Blues supporters mocked the former Villa boss, whose side were heading towards the third tier. Albion fans jeered and targeted their manager with an abusive, industrial chant. After the game, Little might as well have grabbed a pen, a sheet of paper and written his own resignation note.

"This is a very difficult club to be manager of," he said in the Sunday Mercury. "There are too many bosses poking their noses in. I know I can manage if allowed because nobody has wanted me to leave wherever I have been. But this club is riddled with problems. A fax was sent this week which I know nothing about and yet I'm the manager. I've been told too many lies and I don't see why I should carry the can. I'm not going anywhere. I won't walk away. I'm here to stay unless they get rid of me. We made a £1m bid for a Premiership player this week that was going through until the player decided he was better off where he was. There are things going on at this club that simply amaze me."

The decision was taken out of Little's hands. He was dismissed two days later. Sneekes wasn't surprised. "When chairmen come in, they come from a business environment and have their own views on how managers should be, how companies should be run," he says. "They often want managers in their own fashion. Brian was old enough and wise enough to know it was coming. We are in a results business. When your time is up, managers know it.

"All the boys were sad but, having a good hard look at ourselves, it didn't reflect well on us as players. We knew we'd allowed him to go. If a manager's hands are tied in terms of resources, there is little he can do. Sometimes, if there is a job at a lower league club, you have to evaluate whether you can actually do the job you can – it can only reflect badly on you if you fail. We weren't aware of how bad things were off the field. The fans were there – maybe not 22,000 but we still had support [17,029 attended the Birmingham fixture]. We didn't have massive earners, so it surprises me that we struggled for money."

John Trewick took the reins. And so Albion began the search for their first new manager of the new Millennium.

According to polls at the time, the fans' choice was Ron Atkinson. But there was to be no third term for Big Ron, who managed the club from 1978 to 1981 before returning for a short spell in 1987. "I've retired," came his blunt reply. "I haven't given it a thought." Colin Todd, Jan Molby, Joe Kinnear, John Rudge and Ossie Ardiles were mentioned. John Trewick, fellow coach Cyrille Regis and veteran player Andy Townsend also got linked. And so did the likes of Peter Taylor, Steve McClaren, Steve Cotterill and John Gorman. Previous boss Denis Smith – dumped just a few weeks before the 1999-2000 season – was in no doubts as to where the issues were.

"There will be faxes and phone calls going off like you wouldn't believe," he said at the time. "That's because there are still people out there arrogant enough to think they can turn things around. But they want someone who won't answer them back. It should be a good job but managers never get the chance to get on with it. I came close to quitting and I'm one of the most loyal people around. If it can push me that close, what's it going to do to others? They should let the manager get on with the job and give him the support he needs. The trouble is: they don't want anybody other than themselves be to be the top dog."

On Tuesday, March 7, Albion played Tranmere. Managed by Trewick, they won 2-0. Brian Jensen made his debut, Sean Flynn and Lee Hughes scored the goals. Watching in the stands was Albion's next manager. Gary Megson was to become the 31st boss in Albion's 110-year history. It wasn't a popular appointment among fans. The most positive spin to come out of views in the Birmingham Mail's letter pages was that at least he wasn't Brian Little.

Megson's charm offensive started. "I'm just like the fans," he explained. "I don't sit and just watch the game, I get involved and want the team to do everything they can to win. If players always give their best and with a great deal of honesty, they won't get any complaints from me or anyone else. We've got to wake up and smell the roses a little bit. We really are walking a tightrope. We are in a situation where every game is critical, every point is critical and every goal is critical. Everything I do is geared to winning, not just entertaining. But we want to win and be entertaining if we possibly can."

Megson signed a three-year contract. As luck would have it, Albion travelled to Stockport for his first game. Sacked acrimoniously by County nine months previously, Megson had unfinished business as Albion headed up the M6. Sneekes remembers the occasion, although he wasn't playing. "I knew nothing about Gary," he says. "The thing I remember is James Quinn saying 'Brilliant, I worked for him at Blackpool, he's going to be great,' only for him to get bombed out after two months, made into a scapegoat and told to train with the kids. He wasn't so keen on Gary after that.

"Gary made Flynny and myself travel to Stockport, which was strange to us as we were both suspended. He told me that he tried to sign me for Norwich from Bolton and said: 'I want to build the team around you', yet here we were having to run and run before and after a game which we're not going to be involved in. Afterwards, there was this perception that Flynny and I didn't want to do it. But we did do it, although I can't work out why we had to do it. That's where the first bit of friction started...Gary's first game. I generally got on well with him at first but then it started to unravel."

Following Albion's survival in 2000, Sneekes noted a change in landscape. Gary Megson's ability to revive Albion came, in the midfielder's opinion, at a cost in the longer term. In the short term, alterations were to be implemented. They worked. On a frenzied transfer deadline day in March, the manager brought in five players. Bob Taylor moved back from Bolton for a low fee and was joined by experienced right-back Des Lyttle, robust low-cost centre-half Tony Butler, powerhouse midfield loanee Georges Santos and rookie left-back Neil Clement, who arrived on loan from Chelsea.

Sneekes smiles as he recalls the dramatic day and the effect it had. "It was a strange time," he said. "When Bob left, he was getting a bit of a tub, then he went to Bolton and was ripped. It was good to have him back. But, in any team, if you get five players coming in, the fears start. Are you going to lose your place? Five blokes, all wanting to play – they've not come to sit on the bench.

"Ultimately you can say what you want but we stayed up. A new manager is never a good thing because you lose the old one and you're on high alert. When five players come in, you do start to see a lot of panic. It's a sledge-hammer approach. You don't often see five come in straightaway. But it worked for us in that season. We stayed up."

It was in the summer of 2000 that Sneekes started to lose his thirst for football. The demise began. "We went to Denmark in pre-season," he recalls. "I was 32 by then but running the Chambers (Adam and James) lads off the track. They were considered the fittest. I was doing well. Then my best friend's dad died and Megson let me go home. It was all cool. He was fine about that. But then, as the senior player, I went in to see him and handed the players' bonus sheet and it got ripped up straightaway. From then on, he and I went into decline in terms of our relationship."

Sneekes continued: "His pre-season was tough. For the first ten days, you wouldn't touch or see a ball. We just ran and ran and ran. We went to a stadium in Denmark which had a track. We did two 800s, four 400s, eight 200s and 16 100s. Clem had come to us on loan and then signed for us properly that summer. He just lost it completely. He'd come from Chelsea, seen how things are done and totally lost his head. He wasn't having it. He said he couldn't do it anymore. Megson just yelled: 'Shut the f*** up.' Looking back now, it was hilarious."

Sneekes noted the disparity in summer training between English and Dutch clubs. "When I was in Holland, we'd have pre-season for ten days, go to Germany perhaps and have three sessions a day. We'd have running at 7am, then football sessions. In the first week, we'd have conditioning, do work with the ball, then, in the second and third weeks, we'd play games every night.

"Even if it was against the lowest of the low, it was good, just to get you into the groove of playing and working the ball again. Over here, you do nothing for two weeks, then play Saturday, Wednesday, Saturday. I hated running but I was good at it. Once you got the ball after two weeks, you'd be falling over it like Bambi on ice. You'd forgotten what it was like."

The relationship between Sneekes and Megson was deteriorating. The player felt he was being asked to play an unfamiliar midfield role. Albion were to make a charge for the top six but Sneekes was no longer enjoying the game. He was witnessing change and a sense of paranoia around him. "There were eyes and ears everywhere," he added. "You came in, did your job, went home and moaned about it to someone else. The one time, the club chaplain came in and asked someone for some tickets. He needed some quite urgently for someone. This particular player he asked hated Gary with a passion at the time – even now he can't stand him. But he told the Rev: 'Yeah, no problem. I'll make a call for you.'

After 10am, we weren't supposed to call but he was just trying to help a friend out. Someone on the staff saw him and ran out to tell Megson. When we got to training, he started on about Big Time Charlies using their phone and he'd go on and on and on. Come on, have some common sense! My team-mate wasn't doing anything wrong. He was trying to help someone.

"It was all about fear. You couldn't relax. He had people within his staff watching you all the time. That still sticks. He would moan about people buying cars. After one game – I can't remember who we'd played – he wasn't happy with our performance. He burst into the dressing room and said: 'Right, you've got one hour to go home, pack your bags and come back. We're going to Exeter for four days.'

"So there I was having to phone my wife Shirley to tell her I was going home to pack and wouldn't be back until the Wednesday. That was lucky. Normally, if you crossed him, you'd end up training with the youth team. And the youth set-up certainly wasn't his highest priority. Why do people think John Trewick and Richard O'Kelly left? The Chambers lads would run through a brick wall for him yet they were never given a fair chance. We had a young keeper Chris Adamson. Megson didn't seem to get on with him. God knows why. But he got the brunt of everything. It was sad for Chris. There was no middle ground with Megson. You were with him...or training with the kids."

After the quick fix in the transfer market in 1999-2000, the following season was a little more structured. The summer was a key time for the club in many ways. Jason Roberts became their record signing when he arrived for £2m from Bristol Rovers. He was joined by Tottenham's Ruel Fox and Jordao from Sporting Braga, with Neil Clement's move from Chelsea made permanent for £100,000. Igor Balis, Russell Hoult, Michael Appleton and Phil Gilchrist were added during the season. All were to play key roles.

Perhaps the seminal Gary Megson signing was Derek McInnes. Arriving from French club Toulouse for £450,000, he was the captain Albion needed; a warrior, fit to wear the armband and lead his team out. Sneekes, although gradually dispirited by his own predicament, was impressed with the evolution around him.

"Derek and Appy were in the Gary Megson mould as players – the way he played football," he added. "They were great acquisitions. Derek played the Jan Wouters role, the Roy Keane position. Such players are so valuable. He had vast experience and Appy had great spirit. They were similar players and Derek was a true leader. Jason Roberts was a funny guy, too; strong as an ox but maybe he didn't score as many goals as he should have. He scored 16 or 17 for us in 2000-01 but wasn't prolific. He had pace, power and was strong. He was a great player. He and Hughsie complemented each other well. Some decent players were arriving."

The rebuilding process meant others were sacrificed. Leaving the club were Paul Raven, Daniel Gabbidon, Micky Evans and Andy McDermott. Local lad Sean Flynn and Fabian de Freitas also departed. The Dutch striker's reputation was never restored after he missed a Spring Bank Holiday home game against

Crewe in 1999. Albion lost 5-1, with De Freitas blissfully unaware that the game kicked off at 3pm rather than the usual 7.45pm for week-day games.

Sneekes, who had played with De Freitas at Bolton, still laughs at the memories of Flynn and De Freitas – the mention of the latter prompts him to amble around his living room lethargically. "Flynny wasn't Gary's cup of tea, although you would have thought he would be," he recalled. "When Flynny first came, we clashed as personalities but, the longer it went, the better we got on. There was good chemistry between us and we've become good mates, especially now on the Masters circuit.

"I would hate to play against him. He made us laugh. If he put a ball in Row Z, he would do five press-ups – that used to crack everyone up. That's what he was like. Fabian? Oh dear! That game against Crewe.....I was trying to ring him and couldn't get him. But he'd done it before. At Bolton, he saw his name wasn't in the squad, so he went home. We lost a player through injury and we couldn't get hold of him. He used to come in one minute before training. A lovely bloke but he was so laid-back. He would have driven Gary up the wall. And he probably did."

On the pitch, Albion were making progress. Back-to-back hat-tricks from Hughes – against Gillingham and Preston – were early-season highlights, and were followed by a win against Wolves in October. The return wasn't as memorable. Albion froze during a wintery Molineux game. The 3-1 defeat was notable for George Ndah's brace in his first appearance against Albion since breaking his leg at The Hawthorns the previous October. Megson was distinctly unimpressed with his team's performance.

"As extinct as a dodo," was how Megson described Albion's tackling. "I'm not disappointed. I'm flaming furious. Not one player can expect to be in the team against Tranmere after that. This defeat was purely and simply down to the way my players went about their jobs. It's embarrassing to bring 3,000 fans away and perform like that. We should be ashamed of ourselves. Appy did something very strange. He put a challenge in and got injured."

The mood wasn't good. One journalist felt the wrath of Jordao after writing in his match report that he had not fancied the cold weather. The Portuguese midfielder's response was to angrily apprehend the reporter after a training session and suggest a way of settling the argument which would prove his fighting qualities. The shocked media man declined. Sneekes, meanwhile, soldiered through the game after taking a typically hefty Kevin Muscat challenge. Albion improved to finish sixth – their highest final placing at that level since being relegated from the top flight in 1986. But, while the club's fortunes were improving, Sneekes' mood was heading south.

"Fear got us into the play-offs," he added. "I grew to hate Gary. I started to do things I wasn't used to – just to stay in the team. He wanted me to chase the ball for no reason. It was running for the hell of running, chasing lost causes. I've got no problem with hard work but it has to be channelled correctly. I can honestly say that as soon as we played on a Saturday, I'd hate coming in on a Monday and I dreaded the following Saturday. I hated it. I lost my love for football.

"At the end of that season, I should have retired, although I was only 32. But I carried on. I went to Stockport and Hull and it wasn't the same. Even now, Daryl Burgess and Ian Hamilton say: 'You should be playing.' But I lost my heart. I'm 42, so maybe not. I could have played on after 32, though. We played Swansea in the third game of the season in the League Cup and Megson dropped me. I said: 'You could have told me out of courtesy and respect.' He just blew me away. He said: 'I've got no respect for you' and told me where to go. I knew it was going to be a tough season

"We became more and more successful but the fear remained. One bad game, maybe two, and you'd be out. It was like a dictatorship. Yet he got the club into the Premier League and you cannot detract from that. No matter what I think, or say, will detract from his success."

The Premier League would have to wait for a further 12 months as Albion faced third-placed Bolton in the play-offs. With the Rainbow Stand demolished, a crowd of 18,000 and a few builders on the construction site watched Albion take a 2-0 lead, with Jason Roberts' opener followed by a Lee Hughes penalty. From there, it unravelled. Sneekes remembered the game and the return and pointed the finger at Megson for his failure to retrieve the situation.

"It was 2-2 at our place, yet we murdered them," he recalled. "That was a killer for us. Absolutely soul-destroying. What cost us the game at Bolton was what he said to us. We were on £6k pro-rata to get into the Premier League and before we did the warm-up that night, he said: 'You know that bonus...that team in the other dressing room is trying to take it away from you.' It utterly deflated us. We were poor, got well beaten and I was taken off. That was my last game for the club."

In the boardroom, all hadn't been well as Albion moved from one Millennium into another. In 1999, there had been an ugly boardroom tug-o-war between South Yorkshire businessman Paul Thompson and then chairman Tony Hale. A bitter verbal dust-up came to a head in an EGM at the Gala Baths in West Bromwich in the summer. Claims and counter-claims were made. Hale survived by a slim majority.

In December, 1999, Albion travelled to Grimsby. Supporters arriving at the game were to hear that Kevin Kilbane had been sold. Brian Little and chief executive John Wile claimed they knew nothing about it. Thompson declared Albion needed to sell their best players to finance short-term debt. Hale resigned as chairman a few days later, with Thompson appointed on Christmas Eve – the first 'outsider' to take up such a post. Hale was to resign from the board a few months later, completing the changeover. During this unsavoury period, the Albion Shareholders Association came in for criticism for a lack of action, involvement and interaction with shareholders.

In March, 2000, a new organisation were formed: Shareholders for Albion (S4A). Their aims were to maintain regular communication between the board, club executives and the independent shareholders. They were to provide a voice for the small stakeholders and a forum for debate, with regular newsletters. Paul Thompson endorsed and cooperated with the idea.

Richard Sneekes struggles at times to rein in his resentment towards the final Albion manager he played for. Twice since, he has been in his company. Both times, they managed to avoid any verbal exchanges. Even now, as he sits at home, Sneekes pulls the kind of face usually reserved for lemon-tasting contests.

Back in 2001, Megson revealed the determined thinking behind his summer cull. "This season has been miles better than the last but it still wasn't good enough and we need to crank it on," he said. "In my view, we've done 'bigger club' things by moving on a few players who have done okay here. We're now saying that 'okay' isn't good enough and we're trying to move West Brom forward. The standards and expectations have risen, to the extent where we're releasing players like the ones we did yesterday. But that's the easy bit. Now we've got to replace them with better ones, otherwise we will go backwards again."

Sneekes' release at the end of the 2000-01 campaign was hardly a surprise. Being called into the office to be given the bad news was bad enough for him. But the gesture hurt, as did the finality of it all. "It wasn't a shock," he said. "I knew before the Huddersfield game [the final home fixture] that I'd played so many games – pretty much every one – but still wasn't going to get a new deal. I went to see John Wile. I wasn't going to give him (Megson) the pleasure. John said: 'You're my Player of the Season. It's just that he wants to clear the decks.'

"I was gutted but, equally, I didn't want to play for Megson again. I gave my boots to Dave Matthews and drove home. I was by Mere Green island near my home when Shirley rang and said the manager wanted to see me. I said: 'He can f*** off.' I was ready to jack it in. I lost my appetite, heart, everything. I didn't want to play. At 32, you're still fit but, in your heart, you want to shut down.

"People, even at 70, want to be footballers in their own imagination. It's a dream job. But if you've been in a job for 20 or 30 years, it can be more than enough if people are making you unhappy. I started at 16 and got my first pro contract at 17 but it wasn't right any more. Flynny was devastated the year before when he got released. I didn't even say goodbye to my team-mates. They were in the dressing rooms, I was outside waiting in the corridor and I got in my car and left."

The drama didn't stop there. Sneekes contemplated his future, taking his family on a break to America. As they travelled back to Holland, a fire broke out in a kitchen at the rear of the plane, forcing the pilot to make an emergency landing at Washington DC. "I knew something was wrong when all of a sudden the pilot rushed to the back of the plane," it was reported at the time. "My heart was in my mouth when he announced what was happening. The crew didn't know whether the fire had crept through to the back where all the wiring was. It could have short-circuited everything. The plane then started acting strangely. It was really scary.

"From the minute the fire was announced, the pilot had to shut down the power at the back and the plane felt like it was shaking. My kids were just playing among themselves and were unaware of what was going on but all sorts of things were going through my head. We had to wait 25 minutes before we landed. That's how far we were from Washington. My wife wondered what would have happened had we been flying miles out over the sea at the time. Shirley didn't sleep after we took off again. She didn't want to get on the same plane."

Long before the mid-air traumas and the Hawthorns acrimony, Sneekes was one of Albion's stellar players and his career whittled down after he departed. He played a combined 36 matches for Stockport and Hull (with no goals) before moving to Herfolge in Denmark. But two of his team-mates from the late 1990s were to take a different route. At £2.2m, Kevin Kilbane proved to be Albion's final depature of the decade when he joined Sunderland. Then there was Enzo Maresca, who had arrived on a free transfer from Cagliari in August, 1998.

The teenager's car, at the time, was a red Rover Metro. He made 53 Albion appearances and scored five goals, before leaving for Juventus for well over £4m at the end of January, 2000 – two weeks short of his 20th birthday. Sneekes smiles when he recalls his fellow midfielder, who went on to play for Fiorentina, Sevilla and Olympiakos. "I spoke Italian and used to translate for him and Mario (Bortolazzi), who was here earlier," he explained. "Gianni Paladini was Enzo's agent and used to turn up at the club a lot. He was trying to get him a move to Italy. I laugh when I think back.....whenever Juventus came to watch him, you could see Enzo was trying to do everything himself. He was like a kid in playground.

"We played Sheffield United – a 2-2 game in which he scored. He was taking everyone on because he knew Juventus were in the stand somewhere. He was trying to take on the world. But he was a great player, a great talent. He has gone on to play at the highest level. They knew how to live for football, he and Mario. They knew how to prepare for games. When I first came to England, you'd see some players more worried about when their next night out was. Enzo was a kid but, as young as he was, he showed how good he was. He was a brilliant little talent."

Sneekes, meanwhile, is back in training, coaching youngsters. He has owned a restaurant, dabbled in property ownership and is now in an environment he knows well. Crucially, he is back in love with the game. "I never thought I would go into coaching but I have and I enjoy it," he admits. "Would I like to coach at a higher or professional level? Why not? Let's see."

*Sneekes joined League Two club Hereford United as first-team coach in June, 2011. He left his post in May, 2012 following their relegation to the Blue Square Bet Premier.

Des Lyttle

"I walked into this Wolverhampton pub with my West Brom suit, my white shirt and my West Brom tie and I got loads for it. But we'd done it, they hadn't."

DES Lyttle beams the broadest of smiles as the waitress asks him: "Excuse me, are you a footballer?" As chat-up lines go, it's up there with the best.

We're sat in the Three Hammers Golf Complex, near Wolverhampton. Both of us are nursing coffees. Golf isn't on the agenda. We're talking West Bromwich Albion. But only one of us is capturing the eyes of the waitress.The lady follows up her initial question by asking whether Lyttle was a goalkeeper. He doesn't look 41, nor, at about 5ft 9in, does he look much like a keeper. Apart from a different hairstyle, he has barely changed since the day he moved from Watford to Albion in March, 2000, as a right-back. The very notion that he's asked whether he's fit enough might owe something to his time under Gary Megson at West Bromwich Albion. "Megson turned me into a runner," he says. "He made me fit."

Lyttle was born and brought up in 'enemy' territory in Wolverhampton. Yet he tuned into Albion during one famous night across the Black Country. It was spring, 1993. Swansea City were playing under the Hawthorns lights in the Division Two play-off semi-final. The Welsh side were 2-1 to the good from the opening leg. Lyttle was part of that Swansea side, managed by Frank Burrows, the man who would eventually become Megson's no 2 at B71. The defender remembers the return – played in front of a full house, in a stadium which had yet to be redeveloped into an all-seater. Few of the players who performed that night – or the fans who were there – will ever forget the unnerving experience of a stadium that was almost trembling around them. It was the night The Hawthorns rocked to the Boing and is still regarded as a seminal occasion among those supporters lucky enough to have been present.

Albion won 2-0 on the night, 3-2 on aggregate, clinching a place at Wembley and eventual promotion. They beat Port Vale 3-0 in the final. "West Brom made a big mark on me that night," said Lyttle. "We should have been home and dry after the first game but we went to The Hawthorns and it was obvious we were up against it. The noise was incredible. Being from down the road in Wolverhampton, I knew all about the rivalry and what fans are like in this area but it was the first time I'd encountered the Boing Boing.

"The whole stadium was shaking around us. That stuck in my mind. There was talk of me going to West Brom before I went to Nottingham Forest in 1993. That speculation stuck in my mind, as did that particular game. I never forgot what the club was about that day."

Roll forward seven years and Albion have stayed up. Just. After arriving as one of Gary Megson's gang of five, Lyttle was a key member of their successful survival battle. Chairman Paul Thompson made it clear that the days of the club handing out long contracts to unproven players were gone.

Names were not disclosed but it was clear there was no future for the likes of Fabian De Freitas, who was on a lucrative three-year contract, and Micky Evans, who was struggling to convince Megson that he was fit enough for his first team. The club were losing around £25,000 a week. The sale of Kevin Kilbane and Enzo Maresca during the previous six months had eased some of the debt but not all. Thompson, just five months into his reign, spelled it out at the time. "A lot of money has been wasted in the past and we've got to make sure we don't keep doing it," he said. "You don't run a football club to make a profit but you cannot afford to incur debts like we have been."

Evans was sold for a cut-price £250,000, Andy Townsend retired. De Freitas, criticised by Megson for 'not knowing who our games are against,' was swiftly released along with Mark Angel, George Santos, Paul Raven, Andy McDermott and Sean Flynn. The Baggies had thus made a dent in their estimated £3.5m wage bill.

Speaking about the summer of 2000, Lyttle reflects on a period of transition instigated by the cuts – and Megson's desire to shed players he had no intention of keeping. "Every manager wants to come in and build his own squad," he said. "I realise that now I'm a gaffer myself. Decisions need to be made that aren't always popular. We'd survived and he (Megson) wanted to change the culture of the club.

"Some players stick around, others don't. I remember Sean Flynn. He was a character who liked to shoot from the hip. He and Gary had words a few times, so it was almost inevitable he would be on his way. I recall he once got a real rollicking for reading a paper in the physio's room. The managers of all clubs have a rule where only one or two players at a time are getting treatment. Gaz walked in and spotted Flynny lying down reading a paper in the physio's room. The physio got a telling-off as well.

"Fabian was another one. He was a laid-back character. You had to tow the line with Gary...and there was Fab strolling around all relaxed without a care in the world. He was never going to last long while Gary was in charge."

Megson's revolution was under way. John Trewick was to leave the club in January 2001, quitting as youth development manager and citing his ambitions to become a manager. Nutritionist John Williams was recruited to govern the players' diets. Alcohol was banned from their bar at The Hawthorns.

"I'm just trying to make the place more professional," Megson said. "I'm hoping that each of these four things will improve the players by five per cent. Booze certainly has no part to play in football these days. I can't stop the players having a quiet drink away from the ground but gone are the days when you can go out and get sloshed. The rewards from a football career have absolutely gone through the roof. But it's a two-way thing. Players have also got to behave more professionally.

"Before I joined the club, all I ever read in the newspapers about West Brom was turmoil and upheaval. We had a real fight on our hands to stay up but we had the laziest group of players I'd ever been involved with, both as a player and manager. They had it really easy. They didn't start training until 11am, which was a pop star's lifestyle. There was no accountability for what they were doing and there was no spirit or togetherness.

"We let quite a few players go in the summer but not one has joined a higher-placed team. They were being paid by the club but weren't really giving anything back. I want players here who hurt when we lose – and that wasn't the case last year. I don't regret moving out any of them, apart from Andy Townsend, who would never have left had he been a couple of years younger."

Lyttle's initial loan spell from Watford was turned into a permanent deal. He was followed by Neil Clement, who arrived from Chelsea for £100,000. Jason Roberts joined for a then-record £2.1m, with Derek McInnes signing for £450,000 on the final day of July. His capture was significant, as was the gesture of his decision to leave behind southern France for the Black Country. The ex-Rangers man took a 60 per cent pay cut to move from Toulouse. Wiry Portuguese midfielder Jordao was transferred from Sporting Braga before Ruel Fox finalised a deal following his release from Spurs.

Lyttle continued: "Jason Roberts cost a lot of money for West Brom. Robbo wasn't well known at the time as he'd been at Bristol Rovers but he has gone on to have a great career. It was a changing of the guard. It was good the club trusted Gaz (Megson) to go out and spend that money. Dekka was a brilliant personality. I knew nothing about him apart from the fact he'd been at Rangers. He came in as a ready-made captain. He was a strong character. He was smaller than me, mind, but his leadership and character were massive.

"Appy lived around the corner from me in Brewood and Dekka lived in Telford, so on we'd travel in together. He was a great man. Off the park, he was a good bloke. On the pitch, he was like a Gary Megson. He brought some of his Glaswegian traits to the party. He was raw, would take the piss out of others, loved banter, liked a beer. But he made you win football games. Not many players carry that on to the pitch as well he did."

For Lyttle, it was the start of a new era in his career, although it didn't go down well with some his pals. "It was a great period for me," he added. "I had two years left at Watford and Graham Taylor was boss there. Graham and I had a bust-up, which we've since forgotten, but it was also a chance to move back to the Midlands. Mind you, I got some stick for it. My mates are Wolves fans and I got a fair bit of banter from the Subway Army (the hooligan 'firm' associated with Molineux).

"I was from Wolverhampton, I was brought up in Low Hill, which isn't one of the best areas around, and they were asking me: 'What the hell are you doing going to play for that lot down the road?' I was off to play for the enemy but that's football. I was just pleased to be back in the Midlands at a club I felt were going places." Yet the only place Albion were heading for during the opening month of the season was the bottom of the First Division. Bookies' predictions that they would struggle seemed correct.

Megson was having none of it. "I disagree with it and I'll be bitterly disappointed if we finish down there again," Megson told the Sunday Mercury. "But if I was looking at it from the bookies' angle, I'd have West Brom down there as well."

An opening-day defeat at Nottingham Forest was harsh. Albion dominated but were denied a point by Jon-Olav Hjelde, who could earlier have been sent off for a cynical foul. What followed owed more to bad play than misfortune. A 2-0 home defeat against Bolton was made worse by a 4-1 battering at Barnsley. All was not well, as Lyttle recalled. "Gary would have this saying 'The lunatics are running the asylum' whenever we lost. We were those lunatics and we weren't doing it his way.

"But, slowly, things came together. New players had come in and we were trying to gel. We had a few young lads. The two Chambers twins (Adam and James) were coming through. I couldn't tell them apart. They even ran the same. Adam Oliver was also emerging. He had great ability. Gaz loved him at first. It's a real shame he didn't make more of what he had. Gaz had to put him on a fitness programme because he was a bit heavy and struggled in the running, which was never a good thing with Gary. You knew you couldn't have a blow-out at the weekend. If you did, you'd be trying to sweat it out as quickly as possible.

"We had our body fats taken every Monday and if you weren't under 12 per cent, you weren't an athlete, according to him. And, yes, I fell into that trap a few times. We went to Denmark just before that season started and I ended up in the 'fat couch' with Brian Jensen, Adam Oliver, Micky Evans and one or two others. But it made me into a runner and I have Gary to thank for that. Never before had I been so fit."

Albion's form turned. Jason Van Blerk and Lee Hughes helped them to a 2-1 win over QPR before Crystal Palace arrived at The Hawthorns for a game switched to September 3 to exactly mark the 100th anniversary of the first game ever staged at the Baggies' home. McInnes' first goal for the club sealed the 1-0 win.

Lee Hughes had missed the final weeks of the previous season. He made a slow start to 2000-01. By the end of September, he had featured in 14 matches and scored four goals. And then he clicked. Three goals in back-to-back games during October were followed by an incredible November which saw him net at Huddersfield before scoring hat-tricks at home to Gillingham and Preston in successive games. In doing so, he became only the second Albion player since Jeff Astle, in 1968, to net a treble in consecutive matches.

Hughes' profile was growing. Off the pitch, he was leading a celebrity lifestyle. He managed to incur the wrath of Ruel Fox when he bought one of the recently introduced BMW X5s – knowing that his team-mate had, too. Fox, never one for understatements, wasn't impressed to see Hughes arrive in the same car to training. Hughes had been subject of a hostile pursuit by Birmingham City during the summer, with Albion fighting to keep him at the club.He also had a clause which meant he would net £25,000 if he scored 25 goals during 2000-01. He finished on 23. His contract at Albion had one crucial caveat – a release clause which could trigger his departure should anyone offer above £5m. It was to eventually lead to his move to Coventry in summer, 2001, for £5,000,001.

Lyttle, a team-mate and friend of Hughes, watched his development with interest. "Hughesie was always the instigator around the club," he laughs, shaking his head to imply there is a 'but' looming. "He knew the local area, where to go and, put it this way, he seemed to know the lap-dancing places pretty well. He'd collar the single lads and take them out. Nothing silly ever happened when I was out but we mixed well as a bunch. We were starting to pick up on the pitch and enjoyed each other's company off it. Lee's profile was big then. His career was kicking on and all you'd read about is this club or that club watching him.

"I'd seen it at Nottingham Forest when I was there. Stan Collymore was getting attention from other clubs like Liverpool. It's inevitable. We wanted to keep Lee. We needed him to stay and be part of our club. We felt we were going places under Gary and all of us were keen that he was part of it. But, ultimately, money came into it. Coventry put a good offer on the table. He went and was getting a lot more, so we couldn't blame him, but we tried to persuade him to stay. He was a normal street lad. He and Robbo had forged a great partnership and he was sadly missed."

New Year, 2001, brought change at The Hawthorns. The Rainbow Stand, built in 1964, was in place for its final match on January 1, when Albion overcame

Barnsley 1-0, before the demolition crews moved in. The £5.5m East Stand was completed for the first home game of 2001-02, costing 20 per cent above the estimated figure. The plush new structure had 8,000 seats, compared with its outdated predecessor's 6,100. A new club shop and ticket office, either side of an executive entrance for directors, sponsors and hospitality guests, were among the features. The East Stand also included conference areas, banqueting facilities and parking for about 200 vehicles.

There were now 126,500 shares in the club. Turnover increased to £8.5m, with a profit of £1.7m. Dividends were paid to the shareholders for the first time. A rights issue was proposed to help finance the East Stand project. A 'buy a brick' scheme was mentioned, whereby supporters could have their name on the wall of the new stand. That did not go ahead but S4A supported the rights issue and encouraged shareholders to follow suit. It proved a success, offering shareholders the right to acquire three new shares for every five held. Any unsubscribed shares were made available to new investors. Shares were trading at £70 each and director Jeremy Peace invested just under £1m in those available shares. The price gradually rose towards £80 as the year wore on.

A forum, chaired by Adrian Chiles, was held by S4A at the end of the season. At that time, only 25 football clubs were listed on the Stock Exchange. Albion were one of seven who paid a dividend to shareholders. The theme of the evening was to discuss how Albion could compete in future as football evolved into a big-money business.

Peace attended, explaining that he had invested in Albion 'because I am a fan.' He had acquired 29.5 per cent of the available shareholding in the club. Paul Thompson, meanwhile, explained that he believed there was a balance to be achieved between running the club well enough to achieve success while also rewarding shareholders for their investment in it.

Albion were also making progress on the field at their three-sided home. In December, 2000, they signed Igor Balis. The modest Slovakian spent the first few months of his Hawthorns career based at the Moat House Hotel (now the Park Inn) next to the M5. His journey to work every day was a walk, with his boots neatly wrapped in a brown paper bag. Premier League football this was clearly not.

Little was known about the right-sided player, a £150,000 buy from Slovan Bratislava. He later moved into a house in the Wigmore area of West Bromwich

– perhaps the last case of a Baggies first-team player living in the town. He drove a modest, bright green five-door Mazda 323. Elsewhere, Megson added experienced Portsmouth goalkeeper Russell Hoult for £450,000 while Michael Appleton arrived from Preston for £750,000, just six weeks after being dismissed during North End's 3-1 defeat at The Hawthorns at the end of November. They were joined by Phil Gilchrist, who pitched up from Leicester for £500,000 in March. The manager was pleased with the squad he was assembling.

What had once been one of the 'laziest' squad he had worked with was now anything but. "I've been delighted with the attitude and application of every player I've brought in," he told the Express & Star. "Some have played better than others but I don't regret signing any one of them. They have been good additions."

Appleton's signing was significant. Derek McInnes's knee collapsed during the October game against Wimbledon. He was to miss the rest of the season. 'Appy' was brought to add midfield steel in the absence of the captain. Megson's plan was for the two to play together in the following campaign. It was to be a short-lived union.

Lyttle, by now a travelling companion and close friend of Appleton's, was involved in the incident which was to lead to the robust midfielder's eventual retirement. The two collided during a routine 50-50 challenge on Albion's training pitch in November, 2001. Appleton ruptured his cruciate ligament and subsequent surgical mistakes forced him to quit. Lyttle, more than a decade on, winces when reminded of the incident. Although absolved of blame, he found it weighing heavily at the time. It still does.

"It was a horrible day," he recalled. "It was a normal training morning and one of those moments when the ball was there to be won. It happens every day but my knees fell on top of his knees, my weight went on top of him, he fell backwards and, at the time, I thought nothing of it. But it was clear he was badly hurt. It was awful because we travelled in together. I still speak to Appy but, at the back of my mind, I know I started the whole process that was to end his career. He was my neighbour and I ended up ruining his career. I know the operations were unsuccessful but it started at the training ground that morning."

Did Appleton blame him? Lyttle replies: "I don't recall that being the case.

We never spoke about it and it was never raised. We still travelled in after that while he was doing his rehab but you wonder what he might be thinking. We were going well when Appy came to the club. He was a similar kind of player to Derek. He was 'horrible' on the pitch, enjoyed the tackles and was a leader. It's just very sad how his career ended."

Megson, at the time, was unhappy that a club challenging for promotion had no training facilities of their own to call upon. Appleton suffered his injury on a pitch owned by Aston University. A new headquarters was being built just a few hundred yards from where he fell. Lyttle admits that the manager's frustrations were echoed throughout the dressing room. "The facilities we had were shite. There's no other word for it," he added. "We were never sure where we'd be.

"The best place we had was the county FA pitch underneath the M5/M6 junction, over in Great Barr. We'd use that to work on team shape on a Friday, simply because it was a better pitch. Other than that, we'd use Aston Uni pitches or the ones by the stadium. It was all like a Sunday League side. We made the best of it but it wasn't great. I'd come from Watford and, before that, Leicester and Forest. We had decent facilities at those clubs but just had to get on with it at West Brom."

Megson wasn't impressed either and added his discontent. "The training facilities are the worst I've ever had to work with, including Blackpool," he told the Birmingham Mail. "The surface is a joke. It's that bad we're having to train inside the ground. We've got no choice but it means we're going to mess the pitch up. Our lack of proper facilities is putting at risk what we're trying to do and I believe one or two of the injuries have been caused by the surface. It's nobody's fault but it's hard to call yourself a big club when you haven't got decent training facilities."

In spring, 2001, Albion were making a surprise charge for promotion. A surprise only to those outside the club, who had predicted another season of struggle. The Baggies took 12 points from their final eight games to clinch sixth spot. They finished on 74 points, four behind Birmingham and two ahead of Burnley, who just missed out on the play-offs.

Albion played Bolton at The Hawthorns in the first leg of their play-off. They opened the scoring through Jason Roberts in the 44th minute – his 17th and final goal of the season. Hughes added the second ten minutes later. Albion couldn't hang on. Bolton, who finished the season on 87 points, four behind second-placed Blackburn, were too strong for them. Gudni Bergsson pulled one back in the 81st minute. Per Frandsen equalised with two minutes left.

Albion lost 3-0 in the second leg at the Reebok Stadium, with Sam Allardyce's side beating Preston in the final. Baggies fans, although disappointed by the eventual outcome, were seemingly enjoying the occasion. Their side had been tipped for relegation yet Megson took them to the brink of being back in the Premier League. At the end, coaching staff and players acknowledged the away supporters, who remained vocal throughout the unsuccessful second leg, and an overwhelmed Paul Thompson marched on to the pitch to salute them.

Lyttle was recently reminded of the play-off game at The Hawthorns. "My lad got the tape out a few weeks ago," he said. "To go 2-0 up at home, in front of a three-sided full house, we thought we were home and dry. Then we let two in and the dressing room was horrible after the game. We knew we'd probably lost it there and then. Gaz gave us a rollicking and rightly so. We had this feeling we'd blown it and we got battered at Bolton. That was that. It was a horrible summer. Play-offs are a bad way to lose. You're still playing when others are on the beach and the nature of how we lost was devastating. It was a low time."

Albion returned for summer training in 2001 against an unusual backdrop. Lee Hughes left for Coventry and Jason Roberts sustained a pre-season injury which was to recur throughout the campaign. Richard Sneekes, a key figure during his six-year spell at the club, did not have his contract renewed. Whereas the summer of 2000 was about the Megson revolution, 2001 was one of evolution.

Sneekes's departure was significant. His technical ability could not be faulted but Lyttle feels Megson had other ideas about where his team were going. "It was a strange summer," the defender recalls. "Richard had great ability. He was a good player but Gary wanted more of a worker in there. Richard was a big character and had been at the club a long time but Gaz was creating a new West Brom. We'd lost Lee Hughes to Coventry and Jason Roberts had broken down – that's 25-30 goals for a start – yet we grew from adversity.

"I'd been at clubs where change hadn't always gone well. At Forest, Frank Clark tried to change a lot one summer and it didn't work. Gary did the same and his change worked. Darren Moore came in. Another leader. Phil Gilchrist, had not long since joined. He, too, was a good, strong player who could be relied on and lead. Gaz wanted to go with people he could trust. You have to admire the players he brought in. Pretty much everyone improved the team in one way or another. That's the sign of a good manager."

Lyttle's period of prominence was coming towards an end. The arrival of Balis in December, 2000 was key. Megson was keen to maintain his favoured 5-3-2 or 3-5-2 formation, which drew its strength from an industrious spine provided by the likes of McInnes, Appleton, Moore, Gilchrist, Larus Sigurdsson and Andy Johnson. On the flanks, Megson expected a touch more creativity and energy via the use of wing-backs. It's a position which requires great fitness levels from the player, who is effectively charging the length of the pitch at frequent periods to support attacking moves but racing back to cover defensively. Neil Clement had the role sewn up on the left. On the right, Megson had options and Lyttle, a defender by description, knew that Balis's presence was unhelpful to his own prospects.

"Igor was a good, technical player," he added. "He was competition for me and he eventually took over from me. The problem I had is that Gaz liked to play with wing-backs and, once he developed that aspect of the team, I knew I'd be up against it. Igor had a great engine and used to play in the most open games, when teams were happy to play football against us. He could express himself more, whereas I'd be called in for the horrible games, where we had to scrap. I was a better defender than Igor in terms of one v one but he was more of a technical player; almost an ideal wing-back.

"I had never played in that role before West Brom. It's something I had to learn to do. You have to be a runner at wing-back. I had to battle it out with Igor as a result. I was always going to stay and try to prove I was better than him but Gary opted for him. I could understand that."

Promotion followed in 2002. Despite the setbacks resulting from loss of personnel and injury, Lyttle was not surprised by Albion's success. He said: "We were so determined to put right the disappointment of the play-offs and Wolves were our incentive that year. They did so well in the early part of that season. They were scoring loads of goals and, around February, were about 11 points ahead. They had already booked their trips away as part of their promotion win. It was all done and dusted for them.

"Not only did they think they'd go up but they wanted to win the League. That was the feeling they had in their camp. It was between them and Man City for the title, then the rest. I lived near (Wolves midfielder) Tony Dinning. I made sure I gave him loads of grief after that. I got some myself mind. When we went second, I went to a pub up in Wolverhampton where all my mates used to drink. I walked in with my West Brom suit, my white shirt and my West Brom tie and got loads for it. But we'd done it, they hadn't."

Lyttle's time at Albion ended in the summer of 2003. He made just five appearances during their Premier League campaign and joined Northampton Town on a free transfer following his three-year Hawthorns spell, in which he clocked up 76 appearances and one goal. He retains admiration for Megson, even though he barely played following promotion.

"You couldn't knock Gary," he added. "You did it by his book or you were gone. My last 18 months weren't great but I respected the way he managed. He'd given me a chance to leave Watford and, when we got to the Premier League, I had a chance to leave for Swindon. But I stayed to fight for my place. You needed a strong mentality. He made those demands of his players. Your career at West Brom was finished if you weren't respectful of his ways and methods. Some players couldn't abide by his rules. They were soon gone. Others were simply not mentally strong enough to cope with him. Again, his reasoning was that if they couldn't tune into him on that basis, he wasn't sure you could do it on the pitch for him.

"Gary Megson would shout at me and get a response. A few were very nervous....they couldn't cope mentally or physically. Scott Dobie was one. He actually had a good career there and did well but was always physically sick before a game. He was one of these players who wanted to be 'loved'. He was a young, raw lad and that nervousness, brought on by his desire and need to impress Gary, made him throw up. Not nice but that's the effect Gary's style had. I'm delighted I got to play for him because his demands were tremendous and asked a lot of you.

"I'd come from Watford, been in the Premier League and Championship with Forest and recognised straightaway that Gary was trying to build something; not with household names, apart from maybe Foxy, but with hungry, young players. I took the chance on staying in the Premier League in 2002. By then, Gaz wanted me out but I played a few games and did all I could to prove him wrong. I was never bitter towards him. He had a job to do.

"I thought I was better than some of the players he picked but he thought otherwise. That's football. I had been playing for a club where, even as a Wolverhampton lad, I had been accepted. They were three good years of my career. Gary was there to bring success to a club which had been in a mess for so long. And, you know what? He did it."

Andy Johnson

"Sheffield United's players and staff turned up at the airport and I thought: 'Oh no, not again! We've had the Battle of Bramall Lane, now it's going to be the Battle of Heathrow.'"

THERE is no point in trying to make Albion fans feel better. The brutal context of the official club website's match report is a stark reminder of their plight. "Albion's automatic promotion hopes lie in tatters following a night of pure drama in Lancashire." The Baggies have lost 1-0 to Preston. Dickson Etuhu has scored the only goal after 57 minutes.

Jason Roberts is out for the season. His yelp of agony can be heard around Deepdale as he breaks his left foot for the third time in 2001-02. He clutches his ankle, grimaces and flicks his head back in despair. Club legend Tony Brown, commentating for local radio, exclaims: "It's happened again...you can just tell by his reaction. He's had it." Roberts knows it's over. For this season at least. He will leave the ground with difficulty, on crutches.

Albion are limping, too. Predictably, the press are even more down-beat than the Baggies website. "So it's the play-offs then," the Express & Star's man Neil Johnston writes. "Albion's faint hopes of automatic promotion were blown away in the swirling wind and rain at Deepdale last night.........after the blundering Baggies had squandered their eighth spot-kick in 11 attempts this season. There are still 30 points to play for but Megson's shattered side – now ten points adrift of table-topping Wolves – appear to have left themselves too much to do in too little time."

Scott Dobie is the latest culprit. The Birmingham Evening Mail catch up with Darren Moore after the game. "Let's win promotion for Jason," roars Big Dave. It's a statement of hope. Hopeless hope. A few miles up the A41, all is well. As Albion lose at Preston, Wolverhampton Wanderers beat Walsall 3-0. A Dean Sturridge double and Nathan Blake goal have put Wolves five points clear of Manchester City at the top and ten ahead of Albion. "Wolves' march towards the Premiership continued in style as local rivals Walsall became the Molineux team's sixth successive victim," says the Wanderers website. The match report concludes: "At the final whistle, the gold and black section of the 27,000 crowd were well satisfied with their team's work, especially when they heard other results had gone in Wolves' favour."

Wolves are busy making plans. A celebratory dinner is pencilled in to take place at Dunstall Park racecourse, followed by an all-expenses trip to the Bahamas. Then there are the promotion-related bonuses to every player. Reports claim that each will receive £50,000 for winning promotion. Sir Jack Hayward is happy to pay. His dream of reaching the Premier League at last is just two months away. Easy meat for Wolverhampton Wanderers. This is their year.

Consider the maths: Dave Jones' men are jockeying for top spot with City. They have a four-game swing over Albion. There are nine games to play for Wolves, who have 76 points. Kevin Keegan's side are five behind but with two games in hand. Albion are third, like Wolves on 37 games, but with only 66 points. In the first half of March, Wolves take five points from three games. But that's ok because Albion have played two League games and gleaned four points – by beating Wimbledon and drawing with Watford. Surely nothing can go wrong for Wolves?

On Sunday, January 20, 2002, Albion fans woke to the grim news that club legend Jeff Astle had passed away. Astle, aged just 59, collapsed at his daughter's home and was taken to hospital in Burton-on-Trent, where he died. Albion's programme editor Dave Bowler was told the news by his father as he prepared to leave for The Hawthorns. The Baggies were facing Walsall in a televised Sunday afternoon game. Before leaving, Bowler dug out a t-shirt with a photograph of Astle across the front. A colleague suggested he should ask one of the players to wear the item under his Albion jersey. His choice was fitting. Jason Roberts was called out of the dressing room and handed the shirt.

Albion won 1-0 – their first-ever League win against Walsall – with Roberts scoring the only goal of an emotional game and removing his no 11 shirt to reveal the tribute. Grinning broadly, Roberts stretched his t-shirt to reveal the Astle image. As iconography goes, it's up there with any Albion photo of the decade.

Baggies players past and present, supporters, household names from football, showbiz and elsewhere attended Astle's funeral in Netherseal, south Derbyshire. The club immediately planned a permanent tribute to The King. That would eventually come in the form of the Astle Gates on the Birmingham Road at the entrance to the East Stand. The cost of £40,000 was met by a number of organisations, including the club themselves, the supporters club, Boing internet group and S4A. John Whitehouse, a committee member of S4A, using all his experience in the metal forming business, was responsible for the design and specification of the finished article.

Meanwhile, Bob Taylor planned his own tribute. Astle's death came just a few months after the club had mourned the loss of Ronnie Allen, another club legend and iconic Albion centre-forward. Taylor, then wearing the no 9 shirt, was happy to 'retire' the number in honour of two men who had become mentors and friends of his during his spell at the club. "I'd be very happy to give up my no 9 shirt for Jeff and Ronnie," Taylor told the Birmingham Mail and Express & Star. "I met Jeff many times and knew Ronnie quite well from when he used to come into the club. I know what both players meant to the supporters.

"Ultimately, it's up to the club but I wouldn't stand in the way of that – it was the number both players wore week in, week out. It's the number the fans associate them with and if the club want to retire it or hold it back for a season, I would be very happy to go along with it as a tribute to both men." Albion opted against such a move but the loss of Astle became a poignant backdrop as the season gathered momentum.

On March 16, Albion head to Sheffield United. The side-shows to the main event are intriguing. Gary Megson versus Neil Warnock. The two men hate each other. Megson might be wearing a navy blue and white West Bromwich Albion tie but his roots remain in the Steel City. Two years on from taking the Hawthorns job, he still commutes from south Yorkshire every day.

For Andy Johnson, it should be an ordinary game. But it isn't. Twelve months earlier, Johnson – then at Nottingham Forest – was involved in an incident with Sheffield United's Georges Santos, who was caught by Johnson's stray elbow in an aerial challenge. He suffered a double fracture of the eye socket. The Frenchman underwent a five-and-a-half-hour operation at

Sheffield's Thornbury Hospital to have a titanium plate inserted in his face.

Johnson, speaking at the time, protests his innocence. "If anything, their boy was late on me," he claims. "There was no bad reaction from the United players and I am quite happy that I am totally blameless. It wasn't my fault." Santos considers legal action. Instead, he opts for a slightly more medieval and rudimentary response. No solicitors necessary.

March, 2002, Albion are leading 2-0 against the Blades, who are down to ten men following the ninth-minute dismissal of Simon Tracey for handling outside his area. Scott Dobie has already scored and Derek McInnes strikes the best goal of his career to make it two. Then United make a double substitution. Off go Michael Tonge and Gus Uhlenbeek. On come Patrick Suffo and Santos. Johnson is about to become a tabloid story.

From Albion midfielder to the subject of a Sunday newspaper headline: 'Is this the worst challenge ever?' Pretty, it wasn't. Dangerous, definitely. Even now, speaking at the Hilton Hotel in Bromsgrove, Johnson recalls with clarity. "Oddly, Georges had been at West Brom two years before and a couple of the lads knew him," he said. "I remember Beast (Brian Jensen) telling me what a lovely lad he was. I'm sure he is.

"But there was an incident when I was at Forest. These things happen. He thought I did it on purpose – that's crap, I didn't. A lot of rumours came out, like the story that he was being released that year and was put on solely to do me. I don't know whether that's the case but I recall Derek McInnes rolling me a pass with flashing red lights over it. It wasn't Del's best pass and Georges just went through me."

What followed was mayhem. Johnson needs little prompting. "It was a circus – Del (McInnes) got head-butted by Suffo, and Mooro (Darren Moore) had the devil in him trying to get hold of their players. I thought I'd broken my leg because the bottom half, below my knee, was completely numb. I remember Nick Worth (Albion's physio) coming on and slowly my feeling came back and I was like 'I'm going to kill him' and I was fighting with Nick, who was trying to stop me from getting up.

"Anyway, Georges has been sent off and we carry on. By then, the game's dead but I remember Warnock is yelling things, Keith Curle (United player-coach) is shouting this and that. Meggo, in his wisdom, thought it would be wise to get me off the pitch and out of the way. Fair enough, the game was won. We were two up, heading towards three. They had eight players. Game over. So I came off and went to sit on the bench. But Gary told Adie Stovell (the fitness coach) to take me back in the dressing room out of the way. As we're going down the tunnel, Georges is stood there waiting for me. He runs towards me, I'm trying to run towards him and then I see Adie just dive past with a rugby tackle on Georges. He brought Georges down to the floor, which took some doing because he was a big bloke. I considered jumping on Santos to give him a kick but I thought: 'No, I won't do that, especially as I've got a bad leg and I'm in agony as it is...'

"Instead, I went into our dressing room and grabbed one of the metal crutches and thought I'll get him with this instead. I'll whack him with a big metal stick. So there I was, charging out of the dressing room ready to get him. By then, the police had restrained him and some others grabbed me and pushed me back into the dressing room. They wouldn't let me out, so that was that.

"Meanwhile, there's a football game going on and all I know is there's someone shouting 'break his legs' on the sideline, a player is telling his team-mates to 'get off the pitch,' trying to get the game abandoned, someone has done me, Del's been head-butted and left needing stitches and Mooro, the most gentle man in the world, is running around with glazed-over eyes. It was all a bit surreal. No-one had seen a game like that before. I had some really nice letters from the Sheffield United fans afterwards. They were saying the tackle was out-of-order and a 'disgrace.' They were apologetic."

The 'game' was over. Albion had won 3-0 but the League table couldn't be updated as the end came with an abandonment. Albion had not yet gained any points. They would in due course. The Football Association would see to that. It was a rubber-stamping process.

Off the pitch, the recriminations were under way. The players were barred from speaking to the press. Warnock, who took the best part of an hour and a half to attend his post-match press conference, tried to make light of the afternoon. Albion vice-chairman Clive Stapleton travelled home on the team bus. He spoke to Richard Littlejohn, presenter of Radio Five Live's 606. That day's Premier League fixtures were taking a back seat. The only story was the Battle of Bramall Lane.

Referee Eddie Wolstenholme was close to tears after the game, according to anecdotal recollections. One United coach called Megson to apologise for his side's behaviour. Santos and Suffo were moved on. United were cleared by the FA of cheating. Their football executive Terry Robinson said: "We always knew there was no evidence to support the allegations of cheating and feigning injuries to get the match abandoned. We will now be considering our position on the cheating allegations and take appropriate advice. We have to consider all the circumstances as we seek to preserve the good name of Sheffield United."

Despite Megson's post-match accusations, the FA said that "no independent evidence was forthcoming to indicate that there was a deliberate attempt by any Sheffield United player or official to force the match to be abandoned." Warnock was eventually cleared of a charge of improper conduct by an FA disciplinary panel. He was found guilty, though, of a minor charge of misconduct pertaining to the match, in relation to his behaviour towards the fourth official, and given a reprimand of a £300 fine.

United were fined £10,000 and, as well as Warnock, Curle, Santos and Suffo were all punished individually for their parts in the debacle. Santos was found guilty of a reckless tackle and handed a two-match ban, on top of the four matches he missed as a result of his sending-off. However, allegations of a tunnel bust-up involving him were not proven. Curle admitted improper conduct in an incident involving a match official and was fined £500 and given a two-match ban. Suffo was found guilty of violent conduct. He was fined £3,000 and banned for three games in addition to the three-match suspension already completed.

Few others were willing to shoulder responsibility. Former Sheffield Wednesday hero Derek Dooley was a Bramall Lane director. The Dooley and Megson families, who had enjoyed a close friendship for many years, were to fall out over the incident. Dooley died in March, 2008. The two families' relationship never properly reconciled.

Johnson, meanwhile, was in demand. Warnock had blamed him. A Sunday newspaper traced his number. The reporter got little out of him, although the Albion man used an Anglo-Saxon response when told of Warnock's allegations. Bizarrely, Warnock wasn't done. Barely ten weeks after the Battle of Bramall Lane, United invited Albion for a pre-season game in early August. The Baggies, already committed to a friendly against Port Vale, kindly declined in quicker time than it takes to say 'insult' and 'injury.' But it didn't end there.

Albion and United, although by this point Santos was gone, were to share an airport terminal building at the end of that season. Johnson added: "We went to Spain as a thank-you gesture (from the club) for doing so well. As we were going out, Sheffield's players and staff turned up and I thought: 'Oh no, not again! We've had the Battle of Bramall Lane, now it's going to be the Battle of Heathrow.'

"Big Mooro came over to me and just said: 'Johnno, you'll be ok. Stay with me.' You know what? Looking back, I hold no grudges towards Georges and I hope he doesn't towards me. We're old men now. Yes, it was a talking point and now I laugh about it. Nobody's career was ended. I look back on that whole incident with fond memories."

Yet the tale of the season starts much earlier. September, 2001. The western world changes forever. The Twin Towers of New York's World Trade Centre are destroyed on the 11th day of the month. Simultaneously, Washington DC has been targeted by terrorists. Elsewhere across the US, passengers have averted a fourth attack by heroically challenging hijackers. The plane crashes but never reaches its target – thought to be the United States Capitol building in Washington DC. Thousands of lives are lost as a result of the attacks. And so September 11, 2001 becomes known as 9/11.

Albion play, and beat, Swindon on that dreadful Tuesday night. Scott Dobie and Jordao score during extra-time on a Worthington Cup evening on which nobody really cares about football. It is usually deemed as a form of escapism but people wanted to be at home with their families. This was a time for kissing your children goodnight and wondering what lay ahead.

Gary Megson, whose brother lived in the United States, wanted the tie called off. The US atrocities began during the early afternoon UK time. The football authorities deemed it too late to postpone matches. The Baggies official website summed it up well. "On an evening where football came pretty low down on most people's list of priorities, Albion huffed and puffed their way to victory...," stated the match report. "Albion boss Gary Megson had hoped the game would be postponed in the wake of events in America and, following the minute's silence in honour of those who perished, the game was played in a rather surreal atmosphere, not unlike a friendly, with the players seemingly unwilling to further blacken the day with hostile challenges. It was a night when our thoughts were half a world away and we were reminded that football is not a matter of life and death."

Ken Hipkiss, Albion club chaplain, had little appetite for it either. Speaking to the Sports Argus, he said: "The performance on Tuesday was difficult. You could sense that something wasn't right throughout the ground. It seemed to be in shock. What happened might have taken place in America but it was an important part of our lives. Gary was picking the team and probably thinking: 'Why am I doing this?' The fans were quiet and the players were subdued. It was like there was a blanket over whole stadium."

The world ticked over. It had to. Albion started the season brightly, although the summer didn't bode well. Lee Hughes left for Coventry after the newly-relegated Sky Blues triggered a £5m release clause in his contract. Gordon Strachan joked that he paid the £1 to take the bid over the magic figure. That deal went through around the same time that Jason Roberts was ruled out with a broken ankle. It meant an early first-team opportunity for young striker Scott Dobie, who had joined from Carlisle in a deal worth £150,000. He started well, netting nine times in his first 12 games.

Off the field, there was concern for Frank Burrows. He spent several weeks from September recuperating after an operation and subsequent treatment for cancer of the kidney. He was to make a full recovery. Albion, meanwhile, were busy making sure Dobie wasn't the only new boy.

Darren Moore and Johnson arrived during the second and third weeks of September. Danny Dichio was also considered following a successful loan spell but the matter was to test everyone concerned. Albion and Sunderland were initially unable to agree a fee. Then there were Dichio's wage demands, along with the fact he was struggling with an injury. The striker was on about £15,000 a week at the Stadium of Light. Clearly, he would need to take a drop.

Megson and chairman Paul Thompson were heading towards a fall-out. Thompson was critical of the club's scouting system while fans were being critical of him. Hate mail was adding to his postman's workload. "Supporters have been claiming that we have lost points because we've not signed Dichio," he said. "It appears some don't trust the chairman of the board and I have grown very tired of it. It has left me thinking seriously about my future. Yes, I have thought about walking away.

"I am here for three years and, at the end of that period, there will be an opportunity for somebody else to do a better job. We have bought 16 new players at a total transfer cost of £7.1m and we have the best playing squad the club have had for years. We now have a stadium we can be proud of, a new 46-acre Football Development Centre and a very good manager in Gary Megson. When supporters do not back chairmen and chief executives in their negotiations with other clubs, they contribute to undermining their own club's position. This leads to pressure on chairmen and chief executives to make bad decisions, which may be popular in the short term but extremely damaging to the club.

"We have bought several experienced players over the past 22 months, significantly strengthening the squad. However, I believe that for the club to progress, we also need to buy more of the younger players. This is one of the reasons why we are determined to see that the club develop an integrated scouting system which will identify the right players to develop the squad – and the key words are availability and affordability. In the past, this club has concentrated on short-term fixes to problems without looking at longer-term health, a policy that has kept us out of the top division for 15 years. We need to balance the immediate demands of the football manager with the longer-term needs of the club."

The comments about the scouting system were taken personally by Megson. The Albion boss's recruitment policy was a paradox. He was accused of deferring only to the opinion of his father Don. Megson Senior, a former manager and player himself, was clearly an astute judge given the success of Albion's signings following his son's appointment. Yet it wasn't scientific. And what of players who fell outside of Megson Senior's remit? Evidence from the period suggests Albion were offered both Matt Taylor of Luton for £500,000 and Peter Crouch of QPR for just over £1.5m sometime during 2001. Both were given the thumbs-down by Albion's manager and, presumably, his father.

Albion's issue was also one of logic – the notion that managers have a short shelf-life, rendering long-term scouting projects as futile if left within their remit. One player they did target was David Ginola. Everton were willing to release him in March, 2002 but the charismatic Frenchman, who was 35 at the time, did not wish to drop a division. Elsewhere, Kevin Cooper and Jason Koumas were also pursued. The former, then playing for Wimbledon, chose Wolves in a head-to-head between the two Black Country clubs.

Koumas opted out of a move after a £2m fee was agreed with Tranmere. Middlesbrough's Hamilton Ricard was also deliberating during March, 2002, Sunderland's Stanislav Varga signed on loan, goalkeeper Andy Petterson moved on a short-term deal from Portsmouth and Trevor Benjamin stopped by on his 18-club journey around the Football League.

Thompson's comments returned to bite him later that season, although Megson won the battle over Dichio, who signed for £1.25m at the end of November. The Albion manager was upset by a Birmingham Post journalist, who had quoted Dichio's wage demands and how they compared with those of current Albion players. The information had been leaked from inside the club and Megson wasn't impressed. The two clashed verbally during a routine pre-match press conference. It was heated. Megson was feeling the pressure. He felt his players would be unsettled by the disclosure of Dichio's demands. The argument descended into near-farce when an increasingly red-faced Megson called the journalist a 'dope' and urged him to 'stick to f***ing cricket.' The reporter sat with his arms folded, perfectly calm, and replied: 'It's tennis, actually, Gary.' It didn't bode well.

Johnson was happy to be at The Hawthorns. And Megson's pursuit of him was of no surprise. The two had played together at Norwich. "Gary was the reason I came to West Brom," Johnson recalls. "I played with him at Norwich when he was player and then manager. He must have enjoyed working with me and I enjoyed working with him. Paul Hart (Nottingham Forest manager) and I never saw eye to eye. He said I'd never play for Forest again while he was at the club, so that was it. After a couple of months of stubbornness, I got the move I wanted.

"I never fell out with Meggo at West Brom but, funnily enough, I fell out with him at Norwich, both as manager and player. We played Wimbledon away when he was still a player and I was doing all the running. I had a go at him for not chasing someone. He went mad at me. But we were team-mates, we just got on with it. Maybe he saw something in that.

"To this day, if I need something, I give him a call. I have so much respect for him still. He and Frank Burrows were a good partnership. Frank would always let Meggo growl away at us but then he stepped in as the old head. He would never let us see it but I know he calmed Gary down. Mind you, Frank could fight you as well if necessary. He was placid, laid-back even, but, if he went, you knew you'd done something wrong. But it worked for us. We were a gang of lads and they led us very well."

A 'gang' is how Johnson describes Albion's class of 2001-02. The Baggies took a hammer and chisel to Wolves. Chipped away, they did. With some force. Having started March some ten points behind, Albion ended the month just three adrift of their nearest rivals. There were four games to play. History tells us the Baggies were to win three and draw one. Wolves lost their first two games in April, then beat Wimbledon 1-0 before drawing at Sheffield Wednesday. Albion took second place by three points. Wolves lost to Norwich City in the play-off semi-finals.

Johnson reclines in his chair and smiles when asked for the secret to Albion's achievement. "It was unique, wasn't it?" he beams. "I mean 'unique' because there will always be great escapes. West Brom did it, Wolves did it in 2011. Other clubs have done it. It happens. But promotion is tougher and we did it from a position of weakness – and against our biggest rivals. I joined the club and, only a year before, they were barely hanging on in the division. The thing about that group of players is that we were all winners. We were driven. We were over-achieving.

"We weren't even a good football team. We were mates who really fought. Gary worked on that. If he saw something nasty or disparaging about us, he would cut it out of the newspaper and stick it on the dressing room wall. That would inspire us. We were just a gang of lads, mates, with Meggo as the leader. Our football wasn't pretty, we broke the record for 1-0s and clean sheets. We'd scrap, fight, bite, kick. Whatever it took to win. You could train naked for all Gary cared, as long as you gave it everything and were never late. Mind you, he hated coloured boots or 'fancy boots' as he called them. One pre-season, we turned up in moulded boots, the ground was like concrete and he made us all wear studs."

Johnson digresses but returns to how promotion was earned. The source came from within – as much as it did from 12 miles away. "A few things came out from Wolves," he recalls. "They'd booked their promotion dinner. These days, I'm not sure you get much passion with derbies. Fans yes, but players? But, back then, we hated them when we played. There was an intensity. And then it was us or them for promotion.

"We knew we would not only catch them but bury them. Their foot came off the gas, our feet were to the floor. Even in training, we pushed, pushed, pushed. Everything we did was intense, games were super-intense. The night we went up, I went home and went to sleep. I was emotionally knackered. I was in bed by half ten after two beers. We got promoted to the Premier League and, to this day, I have no idea how.

"Even now, it seems unachievable. Think about it.....we were favourites for relegation. We were ten points or so behind a club who had spent a lot, our local rivals, with a handful of games left. You wouldn't have got good odds on us. No chance! That's why I don't think it will happen again. What's more, we weren't ready for promotion. But we peaked at the right time. Everything came together. We deserved it completely but none of us saw it happening. Ask me how we did it.....I have no idea. We never talked about it at the time. You couldn't say the word. We were briefed before interviews – don't mention promotion! It was almost banned."

Johnson was a dynamic, forceful character. The Bristolian could look after himself on the pitch. Off it, his sharp wit always ensured his position at the top of the personality table. But there is a human side. A reminder of one incident prompts his eyes to well up ever so slightly. He pretends they haven't, but they have. "The first-team were like a family, with Gary as the father figure. It was about the first-team bubble. We were stuck in this bubble.

"At the last game of the season, he produced this masterstroke. He said: 'Don't do it for me, don't do it for the fans, don't do it for the club, do it for these people.' Then the door opened and all the families walked in. There were kids crying in the dressing room. It was emotional... even now it's emotional. We were like animals that day. There was no way we were losing. Credit to Meggo and Frank.

"We knew we were on a hiding to nothing but we didn't care. We knew we shouldn't have been there. It has taken until 2011 – ten years since we went up – for the club to say: 'Yeah, we're established now, we're not a yo-yo club.' We were the first side to launch the club to where they are now. But there was no way we were going to survive that first year. We deserved to be there but we knew it was tough."

Johnson adds: "Gary treated us properly. It wasn't an adventure. He stopped us swapping shirts and he even took my red boots. We got to the Premier

League and companies throw boots at you. Meggo was one for black boots and he threw away these red ones I received. I never saw them again. I know it was him. He never admitted to it but I know he took them and chucked my boots. The sod."

The summer of 2002 should have been a time of celebration. The Champagne quickly went flat. The problems started during the protracted Dichio transfer, got worse during the New Year and deteriorated during 2002. Paul Thompson persisted with his notion of an 'integrated transfer system.' Megson continued to take it all personally. Bickering between the two went on. Megson sensed he was increasingly isolated and alienated from the board. Thompson felt increasingly powerless to rein in his manager's growing power. Megson had not only been fighting Wolves during 2001-02, but also his own employers. At least that's how it seemed. The media were brought onside. The politicking between employee and employer was gathering pace.

Thompson had one problem: Megson was becoming a coveted manager. He was linked with vacancies at Aston Villa, Fulham, Leeds and Sunderland during his time at the club. He was more than happy to be mentioned. Everton had him down as second choice when Walter Smith left. Their first choice was Preston's David Moyes and he accepted.

Matters reached a head. Nine days after the promotion-clinching 2-0 win against Crystal Palace, there were rumours Megson was about to quit. He held on. Just. On the tenth day, Thompson packed his backs and left. The motives for the chairman ceding to a manager remain unknown to this day. In reality, Thompson simply felt he couldn't work with Megson. The employer was gone, the employee was king.

The Rotherham-based businessman opted out, writing in a long letter to supporters: "It is obvious from Gary Megson's comments in the press, and from comments he has made to me personally, that he wishes to see me step down as chairman. Now he has got his wish. The two issues are: 1. Public comments which Gary makes repeatedly result in almost constant public criticism of the chairman and the board which is totally unjustified. It is never acceptable for a manager to publicly criticise a chairman or the directors any more than it is acceptable for a chairman to publicly criticise a manager. We all have a hard enough job to do without public criticism being inflicted by our senior colleagues. 2. I have clearly stated that West Bromwich Albion's scouting system isn't good enough. Gary has stated that the scouting system was his dad and a couple of Gary's mates. The lack of a proper scouting system has held the club back for years."

Megson simmered away for four days, then came his reply. "I want to make it unequivocally clear that I want nothing to do with the running of the club other than carrying out my normal duties as a football manager," he said. "I want nothing to do with the finances because I don't know anything about them. I never have and never will do. I just want to be able to do my job, like I have been doing for the last two years; during which we've finished sixth in the First Division and then got into the top flight for the first time in 16 years, reached the FA Cup quarter-finals for the first time in 20 years, beat the club record for clean sheets and totalled more League points than any other Albion team." And that was that.

Clive Stapleton, as vice-chairman, became acting chairman. Director Jeremy Peace, meanwhile, was ready to challenge for the role vacated by Thompson. In so doing, he played the most significant card of the boardroom struggle by backing Megson. Peace's public support for the boss was a key strategy as Megson's stock had never been higher, certainly among supporters.

Megson returned the gesture by stating that Peace was a person he could work with. Many shareholders, won over by the prospect of a harmonious chairman-manager relationship, not least with the added incentive of keeping Megson sweet, signalled their intention to support Peace. A PR man named David Bick lobbied the media on behalf of Peace, of whom little was known. It was all carefully orchestrated. Speaking to the Birmingham Post, Peace said: "I've been a fan of West Bromwich Albion all my life and a board member for 18 months. I know the workings of the club and the personalities in it.

"The arguments for taking on the job are persuasive. I love the club; I have proven experience in running public companies; I have the contacts to bring in more investment and I have the makings of a genuinely good working relationship with Gary Megson. Above all, the question I asked myself was this: 'Will you ever forgive yourself if, as the club threatens to disintegrate around you as others play politics with it, you don't go for it when you're sure there's not a better man for the job?' Answer: No. So I suggested to the board that I become executive chairman.

"Three members of the board (Barry Hurst, Clive Stapleton and Bob McGing) chose to vote against me, preferring to spend this vital close season with only an acting chairman (Stapleton) in place, leading to more uncertainty and instability. This I judged to be against the club's best interests. Since joining the board, I've enjoyed, like you, being part of the most successful period in Albion's recent history. I attribute our success mainly to Gary Megson but also to the good work of Paul Thompson, who has always had my full support.

"Paul Thompson is a gifted businessman and I'm 99 per cent in agreement with him as to how to run a football club. But if, in his vision of how to run a club, there is no place for one of the most talented young managers in the country, then I'm afraid his vision is flawed. I've talked to Gary Megson regularly and at length, and realised he is not intent on bankrupting the club, taking control of it, or any of the other nonsense he has been accused of in the past few weeks. Gary wants to do everything he can to keep us in the top flight. We also need a tightly-run and high-performance scouting system. I am confident Gary and I can work together and I believe Gary shares this view. We'll argue for sure, but we'll resolve our differences."

David Bick added: "I know Albion supporters are wondering exactly who this Jeremy Peace is and I would tell them he's an avid West Brom fan, who follows them home and away and has missed just one game out of the last 82 – a fact he wears like a badge of shame."

There would be no need for an Extraordinary General Meeting. As soon as Peace was satisfied he had the backing of enough shareholders to win power, he effectively claimed control. Directors Stapleton, John Wile, Hurst and McGing were swiftly moved on. Joe Brandrick, who had supported Peace, was kept on. Incoming chairman Peace rewarded Megson with a new three-year deal towards the end of the following month. Brendon Batson vacated his job as no 2 at the Professional Footballers Association to become Albion's managing director.

Mike O'Leary, regarded as a dynamic businessman and a skilled administrator, was appointed as the new chief executive. But, while Megson toasted his financial reward, Albion players were dealt a blow. On Wednesday, July 24, Peace and Batson arrived at the team's pre-season training base in Devon to deliver bad news. Thompson had installed a bonus scheme based on results rather than Premier League survival. Players would receive £5,000 each for a first-team appearance, £7,500 each per game if the team drew and £15,000 each for a victory.

The scheme was based on the fact that each player had received a bonus of about £4,000 for winning promotion. The majority of players were on low salaries by Premier League standards and Thompson's plan was to reward them through appearance money. There was a general feeling in the squad that their achievements were being undervalued, all the more so given what they knew had been on the table at Birmingham, who went up via the play-offs, and Wolves. Albion's scheme was scrapped in favour of a lump sum being shared out if they stayed up.

The news was broken to players in the Woodbury Park Hotel, near Exeter. The reaction was overwhelmingly bad, not least as their manager, who was forced to side with the board decision, was still wafting the ink dry on his contract. The players held an impromptu and surreal press conference in the hotel car park on the Friday afternoon. Hotel guests were driving in and out while a group of 20 or so briefed three journalists – one from the Birmingham Post, one from the Birmingham Mail and one from the Express & Star – as to their potential actions. This was a rebellion.

A senior player read a long letter: "We realise that the modern game is changing and that financial situations have affected some clubs. We know this must never happen at Albion. We feel the players have been portrayed as greedy and we want to show supporters this is not the case. We can assure the fans there will be no change in the level of effort that we will give to this club. However, the players feel that we deserve to share in the success that promotion has brought.

"For winning promotion, an Albion player received an average of £4,000. At Blues, each player received an average of £35,000 and it's well known Wolves players would have received between £50,000 and £100,000. Our original bonus scheme for this (2002-03) season was £15,000, with no change to basic wages, meaning Premiership performance-related bonuses and First Division wages. It is now clear the club is offering us First Division basic pay with First Division bonuses. That is the attitude and behaviour of a First Division club. We are all desperate to play for Albion in the Premiership and be successful but we feel we have to put our side of the argument across."

This was unprecedented territory. The gravity of the players' statement could not be underestimated. The fall-out meant that the following day's friendly against Torquay was in immediate doubt. The players were in no mood for football. The game was eventually played as scheduled and Jason Roberts scored the only goal. But it was more out of respect for the fans travelling from the Midlands.

Premier League fever was still all around. Supporters had yet to grasp the enormity of the stand-off. The frustration and contempt remained. Strike action stayed on the agenda. You can tell it was a dire situation. Even now, as he describes the events from a hotel near the M5, Johnson switches from the matey 'Meggo' to the more formal 'Gary' when speaking about this saga. "I remember that whole episode," he says. "Gary called us down to the restaurant. He, Brendon and Jeremy did this big speech, which didn't go down well. We got together and read a statement out to the media a few days later. I felt sorry for Gary. He was caught between his own job, the players, but also the board. It was not easy for him.

"I tried not to get involved too much because of my relationship with Gary. Not only was he my boss, but I knew him from Norwich. I remember he said to me one day after training: 'Thanks for not getting too involved.' He meant the strike action. I told him I was involved but that he needed to know that the players were close to going on strike and if they did go on strike, I would be joining them as I didn't want to alienate myself from the others.

"It wasn't Gary's fault, it wasn't our fault, it wasn't the new chairman's fault. It was a final dig from the old chairman. We were on this massive deal where we were getting paid £5,000 to basically lose. It was crazy. Don't get me wrong, we didn't get a fantastic bonus for getting promoted but then nobody had prepared for promotion. The club hadn't, the coaches hadn't. We, as players, certainly hadn't. Nothing was in place. It was like having a bonus for winning the Champions League: yes, very nice, but it's not going to happen, so no need for a club to worry about it.

"But it did happen. We were tipped to go straight back down. So what we got were peanuts and a holiday. That was nothing compared with what others got. Yet here we were and this blew up. Strikes weren't just mentioned, they were happening. We weren't going to play, simple as that. We were planning to go on strike. It was very much on our agenda. We had a friendly the next day and we had no intention of playing, although we relented on that one later.

And, of course, we were only a few weeks from playing the first Premier League game.

"We weren't going unless it got resolved. Looking back, it was a major thing. I took a back seat in it all. I was never money-motivated. Gary would say that whatever motivated you, whether it's money or love of the game, then do it. But some of the lads needed the bonus. They needed to live off their bonuses. In the end, they gave a bit, we gave a bit and everyone was happy. But, for a while, we were not playing. We were downing tools and strike action was a big possibility."

Somewhere within the inner sanctum of The Hawthorns, common sense eventually prevailed. Sanity restored, talk soon shifted from the potential picket lines to big-time football.

And so Albion entered the Premier League for the first time. This brought new quirks. Brand protection is a feature of the top flight, with all images owned by the Premier League. This led to amusing scenes during the pre-season when Albion press office staff felt obliged to ask fans to refrain from taking photos during friendlies. The stadium was rebranded with the names of the Premier League's affinity partners and new standardised shirt letterings and numbers were introduced. Backdrops bearing the brands of the Premier League's sponsors were introduced for media conferences before and after games. Press facilities needed upgrading to facilitate more print and broadcasting media. Albion had gone big time.

Johnson – Johnno to his team-mates, AJ to the fans – was becoming a leading character at Albion. The Wales international started his career at Norwich in 1992 and played 66 times before moving to Nottingham Forest. He was close to joining Birmingham during Trevor Francis's reign in a swap deal worth £2.2m, with Peter Ndlovu being used as a makeweight. The deal was pulled late on by Forest. By the time Johnson arrived at The Hawthorns, he was in his prime. Indeed, he was to make more appearances for Albion (131, seven goals) than for any of his other clubs.

It wasn't always plain sailing, though, not least as Johnson needed entertaining. "West Brom have always had a big fan base and good stadium," he said. "It was never an issue for me moving there. It was commutable. I was travelling with Phil Gilchrist but had to knock that on the head. Gilly's banter was terrible. We'd be travelling in as two lads and I'd be asking: 'Gilly, what did you get up to last night?' and his answer would be: 'Oh, I just watched Coronation Street.' I had to get out of there. Plus, he drove like Driving Miss Daisy.

"Oddly enough, he had a Porsche but it still took us about two hours. It felt like we'd leave at half six to get there at ten for training, whereas I'd leave at half nine and get us there for ten. Meggo hated Gilly's car, especially if we'd lost. He'd say: 'Look at these big-time Charlies in their sports cars.' He'd give Gilly some grief."

Gilchrist isn't the only one to be on the receiving end of the Johnson wit. When Johnno was in his pomp, nobody was safe. "After we got promoted, we played Bolton and Per Frandsen, a big lump, stood on me and I thought: 'Shit, I've broken my toe.' Because my boots were so tight, I didn't feel it. I scored the goal, bared my backside, which earned me a fine (Johnson had a bet with a steward that if he scored, he'd show his rear), and after the game the lads had internationals. I was due to go with Wales while the rest of the West Brom lads were off to Spain. I was gutted because I was meant to be going with Wales but I was injured at the time.

"I eventually agreed to go to Spain, which I thought was a waste of time for me, after Gary said I could be entertainment manager and could go to keep spirits up. So, basically, I went and lay next to the pitch with my leg raised, sat in the sun, watching them train. I was thinking: 'This is the life.' We were given a night off after a game of golf. "Me and Greegs (Sean Gregan), neither of us golfers, got up early and made sandwiches for the lads and got them a load of beers into a cool box. We loaded them into the buggy and drove around the course passing them to the lads. We got back to the clubhouse for about 7pm for dinner.

"By then, me and Greegs had had a few. I've got crutches and I'm too drunk to stand on them, so Greegs had to carry me back to my room. We all went out on the night and got back God knows what time. I was sharing with Derek, and Greegs was sharing with Mooro. Towards the morning, Mooro was woken up by a bang. He put the light on and couldn't see anything. He walked around the room, had a look in the wardrobes and bathroom and even looked through the eyehole. Nothing. He went to go back to bed and then heard more commotion coming from outside the room. He looked through the peephole again and there's this little Spanish porter trying, and struggling, to pick Greegs up.

"It was like something out of a comedy film. By now, it was about 6am, so Mooro came to our room and asked Derek and me to help because we had to be up for training in a just over an hour. We sat Greegs down on the bed. He was green in the face, eyes closed and just blowing. That's all he could do, puff his cheeks out and keep blowing. It was hilarious. The golden rule was that no matter how bad you were after a night out, you would always go to training. Gary Megson and Frank Burrows respected that. And we never broke that rule. So we took Greegs to training with us.

"It was hilarious. He was missing every ball which came near him. He couldn't control anything. The lads knew he'd had a few, so Deech (Danny Dichio) and Robbo (Paul Robinson) were pinging these balls over to him and they kept flopping over his foot or underneath. I was there at the side, waving at him. He was flicking Vs at me. Frank called us into a circle and said: 'Greegs, you're a f***ing disgrace,' then looked at me and said: 'It's your fault,' so I got the blame. Charming."

Gregan wasn't the only one to fall victim of Johnson's banter. "We went to Odense in 2004 and Gary Megson went home to try to sign some players," chuckles Johnson, hinting at more mischief. "He left Frank Burrows in charge. On the Sunday, we had a day to ourselves after we'd been on a long run. We had coffee at a bar called Froggys. I was with Robbo, Horse (Geoff Horsfield) and Greegs. After that, we had bottle of red wine and then another and some beers. Greegs had to go back as he was injured, so Robbo went with him but Horse and I went to a Chinese restaurant.

"We were there in our West Brom tracksuits, with some fans sat in the restaurant, too, I recall. We had our dinner and lost track of time. Horse then goes off somewhere and I'm sat at the table for about 20 minutes. So I'm assuming that Horse has done a runner. I just thought 'sod this' and legged it out of the door. As I opened the door, I saw Horse behind me – he'd been in the toilet. We got back to the hotel and had to have another meal. Frank had us. He clocked us and thought we were being disrespectful.

"The next day, we had a game and myself, Robbo and Greegs were on the bench but Horse was picked to play. Those beers caught up with him. It was red hot but Frank had the last laugh. He had us running for ages after the game.

We had to run and run and run. We got back to England and Gary gave us a bollocking and fined us a week's wages."

And what of Jonathan Greening, who was to join Albion in 2004 and leave as club captain in 2009? Time for 'Jono' (Greening) to look away. "He is one of the greatest people I've ever met in football but was also the thickest man in the world," insists Johnson. "In Portugal (pre-season tour, 2005), I remember Jono had just kept saying all these daft things and Nige (Pearson, assistant boss) eventually said: 'Jono, if I was you, I'd take a vow of silence.' Jono replied: 'Nah, I'm just not going to say anything.'

"It was hot in Portugal and he said: 'Well, you know why – it's because there's a different sun out here.' By then, Bryan Robson was our manager. He was one of the greatest managers I worked for. He treated me brilliantly when I was injured – a brilliant man. And we had respect for him. He called us in before our trip to Portugal and said: 'If any of you drink without permission, I'll fine you two weeks wages and you'll never play for the club again.' When a manager says that, you listen. Especially if it's Bryan Robson. He had our complete respect. He said he'd give us a date when we could go out. That was fine. Some of the lads played golf and they put a boat out for us. We got back to hotel and we met up with lads who had played golf.

"Trouble is, Jono was paralytic by this stage. He was chatting away to his missus on his phone and he just fell over, so we put him to bed. During that trip, we stayed in apartments, so there was me, Jono, Robbo and Horse in this one. It was chaos on that particular night. We put Jono to bed and the rest of us went out. I finally got back at 2am because I was knackered. I opened the door and there's Jono jumping up saying: 'Let's go out, let's go out.' Although I was ready for bed, we ended up going to this nightclub that didn't open till 3am. The queue was massive. They let us in and we didn't pay for a drink. That's all we needed. We left at 8.30am and were training at 10am.

"We went for breakfast and then went running. Truth is we were still drunk. After training, we slept until the afternoon session. I'd actually forgotten we'd even done the morning session. You could always rely on Jono. Then there was the time we went to Dubai under Bryan. We'd gone out and Jono went missing. No-one knew where he was. I checked the hotel and he wasn't there. His missus is on the phone going frantic and I even looked over the balcony in case he'd fallen off. Thankfully, he hadn't. We were ten floors up. We eventually found him by the road on a mound of Tarmac, just sat there smiling away in the baking hot sun, looking pleased with life and without a care in the world. That was Jono."

These days, Andy Johnson is looking for opportunities outside football. Working in a cotton mill will not be among the options, as he explains while lifting the lid on one of his stranger phobias. "I don't like cotton wool," he insists. "I've had to get used to it but I don't like the way it feels, I don't like the way it rips, I hate everything about cotton wool. One of the lads filled my pockets, socks, wash bag with the stuff. I couldn't touch anything.

"Horse had these trainers he loved, so I super-glued them to the wall because I knew he had something to do with it. But then I decided to get everybody, so I bought lots of mouse traps, set them up around my house in Worcestershire and caught lots of mice so I could bring them into training. I put these mice in their shoes, wash bags, pockets, in their cars. Russell Hoult, who we called Lassie because he smelt like a dog, got some in his car. Jono also had them stuck on his aerial and roof. He even drove home with them flapping in the wind, bless him."

Johnson, who left Albion in 2006, looks back on his spell there with pride. Some players impressed, some clearly frustrated him. "Hughsie was a good lad," he admits. "He was like a box of frogs or a bottle of pop that was shook up. Houltie was a brilliant goalkeeper. He was very old school. He was a good lad. Gilly too, and Larus (Sigurdsson). Proper blokes. Gave it everything whenever they played or trained.

"Greegs was someone I'd played against a few times before he came to Albion. He was a good footballer; strong, comfortable on the ball but not the most mobile. Mind you, he was the type you'd want next to you. Jason Koumas was one of the most naturally gifted players I'd seen. But I just question the kid's head. He used to drive me mad. I credit him with some of the grey hairs I've got today; a fantastically gifted player but lazy as hell. Meggo used to ask me to keep him in check. He'd never track runners and let people run off him but the kid was a genius.

"I was happy to do his running around and get him out of trouble. To this day, I maintain that if he'd sorted his head out, he could have played for Manchester United or Liverpool. I got the feeling he never had much desire or passion for the game. Same with Wales. He should have played every game for Wales. He had everything.

"Lee Marshall was a good lad. He was loopy and so laid-back – everything Meggo hated. We'd have to be in at ten and he'd rock in at 10.01. He'd chance it. He had that look about him. He looked like he was labouring but he wasn't. Meggo just didn't take to him. Ronnie Wallwork came with a big reputation. I think we were in a transitional period. We'd had this bunch of hard-grafting lads and Meggo brought in players to improve our 'football.' These players didn't match our hard work and that used to do his head in. They thought they could tap the ball around a bit. Meggo wasn't having that.

"The big one, of course, was Kanu. He was very laid-back. He was amazing with the ball. On his first day in training, we were just sat there watching him thinking: 'Oh my God, it's Kanu.' He had a heart of gold. You have to take your hat off to the chairman and the board. Earnie (Rob Earnshaw) was frustrating. He was a fantastic player but never seemed to fulfil the potential. It's always like there's more to come from him. I said when he signed he could be our version of Jermain Defoe. He scores goals but you never get a lot more from him. It's frustrating.

"Zoltan (Gera) was hilarious. He was a good, good player. He didn't speak much English when he arrived, so we kept teaching him bits and bobs. I remember him getting man-of-the-match just after he arrived and having to be interviewed by Sky. We were all watching, wondering whether he'd say (in the style of TV character Borat): 'My wife...she dead.' Thankfully, he never did.

"We had great characters throughout the team. You wouldn't have survived if you weren't. We were successful because we had a spirit about us. The thing that impresses me about West Brom is that the club have never moved backwards. The training ground gets better, the stadium gets better. It keeps improving. You have to credit the club for that. I'm proud that I was part of the first generation that got the club where they are now."

At the end of 2001-02, Gary Megson was unsurprisingly named the Nationwide Division One Manager of the Year, as chosen by his peers. Speaking at an awards ceremony, he paid tribute to his backroom staff. While promotion had been sweet, one piece of news particularly cheered him.

"I am delighted," he said. "You get these awards and they mean a great deal.

When it comes from your fellow managers, it's even more special. But I know what I get from my players and they deserve a mention, as do all the other people behind the scenes. Nick Worth, fitness coach Adie Stovell, coach Gary Shelton and Frank Burrows deserve praise, too. We won 31 games in the league and cup and yet the best result we had was when we discovered Frank Burrows had been given the all-clear after his cancer."

What a great likeness! Richard Sneekes admires artwork of himself (above) and, with locks somewhat clipped, oversees a coaching session in later years (top right). Right: Are you a footballer? Des Lyttle, who made 23 League appearances in 2001-02 (including substitute outings) as Albion stormed from nowhere to pip Wolves and win promotion for the first time in the 21st century, takes a quick breather during training.

We're up! Bob Taylor, one of the players electing to remain fully attired in the victors' dressing room, toasts Albion's 3-0 Wembley win over Port Vale in 1993. It was a campaign of success he spearheaded by becoming the first Albion player since Tony Brown in 1970-71 to reach the 30-goal mark in a season in all competitions. The 1990s hero hit 30 in the League alone. Below: The broad smile (eventually) says it all - SuperBob becomes a winner on the golf course as well.

The many faces of Andy Johnson......above, at a wedding; below left, among the honours at a Player of the Year function and, below, producing a playful snarl for the cameras in training.

Give 'em some hammer, 'Horse'! One of the big heroes of the last leg of Albion's 2004-05 Grea
Escape heroics, had no ordinary preparation for the decisive game, at home to Portsmouth. H
hadn't been a prolific scorer that season but came up with a huge goal when it really mattered.

Top: Darren Carter - proud to have been a Baggie after entering folklore across the 'patch' at Blues. Left and above: Simon Miotto, a reserve with a real tale to tell.

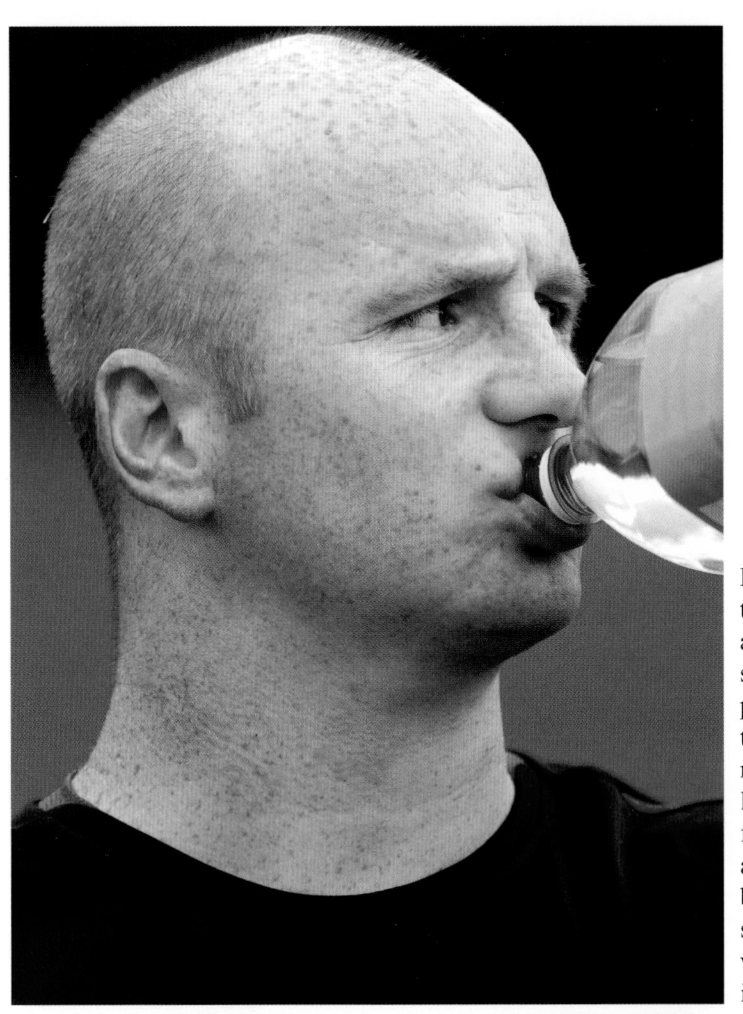

Below: Albion on tour in the Balkans and lining up against Hajduk Split in the summer of 2007. Visiting photographers didn't have to sit this far away but a request did go out for their lenses to be directed away from John Hartson (left) at the training ground. The burly Welsh striker was struggling for fitness and was involved before long in a life-or-death fight.

ame: Kevin Phillips.
ole: Predator.
ission: Scoring goals (especially against Wolves).
rike rate: Very, very high.

mirrorsport@mgn.co.uk DAILY MIRROR, Thursday,

Coca-Cola CHAMPIONSHIP | Play-off semi-final 2nd leg: West Brom 1 Wolves 0

WEST BROM WIN 4-2 ON AGGREGATE

Baggies can Phil the way to glory

KEV HAS FINAL SAY

By JAMES NURSEY

KEVIN PHILLIPS was West Brom's hero again last night as he headed them into a play-off final against Derby at the expense of arch-rivals Wolves.

The veteran former England striker had grabbed two goals in the first leg at Molineux to give Tony Mowbray's men a 3-2 advantage going into the return leg.

Albion dominated and deserved won through Phillips' 22nd of the campaign to move to within one victory of a swift return to the top-flight following last season's relegation.

THAT WAY TO FINAL: Phillips seals a trip to Wembley

BATTLING: Robinson and Keogh

KINGKEV: Phillips heads home for the Baggies to book a showdown with Derby

Jonathan Greening, the accidental comedian of Albion's dressing room, who emerged as a key component of the squad under various managers and was a high-class operator in midfield. So much so that Tony Mowbray made him hi captain before the thir of the club's quartet c promotion triumphs thi century. Greening, a bi part player in Europea finals while with two c his other clubs, admi leaving The Hawthor was a move he came regret.

Bob Taylor

"I thought: 'Why the hell have I done that...going from an FA Cup semi-final and potential promotion with Bolton to being back in a relegation battle?'"

EDWIN Van Der Sar backpedals frantically. He manages to touch the ball over the crossbar. But only just. Bob Taylor, stood some 50 yards away, has been denied his first Premier League goal in West Brom colours thanks to the Dutchman's agility and height. You can see why Sir Alex Ferguson was taking an interest in the Fulham goalkeeper. A lesser or shorter man would have been beaten. And Albion would have defeated Fulham 2-0 on August 31, 2002. It would have been Taylor's 'Beckham moment.'

Instead, Darren Moore's only goal becomes Albion's first Premier League winner while Taylor shrugs his shoulders and smiles. The striker's reaction is the same when he recalls the incident sat, nearly nine years later, in the foyer of the Holiday Inn a few hundred yards from Albion's training ground. He was to never score for the club in the top flight, although his status among the supporters is complete.

Taylor hit 113 goals in 324 appearances spread over two spells – 238 games (96 goals) between 1992 and 1998, with 17 goals in 86 games from 2000 to 2003. He is known as 'SuperBob' to Albion fans. But goal 114 was to never come. And that opportunity against Fulham – surprisingly not included on the 2002-03 season review DVD – remains fresh in his mind.

"It was unbelievable," he recalls. "We were 1-0 up and Gary Megson sent me on and told me to hold the ball, not do anything daft. Van Der Sar was on the edge of the box and booted the ball straight to me. I was in the centre circle and noticed him out of position. I could hear the crowd shouting 'shoot, shoot'...then I remembered what the gaffer had said. I thought: 'Bollocks, I'm having this.' I hit it and remember the shot having a bit of draw on it, like a good golf shot. I thought: 'It's going in, it's going in' but he touched it. I think it would have beaten him had I not delayed it and no other keeper would have got it. The manager said afterwards that had I scored, I could have hung my boots up there and then. He's right."

Retirement then might not have been a bad end to his Albion career. Yet Taylor's reputation was secured over the ten years he spent with the club. Born in County Durham, he was signed by Bobby Gould in 1992 from Bristol City for £300,000 – small change left over from Don Goodman's move to Sunderland a few weeks earlier. During his first spell at Albion, Taylor played for a team who evolved to no more than perennial second-tier strugglers. But, in their promotion from the Second Division to the First Division in 1992-93, he scored 37 goals. Back then, the Baggies were a long way from the Premier League.

Taylor was Bolton-bound in July, 1998. He joined them for a cut-price £90,000, having been offered just a one-year deal by Albion during his final 12 months with them. He returned to The Hawthorns in March, 2000; one of five players arriving on transfer deadline day, signed by Gary Megson. The prize he sacrificed was an FA Cup semi-final.

Taylor recalls: "The whole thing was a bit topsy-turvy. People were asking me if I would go back and, hand-on-my-heart, I didn't think I would. I was at Bolton, things were going well and we were preparing for the semi against Aston Villa. Big Sam (Allardyce) had taken over and, as with all managers, they have their own ideas. For me, it wasn't to be and, as it turns out, Gary Megson and Sam had the same agent. So, whether they had a chat about Bolton helping Albion out, I don't know.

"We'd just done a photo shoot with the Bolton mascot Lofty the Lion, the players and the FA Cup. We were meeting the press before the semi-final like all clubs and players do. I got a phone call from Mike Phelan, who is good mates with Gary Megson, and it went from there. It was merely a call and the silly thing was I said yes straightaway. I didn't think about what he'd said, which is what I should have done. Then I thought: 'Why the hell have I done that? I'm going from an FA Cup semi-final and potential promotion with Bolton to being back in a relegation battle.'

"But it was the last year of my contract and I didn't know where I was going to go from there. I was 33. Who wants an old striker? So we did the deal and I got a contract for three and a half years after they only wanted to offer me a year when I'd been coming to the end of my first spell. It was everything I wanted, plus I was promised a testimonial. You frequently get told to never go back if you've been successful. Yet, lo and behold, there I was, one of five new players."

The Baggies boss was certainly impressed. "He (Bob) has looked after himself, is very fit and loves to train," Megson told the media. "He always puts a great deal of effort into his game and is a credit to himself. I actually think he looks better now than when I was watching him for Norwich maybe five years ago."

Taylor was afforded no settling-in period. The Hawthorns was no honeymooners' paradise in March, 2000. Albion's position was dire. Relegation to the third tier was a distinct possibility. The striker's return came with considerable pressure. Expectation was overwhelming. "A fan came up to me and said: 'The Messiah has returned – we'll be ok.' There I was thinking: 'Oh God, is everyone thinking that?' Coming from the club I had already had success with, to find myself back at that level was quite a shock. And then I remember we played Ipswich and Lee Hughes got injured. He damaged his kneecap. We were down to basically myself and Jimmy Quinn filling in up front.

"Even more pressure came my way through being the only out-and-out striker. It went from there and to score the goals that kept us up was a big plus for me and cemented the love I had for the club. The fans are the heart of West Brom. They always gave me a chance, whatever my form was like. If you've been a player at a club for ten years, there is something going on – an affinity, a feeling for the place. Yes, we were in the bottom three and, to be honest, I'd been there before with Albion. It was before the transfer deadline when I rejoined them. Albion needed someone and now, when I reflect on it years later, I could never have imagined what it would lead to."

August, 2011 is not a civil period. Unrest has returned to our streets. London, Birmingham, Wolverhampton, Manchester and Bristol have been hit. As has West Bromwich. In the High Street, a few miles from where we're sat, the remains of burned-out vehicles are being removed. Spurs v Everton has been called off. White Hart Lane is in a designated crime scene area. Albion against Manchester United, scheduled for the coming Sunday, remains on. United win

2-1 thanks to a Steven Reid own goal. Taylor reflects on a pitched battle of another sort.

Andy Johnson has already given his account of the Battle of Bramall Lane. Taylor brings a different perspective. Sat on the bench for the first half, he had a passive view of the encounter before going on a second-half substitute for Adam Chambers. "It was kicking off when we were warming up on the touchline," he reveals. "We were getting abuse from the fans long before anything happened on the pitch. At Bramall Lane, one of the stands drops below pitch level, so you're sat very low down and the view probably isn't the best.

"The stewards wouldn't let us move elsewhere because the dug-out was also quite low, so we had to stay where we were and it escalated from there. There was an edge to that day. Gary Megson had us up late for a meeting the night before. It was his neck of the woods. We knew what the game meant to him because he was such a Sheffield Wednesday man. He and Neil Warnock didn't get on. That much was clear. It started off as a decent game. Their goalkeeper (Simon Tracey) got sent off for a hand-ball outside the box. Fair enough, it happens.

"Dobes (Scott Dobie) scored and then it all blew up in the second half. Danny Dichio had been up against Keith Curle and, sat on the bench, I could hear things being shouted from the United bench every time Deech had the ball near Curle. He was bullying Curle in a football sense and they didn't like it. The crowd were getting agitated. Gary was having a go at Neil Warnock. Frank Burrows was getting involved.

"When I went on for Adam, I remember him walking up the tunnel and getting all the monkey chants from their fans. Frank again went mad and there was another scuffle. I went on just after Derek scored his wonder goal, then it got worse. Funnily enough, I wasn't aware of Andy Johnson's dispute with Georges Santos. Everyone knew about Warnock and Megson but I didn't know about Johnno and Georges and what had gone on before.

"When I came back to Albion, Georges also signed that day and was one of the first guys I met. He was a lovely, lovely guy – a softly-spoken Frenchman, who went around doing his job. I had no idea he had that in him. Their two subs went on (Patrick Suffo and Santos) and, within a minute or so, they're both leaving the pitch. The ball got squared to Johnno. I'm in the middle of the pitch and all I see is both Johnno and Georges going for it. Georges seemed to win the ball and Johnno did a triple somersault in the air. I thought it was a good, fair challenge. I was looking down the line. It wasn't until I saw the pictures in the paper the next day that I realised and thought: 'Oh my God.'

"The next thing I see is Derek McInnes on the floor courtesy of Suffo. From the corner of my eye, I saw Mooro, Big Dave, running up from our half. He's a born-again Christian but he was legging it up yelling: 'Let me at him, let me at him.' Behind that, I can see Russell Hoult chasing after Mooro, trying to stop him, and one of their players also trying to hold Mooro back. I got hold of Suffo and told him to go off but I wasn't thinking. He could have done me."

Taylor, glad not to have his facial features rearranged, recalls the confusion which followed. "Poor Eddie Wolstenholme was the referee and was clueless as to what was going on. By now, it's 11 versus eight, we're 2-0 up and Dobes scores with another tap-in. I notice Michael Brown walk off the pitch as they're about to re-start the game. I pointed it out and the ref said: 'Don't worry. My fourth official has seen it.' Now it's 11 versus seven and Rob Ullathorne goes down injured, too. I'm convinced there was nothing wrong with him. We could hear them (the United bench) telling him to fall. The referee blew his whistle and said: 'Game abandoned.'

"In the dressing room, we were told to shower, say nothing and get straight on the bus. We ended up in the car park on the bus for what seemed like another hour because people were upstairs trying to work out what was going on and what would happen. We had to wait a few days for the result to be confirmed but what a game that was! You could watch football all of your life and never see that again. We had to make sense of what had gone on. There was stuff going on on the pitch, on the touchline and even in the tunnel. We were never going to replay it. How would we replay it? Seven versus 11? In my opinion, they got off very, very lightly. Something should have been done against them. But, for whatever reason, it wasn't."

The Baggies were awarded three points on the following Thursday. On the Friday, they travelled to Nottingham.

Albion were to famously win promotion in 2002. Taylor remembers with fondness and remarkable clarity the games which followed the one at Sheffield. Albion were chewing at the lead Wolves had at the top of the table. The shift of power was well under way. "I was sub again at Forest," he said. "It was one of the dullest games I can remember; a 0-0 with little going for it. I got a shout to go on in the last few minutes.

"We get a free-kick. Clem (Neil Clement) strikes it well. The keeper didn't collect it properly and, as a striker, you're told to spin for any knock-downs. Luckily for me, I just had to dive in and stick it in. So we made it six points from two days. We had the weekend off and waited to see what Wolves would do. They could only draw with Norwich, so we drew nearer.

"I started in that game a few weeks later at Highfield Road and we really went for Coventry. Lee (Hughes) had a few shots for them but nothing went for them and we stamped out their threats. I got another tap-in and we came away with the win. Just after that, we had Rotherham. We got a corner, I jumped with goalkeeper Mike Pollitt and, as he caught the ball, my finger caught in his jersey. I dislocated my finger and had a spiral fracture. I came off for treatment, got it strapped up, went back on and got a cracking goal. Then they equalised and we lost Phil Gilchrist, who fell awkwardly and dislocated his shoulder.

"We then go up the pitch and score the goal that never was. Jordao's shot was about two yards over the line. That decision (not to give the goal) kept Rotherham up and Crewe went down instead. Had we won that game, we might not have needed to win the Bradford or Palace games."

Albion prepared for Bradford away, knowing their destiny was in their own hands. The Baggies had missed eight penalties out of 11. From somewhere, they required another volunteer, as Taylor explains: "I went for x-rays (in the days before) and the worrying scenario for me was that my hand might need to be wired up. Had that happened, my season would have been over. Luckily for me, I just needed a special plastic guard.

"At Bradford, I should have had a hat-trick. Their keeper Alan Combe played well but I missed a few. He pulled off some great saves from Trevor Benjamin, too. Then, in the last few minutes, Derek sends a ball over the top and I tangled with Myers. People ask whether I dived. I didn't dive. He made contact with my knee. As a striker, you're told that if there's any contact, you go down. But I like to think I might have scored had I got past him.

"After cheering the decision, everyone went silent. It's as if everyone in the away end suddenly remembered we'd missed eight out of 11 penalties that season. I had missed the first of those. I was wondering: 'Right, who's taking this one?' I needed treatment and thought: 'There's no way I'm taking it.' What we didn't know is that we had one guy, who has had a cracking season who takes penalties for his country but hadn't bothered to tell us. Igor Balis. I'd taken one, Dobes, Clem....we'd all had a go. Igor used to come into the dressing room, train and then go home. He'd barely speak until, that one day, he said: 'Oh yes, I take penalties.' All of us are like: 'Igor, why didn't you tell us earlier?'"

Balis's revelation should have come as no surprise to those with a decent memory. In August, 2001, Albion took on Cambridge in the first round of the Worthington Cup. The game went to penalties following a 1-1 draw, with the Slovakian converting a convincing and, ultimately, decisive kick. By the time Albion reached Valley Parade, the obvious takers had all fluffed opportunities. So Balis stepped up as the latest protagonist.

Watch YouTube clips and Scott Dobie walks across the pitch, looking away. So he might. All good stories are played out to drama and its timing. And so Balis's moment was delayed. "I'd been getting treatment, so it must have been a good four or five minutes before he took it," adds Taylor. "But it turned out to be one of the best penalties I've ever seen. Right into the bottom corner. Everyone went mad. The whole stadium was boinging. There were Albion fans everywhere."

Wolves faced a trip to Sheffield Wednesday in their final game. Albion hosted Trevor Francis's Crystal Palace side. Not everybody was convinced of Albion's credentials to complete the job. Palace striker Clinton Morrison promised to help his Republic of Ireland international team-mate Mark Kennedy, who was then playing for Wolves. He remarked: "Mark was asking me to do him a favour and I don't really like West Brom. None of the lads in the Irish squad do. I hope Wolves go up and we can show everyone we are still a good side by helping them do it." Gary Megson's supply of Blu Tac was dwindling.....

"For some reason, Clinton Morrison wanted to humiliate us," said Taylor. "He'd come out with some rubbish during the week and the manager stuck the clippings on the board. Mooro put Morrison in his place before the game. He was heading off to Japan and Korea with Ireland for the World Cup and Mooro just went over, glared at him and said: 'Do you want to go to the World Cup or not?' Mooro didn't need to say any more. He just glared and that was it. Morrison barely touched the ball.

"Before the game, Megson was giving a team talk as usual. He said: 'Go out there and give it your best...but don't just do it for yourself, do it also for these people.' With that, the door opened and all the kids and women came in. 'Do it for these,' he said. It was great management. It was emotional. We went out and finished the job.

"Mooro got the first and I scored the second. Oddly, Derek McInnes had told me I would score a goal that would take us to the Premier League. Clem hit the worst free-kick of the season, yet the keeper made a mess of it. I followed it in and scored. My other memory was being substituted. Just before the end, Scott Dobie was running through one-on-one with the keeper. Everyone in the ground was willing him to score... everyone apart from me. I was like: 'Please don't score, please don't score.' Yes, I was being selfish. I wanted that milestone. Mind you, if we'd won 3-0, it would still have been fantastic. I was going to wear the blue and white striped shirt in the Premier League and that's all that mattered. I can never have imagined being there two years earlier. That day was also my daughter Chantelle's birthday, so it was extra special for me."

The joy didn't last. Albion's summer was ripped apart by in-fighting. Chairman Paul Thompson went, as did chief executive John Wile, vice-chairman Clive Stapleton and director Barry Hurst. In came Jeremy Peace, new managing director Brendon Batson and chief executive Mike O'Leary. Albion were Premier League-bound but it was a rocky road that close season.

As the squad numbers were released, Taylor was not pleased to find himself 'demoted' from no 9 to 15. Danny Dichio was elevated to the traditional centre-forward's number. Was it the beginning of the end? Seemingly so. Taylor, brought up long before the Premier League and its quirks were established, felt overwhelming disappointment. "Everyone asks you where you play and you reply. 'Striker! Oh, so you're a no 9?'" he said. "It's the number everyone associates with strikers, especially at Albion. I was mentioned with Astle, Allen, Regis and, for me, it was an absolute honour and privilege. I didn't want that number taken off me so, when you see someone else get it, you know you're not going to figure much. It had always been my number."

A shirt number is, at best, symbolic. It can also be irrelevant. Yet Taylor's hunch proved correct. He was to start just once in the opening half of that season, in the 2-0 home defeat against Blackburn. He appeared off the bench twice. Albion were struggling and Megson was taking measures to stop the rot. Taylor might have been an icon among the fans but the manager was in no mood to take any notice of public perception.

The no 15 for the 2002-03 season remembers where it all went wrong and gave an insight into Megson's psychological traits. "We never had words in so much that he pulled me into an office. That simply never happened. But you have to understand that Gary had to know everything. He had to know what was happening in the dressing room, outside the dressing room, even behind the scenes. So he brought in people who were close to him. The physio would listen to your chats and just tell him bits or bobs, give him the vibes. Others did the same. Gary fell out with people. During that season, he fell out with Jason Roberts, Danny Dichio, Lee Marshall. Lee barely played again after that.

"When you're not playing, you get angry and wonder why. We were struggling, we weren't scoring and he never ever gave me a chance. He always thought I was too old or didn't have the legs. Football isn't like that. Yes, I was getting on but I could hold the ball up, score goals, bring others into play. I got the hump, although I was always for the team. The press were asking questions, as were fans on phone-ins and in fanzines. Maybe he thought I was fuelling that. I remember going to Newcastle. We were on the coach when the team was read out. I wasn't in it. I wasn't even on the bench. It was the same old faces in front of me. I thought I deserved a chance.

"I was sat there tapping a pen on the table when Frank Burrows turned round and had a right go at me. He spoke to me like I was a kid. I lost patience and said: 'Who do you think you're talking to? I'm not 18.' He went mental and started yelling but I refused to back down. Gary Megson walked over, looked at Frank and said: 'Just leave him be.' After that, I was put in the reserves, along with Marshy and the others."

'Marshy,' Lee Marshall to be exact, was a curious case. Signed from Leicester for £700,000, the Islington-born midfielder was to score the club's first Premier League goal. He was to make just two more appearances after that game at St James' Park on October 5, 2002. He was to play only 11 games for Albion. Such was the ferocity of the Marshall-Megson fall-out that one journalist was admonished for raising the subject of the player's absence during a routine press conference.

Innuendo remains to this day as to the background. Urban myth suggests Marshall made hurtful comments to Frank Burrows when he was substituted against Chelsea. There were reports Marshall nutmegged Megson during a training session and mocked his manager as he did so. Untrue. There were even worse allegations. All false. Taylor laughs off the stories before giving his version.

"A few players fell out with the manager but the main outcasts were myself and Marshy," he continued. "None of those rumours were true. Basically, Marshy has a son who, at the time, was living somewhere down south. He went down to see him but, instead of coming back on Sunday night, he sometimes came back on Monday morning. Once, he got stuck in traffic and was basically an hour and a half late. Megson just pointed at where the kids were due to train and told Marshy to go over there work with them. He got a fine of about 20 per cent of his week's wage but apologised for what he'd done.

"Then it got worse. Megson had this thing where he wanted players to do weights a couple of mornings a week. Marshy was one of them. Again, he came in late but this time by literally a minute or so. Most people would have said: 'Ok, you're here, don't push your luck.' But, instead of overlooking it, the fitness coach Adie Stovell told the manager. So Marshy got another white envelope. He looked at it and read it out to us. The fine was 40 per cent of his weekly wage, for being a minute late. This after getting a 20 per cent fine for being an hour and a half late. Marshy just exploded.

"Our dressing room then was next to the staff's dressing room. Marshy stormed into theirs when Megson was having a soak. They started yelling at each other, with Megson still in the bath. We could hear them. Marshy basically told him he'd get the PFA involved. So that's what happened."

Marshall's days were numbered. Reports at the time, both nationally and locally, continued to suggest Megson was unwilling to play certain players, notably Marshall, no matter what. The manager denied the allegations. Speaking after Albion's defeat to West Ham in February, 2003, he said: "Rumours do get started but there is no player here we pay that I would say isn't part of our plans. I expect all players to be doing their very best for West Brom and doing all they can to get into the starting line-up. Nobody is ever out of contention. Every player we hire is in there with a chance of playing."

Megson also warned individuals with personal agendas to stop undermining his side's survival chances. He did not reveal names but hinted that certain people associated with the club were 'pleased' by the West Ham defeat. "I hope everybody within the organisation of West Bromwich Albion is committed to the cause," he said. "I hope there is nobody here who was pleased with that result."

Marshall never played for the club again. Speaking in March, 2003, he told the Birmingham Mail: "We had a fall-out and the manager told me I would never play for Albion again. I made a mistake but it was something I thought two men could sort out. I have been ignored and left to train with the kids. Fans ask me why I am not playing and I tell them about my row with the gaffer. A lot of them say they just want to see me playing in a West Brom shirt but I can't see it happening. Certainly, the supporters need to be told what is going on."

The Marshall saga was brought up by fans during a Supporters Club forum with Jeremy Peace and directors Brendon Batson and Mike O'Leary. MD Batson made it clear the board would not be interfering. "In terms of my getting involved, it is not an issue between the manager and the chairman," he said. "A manager has to manage the dressing room. As to what will happen in the future, that will come in the close season. If you start to undermine the person who is running that side of the club, you will have a problem. You will lose the manager."

Come summer, 2003, that stance changed. Megson was coming under intense pressure from Jeremy Peace. The chairman was keen to wrestle back some of the power he felt his manager was wielding at the club. He had become unsettled and alarmed during a shareholders' meeting by the growing disenchantment supporters expressed over Megson's style of management.

A group of players voiced their own concerns to the board after a no-holds-barred dressing-down following the final game of 2002-03. Among Peace's requests – by 'requests,' perhaps read demands – was one that Marshall be integrated back into the manager's first-team plans. The player was left confused when Megson showed little inclination to comply with his chairman's wishes. "I'm baffled by all of this," he said. "I never said I wanted to leave West Brom and hope to remain here but I have to admit I thought my future lay elsewhere. The manager told me I would never play for him again while he was in charge, so I'm surprised by this.

"I am happy to wipe the slate clean. It was frustrating to watch the team slip down the division knowing I had no chance of helping out. I doubt I will ever be the manager's best friend but these things go on in football. This is between the chairman and manager but if the chairman wants me to play, I will play. After all, the club pay my wages. If the manager doesn't want me, I don't know where this will end. But while I want to stay at West Brom, I don't want to be sat in the reserves for two years. The last year has been a nightmare but I am willing to stay with West Brom and play a part in their future."

Marshall did get some first-team action. He and transfer-listed striker Jason Roberts played on the left and right wings respectively in the 2-1 win against local team B1909 in the opening game of Albion's 2003 Danish tour. Yet Marshall never returned to competitive action for Albion. During a loan spell with Hull City, he suffered a badly broken leg. The injury forced him to retire in July 2005, aged 26.

Albion found themselves in new territory as the transfer window was introduced to the Premier League. No longer was it open house up to deadline day in late March. Instead, after August, only a period from January 1-31 was handed over to clubs to bring in new players. Back in the winter of 2002-03, Albion struggled with the concept. Macedonia skipper Artim Sakiri was close to joining the club from CSKA Sofia, with Tottenham's Tim Sherwood also targeted. Sakiri's deal never materialised. His time would come several months later. Sherwood ended up moving to Portsmouth.

Valencia's Salva Ballesta, another name on the Baggies' list, moved to Bolton to join his pal Ivan Campo, while US international Tony Sanneh, of German club Nurnberg, also rejected a move to B71. Spanish defender Roberto Rios claimed he was in no fit state to move to Albion. He opted for retirement. Nobody was rushing to The Hawthorns. Nobody, apart from Ife Udeze, who arrived on loan from PAOK Salonika. His move was ill-fated from the start. The press conference to unveil the left-back was temporarily held up while one journalist enquired about the player's health. Udeze was apparently suffering from a fever. He was frenzied, agitated, perspiring, tremoring. He continued to answer questions, albeit uneasily. Perhaps it was an omen.

On March 1, he made a desperate mistake in the eighth minute of the game against Southampton. He was convinced the ball had rolled out of play for a throw-in and, in protesting to the linesman, allowed Paul Telfer to cross. Brett Ormerod passed to James Beattie, who scored. Megson was still seething when he withdrew Udeze 17 minutes later. The manager made it clear where the blame lay for the 1-0 defeat. "What Udeze did – turn round, look at the linesman and let Telfer knock the ball in – has no place on a Premiership football field," he raged. "It was a great strike by Beattie but he shouldn't have been allowed it. That really annoyed me and it was entirely the reason why he came off." Udeze was to make four more starts for the club before returning to Greece.

Albion's first season in the top flight for 16 years, although unsuccessful, gave an insight into where the club fitted into the rebranded Premier League money machine. Turnover reflected the increased revenue from TV and increased to £28.4m. From this, a profit of £5.7m was made, with an increased dividend of £1.70 per share paid to shareholders. Jeremy Peace increased his shareholding to 50 per cent, thereby effectively assuming control. Shareholders were concerned about the impact this would have, with the loss of influence of other shareholders. Brendon Batson was made redundant from his managing director role. Chief executive Mike O'Leary would stand down the following year. Only Joe Brandrick remained of the old guard. Relations with shareholders cooled.

The 1968 FA Cup winning manager Alan Ashman passed away on November 30, 2002. His death was followed by that of Sir Bert Millichip, the former Albion and long-serving Football Association chairman. The season didn't end on a happy note for Gary Megson or his players. The Baggies were relegated – a 2-1 victory at bottom-placed Sunderland not enough to grant them a stay of execution. They finished 19th.

Bob Taylor had also given up hope of receiving a Christmas card from the Megson household. Albion's form was not improving. In 29 games after his last appearance, the Baggies collected just 16 points and scored 22 goals. Only eight of those were from strikers. In one six-game spell between February and April, Albion scored once. Taylor, meanwhile, was on reserve-team duty.

Local media clamoured for his return, supporters asked questions during football phone-ins. The Fanzine Grorty Dick criticised Megson's stubbornness. Such was the robust nature of their editorial stance that sellers and writers were subjected to taunts and abuse from fans backing the manager's standpoint. Taylor shows unease as he recalls the last few months of his Albion career. His contract was running out but the nature of his final hurrah still grates.

"It was my testimonial year," he said. "Gary Megson was invited to many of the dos I had. He never showed once. He didn't bother with the Player of the Year night. Apparently, he was scouting." Worse was to follow. Not only was Taylor bowing out of the club he loved, he was about to be used as part of what he saw as a point-making exercise. For the first time, he now goes public on those painful weeks.

"Two weeks before the end of the season, we played our final reserve game," he recalls. "It was to be my final game for the club – a 2-1 win against Villa and I scored. After the game [on April 28], I came into training next day as normal. The last game of the season was against Newcastle [May 11] but I got hauled into the staff room by Frank (Burrows). The manager was away scouting, again. Frank said: 'Right, Bob, that's it. Your season is over. You don't have to worry about coming in again. Just stay at home.' I asked why and he said it was too far for me to travel. I lived in Lichfield, for God's sake, 20 minutes from the training ground.

"I said: 'No way. This is a f***ing disgrace. I'll come in and keep working, whether it's with the kids or on my own. He told me I was never going to play with the first team again, so to not bother. I felt it was a joke, more so that he (Megson) got Frank to do it. So I spent the next few weeks training with a few kids or on my own. I was nowhere near the level of fitness needed for Premier League football. I trained but I had no intensity. Sometimes, there were just four people training as many had already broken up. It was boring, it was pathetic but I continued as I was still a club employee and, besides, I wasn't going to let him beat me.

"That final game was on a Sunday. On the Saturday, I trained in the morning and got home. I remember there was a rugby game on and, just as I opened a beer, I got a phone call from Alan Crawford, who was first-team coach. He said: 'The manager would like you to report for a pre-match meal tomorrow at the Village Hotel in Dudley.' I couldn't believe it. I told him I was in no condition to play football as I hadn't been allowed to train with the first team.

I wasn't sharp enough or fit enough and I wasn't in the right frame of mind. Alan said it was about giving me a big send-off before my testimonial and to say goodbye before the game."

Conspiracy or not, Taylor raises the obvious question as to why he should be granted permission to break up, only to be brought back for one final game. Yet Taylor was spared the indignity of being forced to complete a game he was ill-prepared for – albeit by a quirk of fate. "I got injured in that game," added Taylor. "Had I not been hurt, I'm convinced he would have kept me on for the duration to make me look a fool. I should have said no straightaway but I let my heart rule my head.

"Two days after that was my testimonial match, so I wanted to say bye to the fans at a proper game and part of me thought: 'I want to score against Newcastle and shove it up his arse.' But I went up for a ball, landed awkwardly and collided with a Newcastle player, so my leg bent the wrong way. That was it. Game over. If you look at the DVD, you can see him (Megson) milking it, telling Andy Johnson: 'Hey, go and tell Bob to give everyone a clap.' It was all crap. I was in tears. It was my last game for Albion and I'd got injured in a game I shouldn't have played in."

The testimonial was played on May 13. An Albion side beat a Bryan Robson All-Stars XI 7-2. Taylor started the game limping and with a heavily-strapped knee. He ended the match in goal. Bryan and Gary Robson played, as did Cyrille Regis, Don Goodman, John Trewick, Wayne Fereday, Richard Sneekes and even Steve Bull. Assistant kit-man Andy Tiernan and club chaplain Ken Hipkiss appeared, too. Gary Megson and Frank Burrows did not.

Taylor was not too bothered by the absentees. But he paid tribute to the Robson brothers, who attended despite the death of their father just days earlier. "Gary Robson was, and is, one of my best mates and Bryan kindly offered to put a team together," he continued. "They didn't want to cancel and we had a minute's silence before the game which was brilliantly observed. His mum and sister were at the game too, all so my testimonial could be played. For that, I'll always be grateful.

"In a way, I'm glad Gary Megson didn't turn up. I didn't want him there. The day after the Newcastle game, we all went in. I went to see him and said it had been an absolute pleasure, which it had because I was thinking about the three years as a whole, not him as a person. I shook his hand and he just said: 'You were never brought back to this club to do what you did.' That's all he said. I've no idea if it was meant as a dig, a back-handed compliment or what.

"I look back now and, as a manager of this football club – my football club, which I feel part of – you cannot knock what he did. He was the right man and was what the place needed. Yet the way he treated me wasn't professional. As a manager, Gary Megson did a job for this club. But, as a person, he's a shithouse."

Taylor reflects on his time at Albion in the same way as Mancunian Tony Brown, French Guiana-born Cyrille Regis and the late Jeff Astle, of Nottinghamshire. Ask the Easington-born Taylor about the club and he refers to 'we' and 'us.' "The two spells are like two halves of football," he added. "They were never going to be the same. The first half was about me coming to a club where I'd never been heard of. I needed to establish myself, win the fans over and be a part of something like promotion. We never got relegated back then but always struggled.

"The three and a half years when I came back were a progression. We were evolving. I also worked for one manager in those three years or so, as opposed to working for six in the first spell, not to mention all the caretaker managers. The new chairman wanted to make changes and Gary embraced that when he first arrived. It had grown stale. Paul Thompson changed that, whittled out people he felt weren't taking things forward. The club were changing and I'm glad I was able to be part of that."

A decade on, Taylor has fond memories of his 2000-03 team-mates. "I have some great memories. I really don't know where to begin," he smiles. "Greegs (Sean Gregan) I remember well. I always had a running battle with him when he was at Preston. Then he joined us and I think he struggled with the physical side at times but he was a strong character. Derek McInnes was a great captain. He was a leader but more than that. He was a mate. If anything happened, he'd be there looking after you.

"Mooro was a softly-spoken Christian, a lovely lad. And then you see him on the pitch and wonder if it's the same bloke. Appy (Michael Appleton) was gung-ho, loved getting stuck in. I was right next to him when he had that sad accident with Des Lyttle and his knee went. It was just unfortunate they collided. That was the day his career ended, even though he fought so hard to get it back. He was a big loss and was in a similar vein to Derek.

"Lee Hughes was a great finisher. A natural in terms of scoring goals. Off the pitch, he was easily led. When the new BMW X5 came out, Ruel Fox had one on order for months. Foxy came in to training the day he got it and the next thing you see is Hughesie pulling in behind him with the same car. Foxy was gutted.

"Then there was Igor, who didn't say anything. He'd do his training and go. It was a chore to get him out. Mind you, once he got a few vodkas in him, he'd be well away and would open up. He was a superb player for us. We had good people at the club. It was a great time."

Simon Miotto

"I won a West Brom shirt in the 1970s. I'd been a schoolteacher until my mid-20s, training on a dusty pitch in Italy, yet here I was being introduced to thousands of Albion supporters stood in front of the town hall."

WHO is Simon Miotto? A good question because he never played a single senior game for West Bromwich Albion. He appeared only in half a friendly and a couple of reserve games. He's a Tasmanian, of half-Italian descent, who was to become one of the closest players to Gary Megson after signing in 2003-04. But there is more to this story. So here's the tale of a promotion that's often forgotten, as told by an Albion player few will remember. Why not...?

All this starts in the late 1970s, with a raffle in Tasmania, an island some 150 miles south of the Australian mainland. A young Simon Miotto wins a WBA shirt. A coincidence. The triple-barrelled name of the club makes an impression. The youngster, born to an Italian father and to a half-English/half-Australian mother, was pursuing his own dream. By 1990, he was a triple jumper. The Commonwealth Games beckoned. Young Miotto had aspirations of representing Australia in the Games at Auckland. He was their no 2 triple jumper. Then his ankle gave way. He spent the summer of 1990 watching a sporting event of a different nature. We take up the story when I catch up with him at the Malmaison Hotel in the bowels of Birmingham's Mailbox.

"I remember the lettering WBA but at the time thought nothing of it," he recalls. "I grew up, went to school, loved sport and played football as a left-winger but went into track and field. I was the silver medallist in the under-20 triple jump nationals and was in line to go for the Commonwealth Games trials in 1990 but got injured. That was pretty devastating, so I went to Italy instead for the World Cup. The Italian side of me drew me to football. Without that, I might not have got interested at all.

"It was to have a massive effect on me. I'd always loved Italy, I'd always wanted to be an international footballer but everyone was saying: 'You're too late, you're too old.' My dad had been ill. He'd had cancer but was making progress. Football has always been in my blood. I was a mad Juventus fan, I used to wear an Italian shirt under whichever club shirt I was wearing. It was a reminder to me of my Italian heritage and love of the game. Because of my late start, I needed reminding why I came to the other side of the world. Every game was going to be important to me. I knew I could very quickly be a fan, not a footballer.

"At the World Cup, we went to watch the first game. Seeing the Italian goalkeeper Walter Zenga playing was special. Back then, you had two TV channels in Tasmania and you didn't get the same exposure to football as now. But there I was in Italy, cheering on my father's nation. That was a special time.

"I was inspired by that World Cup. Dino Zoff was 40 when he won it in 1982. I was 21 by 1990. I thought if I started then, perhaps I could be a professional footballer – maybe only an average one – for 17 or so years. I was qualified as a teacher in Tasmania at the primary school I went to as a kid. But I knew the only way I could chase this dream was to leave the teaching profession and just train and train and train, often during the night. Sometimes, I'd come home from visiting my dad in hospital, go for a 5km run and then go out on to the strip outside my house, with the help of a lamp post so I could see. I'd throw the ball against a wall and practice my handling.

"My house was near a golf course and the casino. The taxi drivers in that area used to talk about it for years after I signed professional: 'Do you remember that man who used to jump on a ball during the night outside his house?' After Dad passed away, I stayed with Mum for a few years before I arrived in Italy in '94 to pursue my dream. That was an interesting experience. I used to ride my grandfather's bike 25km a day to train with what was effectively a league two club for two hours. Then I'd ride the 25km back on a 40-year-old bike. Eventually, they told me I was too old but, because I had an Italian passport, I was required to do national service, so I could either stick with the amateurs for a season or go into the army.

"Then a friend of a friend got me to come to England; a place called Manchester. I arrived and was told to get a haircut. I went to train with a team called Blackpool and the next thing I know I was asked to go and see Sam Allardyce. That's how it all started. I was just 25, sat in Sam's office and trying to get a trial. He asked how many games I'd had. 'None.' 'What's your previous club?' 'Er, I haven't really had one.' He said: 'Look, we've got kids who have come through a system.' So I worked my arse off. I learned very quickly."

At West Bromwich Albion, expectation was high in summer, 2003. Relegation from the Premier League was no shock. Albion were ill-prepared for the rigours of top-flight football but the riches from a solitary campaign in England's elite brought a new wave of optimism. Gary Megson's side were immediately installed among the favourites for promotion.

New signings included Rob Hulse (Crewe, for £750,000, Thomas Gaardsoe (Ipswich, £500,000) and Bernt Haas (Sunderland, £500,000). They were joined by Paul Robinson from Watford for £350,000 and, later in the year, Geoff Horsfield (Wigan, about £1.2m). James O'Connor (around £300,000) arrived from Stoke and Macedonian skipper Artim Sakiri joined from CSKA Sofia after a prolonged battle to secure the necessary paperwork. The Baggies were granted a hearing by the Home Office after a Department of Overseas Labour panel rejected their application for a work permit earlier that month. Among those lending their support were Bolton boss Allardyce, ex-Baggies manager Ron Atkinson and Tomaslav Ivic, Porto's European Cup winning coach from 1987, who knew the player. Each provided written testimonials, along with future England coach Steve McClaren, Peter Taylor and veteran coach Ted Buxton, who had scouted Macedonia on the FA's behalf. West Bromwich MP Tom Watson also threw his weight behind the campaign. Patience was required but the rubber-stamping came just before the campaign started.

Albion lost their opening game at Walsall 4-1, with Paul Merson netting twice on the day ex-Baggies boss Ray Harford died. Merson's double was exacerbated by the revelation that he had turned down Albion after his deal at Portsmouth expired. Albion's style and personnel were key to his decision. "My agent met the chairman (Jeremy Peace). They were the first club we talked to and they were up for it," Merson told the local media after the game. "But, to be fair, you have to play to how a team plays. I didn't think myself and Jason Koumas could play in the same team and he's a good player. But, for me, West Brom will win the league. By Christmas, they will be too strong."

Victories in their next five League games suggested Merson might have a point. A defeat at Wigan – the only goal was scored by Geoff Horsfield, who would sign for Albion in December – was the only other dent. The 2-0 victory at Gillingham on October 4 left Megson's side top, with five straight home wins and 25 points from the opening 11 games. But it wasn't enough.

October was a strange month. The Baggies lost top spot with their first home defeat of the campaign (2-0 against Sheffield United) and, on the 14th, Norwich visited The Hawthorns. A moment of legerdemain from Jason Koumas to ensure a 1-0 win should have been enough to impress the home fans. Not so. Albion fans booed at the final whistle.

The Birmingham Post sympathised with the scornful supporters. "A ghastly and frustrating exhibition by West Bromwich Albion," said the match report. "The frustrating thing is why so many good players are forced to grind out so many points from so many indifferent performances. The more obvious question is this: Why is the finest squad seen at The Hawthorns for 20 years playing the type of football that went out of fashion with Carry On films, Errol Flynn moustaches and terraced houses? For assembling such a talented squad, Megson deserves credit; for employing such dire tactics, he deserves stricture. If, or when, Albion are promoted next spring, it will be in spite of the style of play, not because of it. Of course, everybody is happy when the team has won and it might be considered churlish to criticise a manager who has revived the fortunes of Albion and at last given the supporters something of which they can be proud. One suspects, however, that most of those fans would like their victories to be achieved with a bit more panache and style, just like the days of Cyrille Regis, Tony Brown and Laurie Cunningham."

Wimbledon, making their final visit to the Hawthorns as a south London club before their move to Milton Keynes, brought just 24 fans to The Hawthorns the following Tuesday. Their previous game had been a 6-0 defeat to Nottingham Forest. They beat Albion 1-0. This time, the full-time jeers carried more resonance. For the first time, Megson was feeling the pressure. His relationship with Jeremy Peace was fading.

Behind the scenes, Albion were making plans. Mark Hughes, manager of Wales, was sounded out by Hawthorns representatives. He had gone on record as saying he wanted a job in club football. Calls were made, informal talks took place. Hughes implied that he would be willing to commit to discussions on a formal basis should the role become vacant. That vacancy was yet to arise. Megson was hanging on.

Meanwhile, back within Albion's corridors of power, director Mark Ashton was made head of scouting and recruitment. He was charged with finding a coach to front Albion's youth development. Aidy Boothroyd, head of Norwich City's youth team, was picked. The fall-out of his departure from Norfolk to become Albion's youth development officer was significant. Canaries manager Nigel Worthington expressed his disgust at Norwich's failure to keep Boothroyd.

Megson was equally unimpressed. Used to having a near-autocratic hold over all aspects relating to playing staff, he was less than welcoming to Boothroyd and his brittle relationship with Ashton broke down in the week leading up to Albion's trip to West Ham. The two men exchanged strong words. Megson was losing allies in the boardroom. He was potentially one bad result away from the sack.

By the 18th minute of the clash at Upton Park on November 8, Albion were 3-0 down. It was materialising as the result Megson's detractors needed. Jermain Defoe, scorer of West Ham's opening goal, missed a brilliant chance to make it four. His weak shot was saved by Russell Hoult. Rob Hulse pulled two goals back, with Defoe then being red-carded for a lunge on Sean Gregan just before half-time. Brian Deane, who had scored twice for the home side, made it 3-3 when he completed an unusual 'hat-trick' with an own goal. Lee Hughes made it 4-3 some 13 minutes from time. One of Albion's greatest comebacks was complete. Megson kept his job and Mark Hughes never did get that follow-up call.

In Italy, Simon Miotto was training with a small club called Biellese. He was still chasing the dream. The final destination was no nearer. An opportunity in English football was looking less likely, as he explained: "Sam Allardyce was my first manager at Blackpool. When I went back there some time later, Gary Megson was in charge. Big Sam had moved to Bolton but he let me train for a week. The Albion goalkeeping coach at the time was also working at Bolton and that was Fred Barber. He didn't rate me at Blackpool. He knew I was enthusiastic but way out of my depth. In fact, years later, I heard he had a nickname for me which was 'Tony the Tiger' because, by the time the ball was hitting the back of the net, I was diving after it. After I improved, he told me this.

"Yet after I did a session at Bolton, he was in shock at how much I'd improved in six years. He asked me to come back the next day. And with Fred it was 'Fred's way or no way.' And Fred's way was that I needed to get better. It was about hard training and I ended up training with Bolton for two and a half months. Sam was fantastic. They all knew that when I came from Australia the first time, I was fit, athletic and keen but way too risky because I was in my mid-20s. The truth is I was a good fella. I'd worked hard and I'd improved. They could see that and they told me. That I respected."

England, for now, would have to wait. Or at least it would until somebody needed a goalkeeper. "I was living between Turin and Milan," he continued. "I was holding out for two things at the time – a Scandinavian opportunity in March, or a chance in Italy. I was catching two trains a day to train in the mountains with what was an Italian league two equivalent team who were on the verge of relegation. They trained on dirt and gravel, no grass. It was the land that time forgot. I'd been training with JJ Okocha and Djorkaeff at Bolton. I thought I was making progress. They wanted to sign me but I threw the one in about having 'lots of options but I want to stay in Italy,' which of course you do.

"As it worked out, I got an offer from Sweden and was on the verge of going to Gothenburg. I thought it would be perfect; a well-known club, a change of scenery. It fell through at the very last minute. I was actually waiting for a call from their people in Sweden to find out which Milan airport I'd be using. And then it never happened. Now I was stuck. One of the things I've always done, wherever I am living, is go into town and buy a ball. If I'm not training with a club, I'll hide the ball in a bush and go out for a run, come back and throw the ball at a wall.

"I was doing that and realised I might have a problem. I'd said no to smaller clubs in Scotland and smaller clubs in England. I was wondering whether there would be another opportunity around the corner. And then Joe Murphy rolled his ankle at West Brom.

"Within 48 hours, I spoke to Fred Barber and got a call from Gary Megson, who said: 'We're going for promotion, we have two goalkeepers so come and work your backside off, do what you did for me at Blackpool.' It happened quickly. By the time I got back to where I'd been staying, the club had a contract ready and faxed over with a first-class plane ticket from Milan to Birmingham. When I hopped on that flight, I remember thinking I had been very close to my career being in a bit of trouble.

"You have to keep a level head. All of a sudden, I was heading to one of the biggest clubs outside the Premier League. It happened for a reason. Yes, I'd earned it but it was very close to not happening had other things not happened. I remember being told that flights from Milan to Birmingham were at 2pm but I noticed that I could get one at 6am that would allow me to come straight into training. For me to hang around until the afternoon was a wasted day. So I packed up all my stuff where I'd been living.

"I didn't sleep all night. A mate drove me to the airport [the 'mate' is now a highly-capped Australian international, Carl Valeri, who was then with Inter Milan]. I went straight to training. I didn't want to wait. The truth is I needed to work out that I needed to justify being there. I'd been presented with this wonderful opportunity. I wasn't about to hang around. It was all about work ethic and taking on responsibility and the privilege of being there. So I signed. It was March and there I was. I was coming in, Houltie was on the verge of being named the greatest goalkeeper in the club's history in a club poll and Joe was a talented kid who probably needed a hyperactive, bouncy, excited Tasmanian to bring out the best in him."

December, 2003 was not a time of festive bonhomie for Albion. A 1-0 victory at Bradford City was clinched by a late Scott Dobie goal in a drab game which could have been called off due to heavy fog. It was to be the only pre-Christmas cheer for Megson's side. A home draw with Crewe was followed by a midweek Carling Cup defeat against Arsenal (2-0) and a 1-0 reversal at Coventry. Festive games against Derby and Wimbledon produced 1-1 and 0-0 draws respectively, then Albion opened 2004 with an FA Cup exit at Nottingham Forest. Enter Lloyd Dyer.

Young, sprightly, raw and energetic, the 21-year-old winger made his first League appearance for the club as a substitute in the 2-0 win against Walsall. He set up Albion's second goal – Geoff Horsfield's first for the club – within two minutes of going on. Horsfield was impressed. "I haven't seen anything as quick on two legs. He was like shit off a shovel," he said. "He's only a young lad and I think if the gaffer and the more experienced players can help keep his feet on the ground, he can go a long way with that pace and ability. He absolutely skinned that right-back and I think he'd skin most right-backs with his skill and pace." Skin them he did.

Horsfield's graft, strength and power – knitted with a supply line from the young Dyer – helped Albion to three wins and two draws in their next seven games. Miotto recalls the mood during spring, 2004 in a camp galvanised by Megson over the final third of that season. "I found a very slick machine," he recalls. "I remembered Gary from six years before at Blackpool as a very, very intelligent guy. He was a manager who had grown but his philosophy, mentality and principles remained the same. He took this great club from a difficult position to where they were when I arrived. It was about his high energy, organisation and work ethic.

"If you weren't going to work hard, no matter what ability you had, you weren't going to be in his plans. When I got to West Brom, I saw these winners, these players who didn't flap when it didn't go their way. They were strong players. We went into games knowing that, even at 0-0 with ten minutes to go, we were going to win games. The boss used to structure training specifically to our strengths as individuals. At some clubs I've been to, you have training then sometimes groups of the lads do something afterwards. It wasn't like that with Gary. You came in, you worked, you went home and you rested. And it was done properly. If we went a goal behind, which didn't happen very often, we felt like we could deal with it."

Miotto knew his place in the squad. As third-choice keeper, he was a useful training colleague for the two ahead of him. His application, dedication and desire impressed his manager and created a bond which lasts to this day. Miotto eases back in the soft Malmaison armchair, points to a settee behind me and recalls meeting Megson, by chance, at the same spot just a few weeks before. Sheffield Wednesday, then managed by Megson, were due to play Walsall while Miotto was catching up with friends from Fulham, who were staying nearby before a game in the city.

Miotto's friendship with his manager stems back to when the men first met at Blackpool. It was cemented and it flourished at Albion. "I joined knowing there were two better guys ahead of me but told Gary I'd rather be on the pitch helping them get ready, whether it was kicking balls, warming them up, helping with distribution or even just regulating their own alertness levels," he continued. "I spent a lot of my career in the stands but wanted to be on the pitch in case Houltie hurt his hand in the warm-up. What use am I if I'm in the stand? I've got my shirt on. Joe will go in goals and I'll be on the bench.

"Houltie and I have a great friendship to this day because he saw that professionalism in me. It was tough to be anywhere near as good as those guys. I knew I wouldn't be. But I was determined to be one of the best in terms of application. It was something I was aware of and perhaps it helped me get a new contract after we got promoted a few months later. The mentality was if I wasn't on it every day, I was letting myself and the club down. The others were already this machine. I was brought in to work at the back of that but I was part of it. Gary had this incredible work ethic. As at a lot of clubs, players don't always like managers and certainly Gary wasn't popular with everyone but I thought he was fantastic.

"People like praise but it's about knowing how to take criticism. Fans look to us to get them away from bad days or because they have a good life and it enriches them. They pay good money to give us these good lives. Gary expected his defenders to be ready for scenarios in training, show energy, even when there was no opposition. Darren Moore was exceptional in continuing that philosophy on the pitch. He'd carry it on there vocally. One thing Gary was very clever at was going to the right person when the time was appropriate. Sometimes he needed noise, sometimes he needed calm. We had people like Paul Robinson and Andy Johnson, who would burst down a brick wall. They were Gary's men. They were successful under him.

"The dressing room was full of those. There were people who perhaps didn't always fit into that template. Jason Koumas, for instance, was a brilliant talent. I had a lot of time for him. Koumi was one of few in his generation who, as a goalkeeper, you'd have no idea where he would put the ball. He was a certain kind of character and perhaps not in the typical Megson mould. But what he brought was a quality in a different way. One on one, I found him to be very honest, a great one for conservation, someone very close to his Merseyside roots. The distance didn't help him in that respect.

"In a way, Artim Sakiri was the same as Jason. In Macedonia, he was a legend, yet with us he wasn't playing. The club were understanding of that as well. I'm European-Australian, so I had a rapport with the British guys but I could also appreciate the European mentality. His style wasn't West Brom's style but you wouldn't have found a better left foot in England at the time. He wanted to win. He'd go through it during the game. He lived every moment during a game."

Booed by his own fans in October and within a Jermain Defoe miss of dismissal in November, Gary Megson found himself lording it, yet again, on the Sandwell Council House balcony come May. He's the only manager in the club's history to win promotion twice with them. Between March 2, 2004 and April 24, Albion played ten games. They drew at Norwich, won their next six and drew at Millwall before two more victories – against Sunderland and Bradford. The latter two clinched promotion.

On April 18, Albion travelled to the Stadium of Light. A victory for Mick McCarthy's third-placed Sunderland team would have seen them close to within six points of Albion. The Baggies were battered for the best part of 89 minutes. They defended superbly. Jason Koumas's 90th minute goal clinched the victory. It left Sunderland needing to make up 12 points – 13 if you counted their poor goal difference – in five games. McCarthy's side lost 3-0 at Crystal Palace three days later and drew 0-0 at Wigan in a lunchtime kick-off before Albion hosted Bradford. Sunderland's failure to win that early game ensured Albion's promotion before a ball was kicked at The Hawthorns.

The Baggies players celebrated during the warm-up after watching the closing moments from Wigan on the giant screens. Miotto has fond memories of that success, less so of Albion's failure to challenge Norwich for the title. The Baggies lost their final three games to Reading (0-1), Stoke (1-4) and Nottingham Forest (0-2). "We got promoted on the pitch and it remains one of the best things to happen in my life," he says. "The crowd were watching the game, we were warming up and it was emotional. We were up against Bradford and Bryan Robson was their manager. He looked a shadow of himself. Little did we know he would be managing us later that year.

"We'd just been promoted but we still won 2-0. It goes back to this notion that we were a machine. It's what we were. Part of me felt embarrassed because I hadn't been there that long. The players and staff took me in. I won a West Brom shirt in the 1970s, I'd been a schoolteacher until my mid-20s, been training on a dusty pitch in Italy, yet here I was being introduced to thousands of Albion supporters stood in front of the town hall. There was a strange feeling with being promoted because I think we let ourselves down at the end. We could and should have won the League.

"Gary was very well aware of the fact and you could feel his disappointment. I think the boys wanted to (win it) as well. Looking back, I get the feeling that there was just a release after crossing the line. It's like we'd achieved the goal and everyone just wanted a break. My impressions are that Gary was disappointed by that. We had an awful night at Stoke and we lost to Forest and Reading. I don't think any of us lost sight that we still had three games.

"I still maintain it was that game at Sunderland where we won promotion. That was incredible. Even now, I can hear: 'Lloyd (Dyer), Lloyd, take it into the corner...head for the corner.' Lloyd being Lloyd, he didn't do that and the next thing we know he has passed to Jason Koumas, who scores. Brilliant! Sunderland came at us in droves for the whole afternoon and that game probably summed up Gary Megson, summed up Russell Hoult, summed up the brilliance of Jason Koumas, summed up the raw energy of Lloyd Dyer, summed up Sean Gregan's fantastic defending. This is what our team was about. I remember at one point Russell Hoult coming for a cross and just putting his finger up and wagging it side to side to say 'no, no, no' to the lad putting in the crosses.

"We had 5,000 fans or so up there that day. It also summed up our supporters. You looked at it on Sky and how our fans went crazy. There was a brilliant photo of Houltie going mad. It was magical."

On November 22, 2003, Albion drew 0-0 with Reading. A few hours later, Lee Hughes was involved in an accident. It happened in the early hours the day after Hughes had gone on as a second-half substitute and been named man of the match. He fled the scene of a fatal smash in Meriden involving his silver Mercedes CL55 Coupe and a Renault Megane. Douglas Graham, who was sitting in the back of the Megane, was killed instantly. His wife was taken to the Coventry and Warwickshire Hospital with a broken leg. She was to die in her sleep 13 months later. Albert Frisby, another passenger, was confined to a wheelchair.

Warwickshire Police said the Megane had been turning into Pickford

Grange Road from the A45 Birmingham Road when it collided with the Mercedes, which was heading towards Oak Lane. Hughes, who was uninjured, went into hiding, prompting the police to take the unusual step of naming the person they would like to speak to in connection with the accident. On Monday, November 24, Hughes walked into Little Park Street police station in Coventry at 10am and gave himself up. Detective Inspector Chris McKeogh, of West Midlands Police, said: "A 27-year-old man from Meriden has been arrested on suspicion of causing death by dangerous driving and failing to stop after a road accident."

Hughes pleaded not guilty to causing death by dangerous driving. The case was referred to Coventry Crown Court and, on August 9, 2004, Hughes was found guilty of causing death by dangerous driving. He was sentenced to six years in prison. Within minutes of sentence being passed, Albion issued a statement disclosing they had terminated Hughes's contract with immediate effect.

During the hearing, the court heard that the striker ran away to escape being breathalysed. Judge Christopher Hodson said Hughes had shown 'callous disregard' for the victims. It emerged Hughes had been drinking Jack Daniel's whiskey, fleeing the scene to avoid a breath test. The judge also imposed a four-month sentence for the offences which Hughes admitted at the start of the case – failing to stop at the scene and failing to report the accident to police within 24 hours. He received a ten-year driving ban and was told to pay costs of £8,467. The player was released from prison in summer, 2007 and given the chance to resurrect his career with Oldham Athletic.

He also spent a loan spell at Blackpool before moving to Notts County, where, at the time of writing, he has scored 60 goals in 120 appearances. I made several attempts to speak to Hughes, asking him to give his account of the incident and the rebuilding of his life. The calls were not acknowledged or returned. Notts County felt it would not be in his best interests to speak about the accident. Talking to the press at the time of his move to Oldham, he said: "This the first time I have been able to make a public apology. I only wish I could turn back the clock. I have served the sentence laid down by law but nothing I can do, or say, can change what has happened.

"I've made dreadful mistakes and decisions that will live with me for the rest of my life. I'm so remorseful for what I have done. If I could change back time, I would. But I can't. I can only apologise and keep saying sorry but I know that isn't good enough for some people and that they won't forgive me. I made the biggest mistake of my life and I can't change that. If I can help even one person to avoid getting into the same situation, it will have been worthwhile. I've let my family down and I've been away from my little children for three years. I see their faces, unhappy all the time. It has greatly affected my own family and I will never forgive myself for that."

Hughes continued: "I spoke to a lot of people before deciding I wanted to come back and I'm determined now to do well for them. I'm not here to be a hero and I don't want to be the centre of attention. I just want to play football. I know there are some supporters who won't want me here but, hopefully, I can make myself a better person and show them that I know I have made the biggest mistake of my life but that I can turn it around."

In the summer of 2004, Simon Miotto was aware of the delicate nature of Hughes's predicament. Eight years on, he is reticent about disclosing too much from the inner sanctum of Albion's dressing room on this subject. He is particularly mindful of the hurt and anguish caused. "I didn't know a whole lot about it and, out of respect for Hughesie, I didn't want to pry," he said. "As players, we were incredibly respectful to everyone concerned.

"No-one talked behind his back or even to his face. My own thoughts were that it was incredibly sad and tragic for a family I didn't know. But it was also sad for a colleague who had a family of his own. The club supported him throughout that period. There was a question whether he could perform under that kind of pressure, which he did, and that was quite incredible. It showed remarkable character on his part. I don't know Hughesie well enough to comment on his background but, at training, we saw a positive and talented guy. I found him to be a nice guy.

"I think the club acted respectfully and with dignity. Lee Hughes was a nice guy to me. When Tranmere played Notts County not long ago, he was very warm to me. We spoke about his family. It was great to see him. When he went to jail, I wanted to see him. Darren Moore had already been and I told Mooro I wanted to see him. It wasn't the right time then but I made that effort. No-one really talked about it. There was a dignity among the players. Nobody gossiped about it. We were footballers with other pressures and things on our mind. What happened to Lee was a private matter, albeit one being played out in a public arena. When everything went through, I just think the less talk there was, the better. We had a respect for the people who were affected."

Preparations for the 2004-05 season continued. Miotto was aware that he might find himself looking for a new club. He was to be pleasantly surprised. Approaching his 35th birthday, he had never felt so fit. "The one thing I've had is that I'm really, really fit, I have springs in my legs and I'm agile," he added. "I had been an athlete. I remember signing for Blackpool and no wonder they got rid of me. I was out of my depth. But I put my work in and West Brom gave an incredible opportunity, a great lifestyle.

"I remember we were sat in a conference room in Denmark during our pre-season, just before Gary went home early (on the premise of concluding some incoming transfer deals). He sat us all down and said: 'You're all here because you deserve to be and you're all Premier League footballers.' I looked at Houltie and started grinning. He turned around at the same time and laughed at me, shaking his head as if to say: 'Yeah...except you.'

"The club actually released ten players at the end of 2003-04. They literally released them, shut the door on them and we were told that we were the players for the next season. Some of the lads jokingly said to me: 'What are you still doing here?' And then Gary continues: 'You're here because you're professional, have a winning mentality and are great players.' Then he turned round, looked at every one of us and said: 'You're all talented...really, really talented.' I just burst out laughing. He said: 'Miotto, what's up with you?' I replied: 'Come on gaffer, I've been sat here ticking every single box...and then you turn around and say we're all talented. I said: 'I tell you what gaffer...I have the biggest cross in that box.' I was honestly wondering whether he knew I was there. It was great for me."

Yet Megson was to last just two months into the season. Miotto feels a pang of guilt, even now. "We lost 3-0 to Palace and he was gone," he recalls. "I was disappointed he left. We let him down terribly. I have to be careful what I say because there were boys who were playing and they were better than me. I mean the group as a whole let him down. I let him down because I wasn't a fantastic goalkeeper who kept clean sheets. We were playing against teams who were better than us. It was a transitional period for us. We were aware things weren't right. We could feel it.

"But I want people who are good to me to do well. I always had a lot of time for him. I would have done everything for him. I didn't want to hear that my boss and the chairman weren't getting on great. But it was becoming more and more evident. It's understandable. We needed to do better and didn't."

Megson was replaced by Bryan Robson. It wasn't good news for Miotto's career. "I felt from the outset that Bryan wanted a lot of foreigners out, wanted certain people to stay and for the team to play a certain way," he continued. "You could tell straightaway which group you belonged to. I don't think he was overly happy with the foreign players he inherited. That came across and I include myself in that. Bryan wasn't interested in hard-working squad players. He was interested in players who could make things happen. This was something you had to support him with. He had his own vision and had a job to do. The club were extremely good to me. They were generous. I left in the New Year but you don't hang around for the wrong reasons. You have to see the bigger picture.

"I'd been doing some of the goalkeeper training for a few weeks when there was some uncertainty over Fred Barber's position. I didn't think anyone was vouching for Fred, so I went to see Bryan and said: 'Look, it's none of my business but I wanted to let you know Fred was a great goalkeeping coach and I'd like to say that on the record out of respect for what he's done.' I don't think the gaffer liked me doing that but I felt a duty to say it and I wanted to be respectful. I know Bryan might have had his own plans – he ended up bringing in Joe Corrigan – but I wanted him to know how I felt. I have always been loyal and I thought Fred needed that.

"Joe was fantastic and I loved working with him, of that there is no doubt. So, at Albion, I had Fred Barber and Joe Corrigan, both excellent coaches who developed different parts of my game. Both were very good to me. Bryan needed to change things quickly and he changed things as quickly as he could. That was fine but what I didn't like at the time was how some of the lads were treated. Some players there were experienced and weren't given the best of times. Cosmin Contra, for instance, left West Brom, went back to Spain and did extremely well. He was an exceptional player but he wasn't 100 per cent fit when he came in. He did well when he left. He was a fantastic guy and a player we could have made more with.

"But, with a change of manager, everyone fears what he'll do. Bryan released me but I left on good terms. My thoughts were that he didn't know my worth but I was understanding that he had a job to do. As a bloke who became famous for playing for that club and was coming to a club without having had much success as a manager, I was hoping it would be the start of a successful period for him now he was at West Brom. I wanted him to do well so I didn't take it personally."

Miotto added: "Bryan brought in discipline. He banned us from wearing boots in the dressing room. He told us to treat the training ground like we would treat our home. He wanted things done a certain way. He gave fringe players a go but he didn't have a lot of time to play with. People don't wait. Managers get the sack if they're not succeeding, so he had to be ruthless. Bryan was an advocate of English players, so I don't know how it went down when Cosmin Contra, Riccy Scimeca, Kanu and myself were chatting in Italian...not sure it went down well with him!

"Personally, I thought I should have played more reserve games. I played twice, I played half a friendly. It would have been great to play more but I understood why I couldn't. I am sure had I been around longer, I would have helped. I didn't come through football the conventional way. I was a schoolteacher, lived a good life before football and I live a good life after football. My life wasn't inside a football bubble. It was easy for me to come in and out without any problems.

"Looking back, it was a privilege to work for Bryan. I respected the bloke and what he wanted to do. When West Brom stayed up, I felt a positive emotion. I was part of that squad at the beginning of that season. I was so happy for Bryan especially, because I knew what it meant. Bryan Robson has been and will always be a top name. To have him as a boss, even for a short period of time, was great."

Apart from being one of Megson's closest allies, Miotto was also a bystander to the blossoming career of Tomasz Kuszczak during early 2004-05. Russell Hoult, undisputed no 1, found himself coming under pressure from the young Pole, who had arrived from Hertha Berlin. Kuszczak made his debut for Albion against Fulham in late September. His performance was underwhelming. But he went on for Hoult in Albion's penultimate game of the campaign at Manchester United and produced a display which was to linger in Sir Alex

Ferguson's memory. Albion drew 1-1, secured survival the following week and Kuszczak became first-choice keeper during the latter half of 2005-06. His form earned him a move to Old Trafford.

Miotto detected a rivalry and spoke about the chemistry between Kuszczak and Hoult or, rather, the lack of it. "Tomasz was a very intense guy," he said. "We went to Denmark on pre-season and we'd go out after training. But he'd be resting or stretching. He was completely dedicated. It worked. He ended up at Manchester United. I know a lot of Polish people in Australia and Europe, and I could see that in him. He was a certain character. He had his ambitions and a way of doing things and wasn't giving in terms of his energies or thoughts. He found it very difficult to adjust to the intensity of our training with Fred Barber and didn't really appreciate our sense of humour.

"He wasn't great with the language but body language can usually tell you whether he's in tune with our humour. But Tomasz was a good kid, a great professional. When you've got a mad bloke like Houltie and a loopy Tasmanian and then Joe Murphy – who was often coming out with his Irishisms – then perhaps Tomasz didn't really relate to that. He was a young man who had come from German football, a Polish background and didn't speak English. We were all wary of that.

"We tried to get him into the culture of English goalkeeping but he struggled to adjust. On the flip side, how could you not want the kid to do well? He was sitting on the bench, Joe was on loan and I was trying to help him. Houltie and I got on well and it wasn't that Houltie and Tomasz didn't get on well, but there was simply no chemistry. That's not to say he was a bad guy but he was a different kind of guy. In football, you get some people who provide to a community and team environment. Then you get some people who just look after themselves and are very driven towards that goal. That was Tomasz.

"He wasn't as giving to the club or team environment as some of the other lads, including Houltie and I. You need an ability to laugh at yourself. If you can do that, you contribute to a team environment. Tomasz had his system, he had his agenda. He has done exceptionally well but I just wish he'd gone out to get more football while he was at United because he was professional and fit. It's a waste to see him not playing but fantastic to see him do so well during his loan spell at Watford.

"When he went to United, I dropped him a line to congratulate him. He'd earned that move. He's played Champions League football, he's an international, he's had great success but did I socialise with him? No. He was hard-working, a great kid and a very intense player for all of his reasons. And rightly so. It got him the move he wanted."

Speaking about Hoult, Miotto continued: "Houltie was a big character. He was a funny bugger in some ways. He and I would be the first in training every day, we'd go in early and just had a good laugh. He wasn't lairy in the obvious way but he did have this great presence and confidence. He was very opinionated with how goalkeepers and goalkeeping should be. He had exceptional hands. He was brave, 6ft 5in – but played 7ft in so much as he knew how to cover his goal so well – and played 350 games or so. I now consider him a friend and have great respect for him. We were very close as colleagues at the club."

Relegation in 2003 had meant a reduction in turnover to £20.6m and a loss of £100,000. Dividends to shareholders, however, increased to £2.50 per share. The club announced their intention to develop the Sandwell Academy at a cost of £30m. This was to be funded largely by central Government and a planned opening date was set for September, 2006. S4A, meanwhile, held their usual spring forum, attended by Jeremy Peace, secretary Dr John Evans and fellow directors Mark Jenkins, Jeff Farmer and Joe Brandrick. The theme of the evening was how the club could improve on their first attempt back in the top flight. Peace, now a full-time Albion employee, believed a three-year stint as chairman would be sufficient. He thought small shareholders were still important to the club and also felt new investors would always be considered if they showed intent.

Miotto left Albion in February, 2005, for Danish club Olstykke. He went on to play for AB Copenhagen and Koge BK. Now 43, he pays tribute to the man who brought him to The Hawthorns. Gary Megson remains a friend, a colleague, a boss. "I will never forget what he did for me," said Miotto. "That period was so important for the schoolteacher from Tasmania who took up goalkeeping. Being associated with West Brom has given me a great springboard for the rest of my life.

"I remember one time we had shot-stopping and I was getting lairy, having a yak with the players. Gary had a lot of time for me but, on this occasion, he put me back in my place in three seconds flat: 'Hey, why don't you just shut up and make some saves because I haven't seen many from you yet?' He was the boss. Organisation was big. I've had 13 professional clubs in four countries and have never met a man who before a team go out in such crunch matches – and, remember, we had a few of those – he would speak so eloquently, intelligently and articulately.

"Gary was the best motivator I had as a footballer. I've had Robson, Big Sam, Chris Turner, Brian Laws, Billy Stark, people who had won European Cups, so many...all were good people and a privilege to work with. But no-one could match Gary in that way. He was resourceful without being self-obsessed. He cared about his family. He always had a great priority on his life. When I first met him at Blackpool, I said to him: 'Gaffer, did you ever play?' He said: 'Are you serious?' Mike Phelan was no 2 and killing himself. Here was this strange guy from the other side of the world asking him if he'd kicked a ball. He just replied: 'Have you never heard of Sheffield Wednesday or Manchester City?'

"If you had a go, he'd give you the time of day. If you were not good enough, he would tell you. Half of the reason why people don't like him is because they can't take criticism or they don't like hard work. Two or three hours a day, you have to try your hardest, do as you're told and then deal with the pressure at the weekend – and if you're not selected then, you look at the bigger picture and remain part of the club, part of the team and the community. You can be ruthless and self-centred but I think a lot of people who didn't like him, including some friends of mine, might not necessarily have taken criticism the right way.

"If they were working in an office, they'd probably be frustrated but, for me, this is the most privileged job you can have. I was a hard worker. They could see that. As a result, I kind of let them come to me a little bit. I've always got on really well with lads. When Bryan Robson came in as manager, he got the guys to organise a few of the players who were representatives between the dressing room and the management. There was myself, Kanu, Mooro and Andy Johnson. So I know I was respected. Clem (Neil Clement) was a magic guy, a super-talented athlete. He made a big effort to welcome me. He asked me early on: 'So where were you before coming here?' I'd answer: 'Sleeping on my mate's couch in Milan and throwing a ball against the wall as my training.'

"They couldn't believe I was in the same dressing room. Yet I had a sense of humour about it. I came from an all-boys Catholic background, St Patrick's in Tasmania. School was everything and you did what you could. If you couldn't win, you would turn round and be an advocate of your team. It was about sportsmanship, the spirit of competition. The respect and bond remains for me whenever I come across one of my former team-mates. We all love football.

"I have two different shirts with two different League logos and numbers from my time at the club. I treasure those because it was a big privilege to be involved with this club. Footballers have a shelf life. We can only jump, run, spring for so many years, so you have to make sure you do something about that. There are bad days in every profession. Things don't always go as we desire. But I worked very hard at taking responsibility for my career and my happiness. I did everything I could to be the best I could. A million and one people had better careers but not all are as satisfied with their career as I was with mine. My time at the Albion has contributed to this contentment. For that, I will always love the club."

And that was Simon Miotto.

Geoff Horsfield

"It wasn't often I wasn't involved in a night out, least of all where someone got into trouble. Luckily, Britney Spears saved me that night."

GEOFF Horsfield picks up his finest lump hammer. He smashes it against the wall with venom. Once, twice, thrice. The wall is hurting. Horsfield starts this process in the morning. He ends in the evening. The wall is no more. The West Bromwich Albion striker then heads off to a Chinese restaurant for a meal. This is how prepares for the biggest football match of his life. It's Saturday, May 14, 2005. Tomorrow, he will be one of a dozen or so footballers hoping, aiming, fighting to keep Albion in the Premier League. The former labourer is used to graft. He worked in the building trade before he was taken on as a professional footballer at the age of 24. But now it's time for goodnight. Tomorrow is a big day...

Horsfield was with Birmingham City when Gary Megson first tried to sign him. Both Albion and Blues won promotion in 2002, Horsfield scoring the equaliser against Norwich in a play-off final that was to be decided on penalties at Cardiff's Millennium Stadium. By 2003-04, Albion and Birmingham had gone their separate ways. Megson's men were back in the second tier. Horsfield remained at Premier League Birmingham, whose survival chances in 2002-03 had been enhanced by the arrival of Robbie Savage, Matthew Upson and, notably, Christophe Dugarry.

Back in autumn, 2003, Steve Bruce picks out Chelsea youngster Mikael Forssell as the man to partner Dugarry. Horsfield, signed by Trevor Francis in July, 2000, takes the hint. There are no hard feelings. Megson must wait. Horsfield departs the West Midlands but his next call is more of a pit stop. He signs for Wigan for £1m. His second game is against Albion at the JJB Stadium.

"At the time, they had Jason Roberts, Lee Hughes, Rob Hulse, Deech

(Danny Dichio) and Scott Dobie," he remembers. "Steve Bruce pulled me in and said: 'Wigan want to sign you. You're not going to play here because I'm going to bring Forssell in.' Wigan were in the Championship, so I was happy to talk to them rather than sit on the bench. I always remember the Albion game. I was up against Thomas Gaardsoe. I'd heard he was a bit of a softy; a nice kid but I knew I could bully him. So I said to him in the tunnel: 'Lad, I'm going to beat you to a pulp today. First minute, I'm gonna smash you.' I could see the fear in his eyes. The other centre-half was big Darren Moore but I wasn't going to say it to him. So I played directly against Thomas and we're going one-against-one in the game. I gave him a little nudge. I beat him for pace, somehow, he went over and I slotted it past Russell Hoult. We won 1-0. We were challenging West Brom at the time and it was a big result for us."

Megson had clearly taken note. By December, 2003, Jason Roberts was gone, Dichio was on loan at Derby and Hughes had been charged. He would remain at the club for now but only subject to his court case the following summer. Albion were under pressure to win promotion. Horsfield was very much on the agenda. This was to be no ordinary transfer.

Sat across the table from me in the Bell pub in Walsall, 'The Horse' cuts a figure of responsibility and dignity as he recounts what followed. These days, he is a coach at Port Vale. Back then, he was one of the lads. And it was all a little more frivolous back in 2003. "I knew Meggo fancied me when we played West Brom and, a few weeks later, I got to sign for him," he continued. "It made sense to me. I was travelling up and down the motorway from the Midlands and Paul Jewell said: 'Look, West Brom have come in. If I were you, I'd go. They're a bigger club.' So that was that.

"The day it all got sorted was the Friday before a game against Bradford. Paul Jewell asked: 'Do you want to play?' I said I would. I scored, it was the middle of December and we had our Christmas do afterwards. At some point that evening, my agent called and said: 'You've got to meet Gary Megson tomorrow.' I said: 'Are you sure? I'm sat here in a yellow suit, I've got my face painted green – I'd gone dressed as the Mask – and I'm here on my Christmas do. I'm out on the pop.'

"I knew I wouldn't be getting back until about 4am, then I'd need to travel down to meet Gary and Jeremy Peace. That phone call, as much I was glad to get it, was not the best timing. Anyway, I agreed to go, had a few more beers, then spent all morning trying to get the paint off my eyebrows and stubble. My face was red raw by the time we got to The Hawthorns. Phil Morrison was my agent at the time. I met him in the car park. I told him I wanted the same money as I was on at Wigan. I was just happy to be back in the Midlands and at a big club."

Horsfield, not content with looking a little green, was also feeling a little green and swiftly turned to red. Or, as the colour guides would have it, 'embarrassed red.' He added: "We went into The Hawthorns, walked into the East Stand and were led into a room where we sat around this giant oak table. After a few minutes, this bald bloke appeared with a plate of sandwiches and asked if I wanted coffee. He didn't introduce himself. I said: 'Yeah, cheers mate' and off he went to the kitchen. I tucked into my sandwiches because, by this time, I was getting the 'beer munchies.' You just need food when you've had a few beers the night before. I could feel my agent glaring at me. He had this look of disgust and said: 'You do know who that is, don't you? It's the West Brom chairman Jeremy Peace.' Shit! I couldn't believe it. There's me, still worse for wear, with a red raw face, bits of green paint still spotted around and I'm referring to my future employer as 'mate.'

"After that, I started calling him Mr Chairman and being respectful. Gary Megson wasn't there because he was taking training. I'm glad he wasn't to be honest. It would have been very embarrassing. Everything with Gary was agreed and I was just pleased to come to West Brom. God knows what the chairman thought of me, though..."

Albion went up in 2004. Horsfield remembers it as a strange time. It was a strained promotion. It was enjoyed and toasted, rather than fondly remembered and revered. At times, it seemed hard work. Albion were up before they kicked a ball against Bradford. Sunderland's failure to beat Albion – the Baggies won 1-0 at the Stadium of Light – followed by defeat at Crystal Palace and a Saturday lunchtime draw with Wigan handed the prize to Megson's men.

"Promotion was such an anti-climax," he recalls. "We were on the pitch warming up in the far corner between the Birmingham Road End and the Halfords Lane stand by the families. The ground probably had about 10,000 in as many fans were making their way or were on the concourses. There we were, watching our promotion on the big screen thanks to Sunderland not beating Wigan. It was like watching it at home with your mates. "We beat Bradford who, funnily enough, were managed by Bryan Robson. Hughsie and I scored. We went up but most people expected us to. We had the civic bus ride around West Bromwich but nothing stood out. It just wasn't memorable. It didn't seem like a success, to be honest."

The summer of 2004 was all about preparation for a Premier League return. This time, Albion were more serious about survival. Martin Albrechtsen was signed for a club record £2.7m. He was to become known as 'Two Point Seven' by some of his team-mates. The Dane's arrival from Copenhagen ended a year-long pursuit. The Baggies, with hindsight, perhaps didn't do too badly out of the deal. Twelve months earlier, they had been quoted £9m for a player who was extremely highly rated by Megson's no 2 Frank Burrows. Darren Purse arrived for around £750,000 from Birmingham with Riccardo Scimeca activating a get-out clause in his contract with Leicester following their relegation. A little-known goalkeeper called Tomasz Kuszczak pitched up from Hertha Berlin.

Even then, Albion weren't done in the transfer market but more signings would have to wait. Over in Denmark, the men who would carry their hopes on to the pitch were bedding down on their pre-season tour. Or at least the players and coaching staff were. Gary Megson headed back to England the very next day.

The manager was emphasising the need for new players by tackling the negotiations himself, notably with Jonathan Greening and Kanu. Megson was unimpressed with what he described as Albion's dithering in the transfer market. 'Faffing around' as he called it. Back across the North Sea, Albion players were making the most of their manager's absence by acquainting themselves with the Andersen Hotel in the centre of Odense.

"I remember it well," says Horsfield. "We got to the hotel and the manager came up to us and laid down the law. We looked around the hotel and I remember thinking: We've got a problem here. There was a casino, nightclub and bar underground. Me, Greegs (Sean Gregan), Robbo (Paul Robinson) and Johnno (Andy Johnson) just looked at each other and shook our heads knowingly. Meggo sat us down and said: 'Lads, you might get a night out, but you're here to train.' The next morning, Frank said: 'The gaffer's gone back to England. You're under my control but nothing changes.' We just smiled. The one night, we went out and Greegs threw a load of mashed potato and sprouts at Johnno. Johnno threw them back at the curtains and wall. That was it. It all went off. From somewhere, Johnno found a carving knife and, for some reason, hid it down his trousers. We were drunk when we got back to the hotel, so we asked the waitress to get us four coffees.

"Someone had told Frank Burrows. He came up and said: 'Listen, I know you've been drinking. Don't take me as a mug. I've had confirmation that somebody has been swinging a carving knife.' We told him to prove it and Frank replied: 'Well, he's got long hair.' We looked at Johnno and replied: 'God knows who it is Frank. Must be someone else.' We were sent to bed. Sometime later, Frank came to check on us. Apparently, he opened the door to Johnno's room and there was Johnno lying face down, stark naked, with his face in a pizza – God knows where he got that from – and a big carving knife next to him. We ended up being fined a week's wages."

Away from the fun and games, Albion were still trying to sign players. Speaking at the time, Horsfield revealed the importance of the right ones being brought in. "The players we've already signed are good ones," he said. "Establishing yourself in the Premiership is a gradual thing and not all about spending massive amounts of money. It's about the right players working for each other. Charlton have done it gradually, as have Bolton, and that's what we've got to try and do. This is a crucial year for us. We don't want to be seen as a yo-yo side."

Kanu and Jonathan Greening were unveiled in the same week. The Nigerian arrived on a free transfer from Arsenal and Greening came from Middlesbrough for around £1.2m. They were joined by a Hungarian midfielder called Zoltan Gera. Little was known about the Ferencvaros captain, of whom Megson had no knowledge. His first sighting of him was during a trial organised by the club's hierarchy. He was soon won over. Albion had become aware of his availability only when they were contacted by an agent. The club's due diligence into his background suggested he had been a target for Tottenham the previous year. David Pleat, who had just finished a stint as caretaker boss following Glenn Hoddle's dismissal, was swift to offer a thumbs-up to his contacts on Albion's board. Spurs had been quoted above £3m. At £1.5m, Albion were, in Pleat's words, getting a bargain.

Also joining was Junichi Inamoto. The Japanese international midfielder signed on loan from Gamba Osaka but was unfit. He had broken a leg during a spell at Fulham. His Hawthorns stay would immediately trigger a £200,000 permanent deal when he was first named in an Albion match-day squad.

The list of players linked with Albion that summer ranged from the underwhelming to the ambitious. Lomana LuaLua was too costly, Valencia's John Carew wanted a bigger club and Seyi Olofinjana chose newly-relegated Wolves, who were offering a better financial package. Patrick Kluivert, Marcus Bent, Arsenal's out-of-contract forward Sylvain Wiltord and Anderlecht's Aruna Dindane were all considered. An unsuccessful offer was also made for West Ham's Michael Carrick. Striker Mateja Kezman, meanwhile, who was then at PSV Eindhoven, simply laughed off Albion's pursuit. Speaking on Dutch TV, he said: "I know Charlton and West Bromwich are interested. But West Brom are not big enough. In my eyes, they are not a serious option."

No doubt charmed by Kezman's snub, Albion looked elsewhere. Completing the summer transfer activity were loanee Cosmin Contra, a Romanian full-back, and Robert Earnshaw, who set a new club transfer record when he arrived for £3m after making one of his toughest career decisions in McDonalds. 'Earnie' was on his way to a West Midlands hotel during the early hours when a late call came from Everton. The Cardiff striker, who was travelling with his agents, pulled into an M5 service station to mull over the offer from Merseyside. Following discussions over fries and several cups of tea, Earnshaw decided to continue his journey and join Gary Megson's men. He signed at 3am. "Negotiations had dragged on and we just decided to drive up through the night and do the deal," said Earnshaw. "It was in the early hours. I bet not many transfers have been concluded like that."

The arrival of two front-line strikers left Horsfield under no illusions about the task he was facing. "I remember when Kanu signed – he was like our Christophe Dugarry," he commented, recalling the impact of Birmingham's Frenchman. "Christophe was laid-back, so was Kanu. It looked as though he didn't try or care but he did. The first thing I thought was: He's not a Gary Megson player. But Gary saw something in him. With Kanu and Earnie there, I knew I'd have my work cut out."

The autumn of 2004 was to signal the end of Megson's time at The Hawthorns.

Jeremy Peace and his manager were struggling. Communication between the two was diminishing. On the pitch, results were underwhelming. The opening game, at Blackburn, produced a 1-1 draw that was followed by back-to-back home draws against Villa and Spurs, the latter signalling a brilliant debut goal from Zoltan Gera.

Trips to Everton and Liverpool then ended in defeat. Ominously, the game at Anfield was to make the back pages of the national press on the Monday after. Thomas Gaardsoe reportedly sparked a row on the team coach when he shouted following a 3-0 thrashing: "Taxi for Megson." The Dane's comment alluded to the growing prospect of the Albion boss being sacked. Megson was still inside Anfield and did not hear the comment. But Adie Stovell, the club's fitness coach, did, squirted water at the player and a scuffle broke out between the pair. Gaardsoe denied the allegation, telling team-mates he said 'taxi' and directed it at Earnshaw, who unsuccessfully tried a fancy trick during the game.

Megson tried to defuse the story but the outlook was grim. The Baggies boss was out of contract at the end of that season and Albion would need to pay him only £500,000 in compensation if they sacked him. Megson had reportedly already received two warning letters following comments made to the media. Commenting at the time, League Managers Association chief executive John Barnwell confirmed: "Gary contacted me and I would say something is coming to a head quite quickly. We know he has had words with the chairman and is a bit uncomfortable about it. It is any club's prerogative to change manager but sometimes the next question is: 'How much will it cost us?'"

Megson added: "I can't do anything other than my job. I don't have a crystal ball and don't know what my future is. Nothing's been said to me. It is unpleasant and doesn't help the team or the club but it's part and parcel of football. I just want us to concentrate on the tough game we have coming up against Fulham."

A feisty draw against Fulham, in which Neil Clement was sent off for scrapping with Andy Cole after Papa Bouba Diop had been red-carded, deflected attention away from Megson. A dreadful Carling Cup exit to Colchester was followed by a further reversal at Newcastle but home points were collected against Bolton (2-1) and Norwich (0-0). The inevitable parting of the ways came, though, with a 3-0 defeat at Crystal Palace.

Two days before the game, during a media briefing at which the manager and a senior player would normally be present, a surly Russell Hoult stumbled through his press conference duties, offering one-word answers to questions and sneering at journalists. His mood gave a flavour of a darker backdrop. And Megson provided a revealing insight into how things had regressed further. "You try to do your business properly but, last Monday, Alan Crawford [the first-team coach] had to tell seven players to train properly," he said. "On Tuesday, I was going bananas because training was not right and the players were sauntering about as if the world owed them a living. I gave them Wednesday off but, on Thursday, it was exactly the same as earlier in the week. I scrapped training after 20 minutes because the endeavour and effort just were not there."

Interestingly, Inamoto was named among the substitutes at Selhurst Park. Thus, a condition of Albion's contract with Gamba Osaka had been fulfilled. Inamoto was now technically a Baggies player and they would need to pay his £200,000 transfer fee. His inclusion was a mystery as Megson claimed at the time he had 'no other midfield players' to call upon despite Artim Sakiri, Adam Chambers and James O'Connor all being available and capable of fulfilling that role.

On Tuesday, October 26, BRMB radio's network ran the exclusive news that Megson would not be renewing his contract when the current one expired at the end of 2004-05. Albion took this as his statement of intent to resign. Megson notified Peace of his intentions by internal memo on the Monday but that appeared to backfire, with Albion insisting his written statement was deemed a resignation letter. He would only be entitled to compensation if he was sacked from his post.

A club statement said: "Gary Megson has informed the board by letter that he wishes to leave at the end of his current contract, which expires in around eight months on June, 30, 2005. The club accepts this letter as one of resignation and the board believe it is in the best interests of WBA that Gary Megson no longer remains in charge of team affairs. As such, he has been relieved of his duties while contractual matters are resolved. This is a crucial period for the club, and the board regard the timing and manner of Gary Megson's announcement as extremely unhelpful, particularly following the team's disappointing performance at Crystal Palace on Saturday. Nevertheless, the board intend to move swiftly to appoint a new manager, who will be fully focused on the job of taking this club forward in the Premiership."

Geoff Horsfield remembers the period uneasily. With hindsight, and like Simon Miotto previously, he claims Albion players did not do enough to protect their manager. "When you start losing games and are bottom of the League, you don't feel for the manager," he said. "Not at all," he said. "You just think: 'Right, there will be a new manager coming in soon.' It's only now, as a coach myself, that I look back and think that. Now I'm on the other side, I realise players are very, very selfish. They don't realise managers and coaches have families to feed, houses to run, children to care for.

"Were we selfish? I don't know, maybe. I certainly didn't think like that. But I was very sorry to see him go. I know we didn't do enough to keep him in a job. There was an onus on us and we didn't do it. I got on really well with Gary. I know he was a ranter and raver but as long as you worked hard for him, he was great. Now I'm a coach, I can see a lot of the man-management he used. Some of it I use now. But he got West Brom promoted twice, which is a massive achievement. His theories worked. I only had one bust-up with him. But we were fine after that. He got me success and back into the Premier League, so I can't complain about him."

So the search for Megson's replacement started. Sir Bobby Robson was the first man mentioned, even before Megson had lost his job. Also touted were Gordon Strachan, Micky Adams and Glenn Hoddle. Others, including Gerard Houllier, Paul Jewell, John Gregory and Iain Dowie, were mentioned in dispatches. The final short-list comprised Hoddle, Strachan and former Albion star Bryan Robson. Hoddle's demands were a problem because he was seeking a get-out clause. Oddly, he would end up at Wolves following Dave Jones's dismissal; a job Megson was also linked with.

Eventually, Robson was named as the new boss, with Nigel Pearson as his assistant. The opening few weeks were not easy. Robson, hardly a popular choice among the fans, lost his first game – 2-1 to Middlesbrough. The game was noted for the awful Kanu close-range miss. The second match was an encouraging 1-1 draw at Arsenal, thanks to a late Rob Earnshaw goal, but the following weeks were not good. Albion lost their next three games – 3-0 at home to Manchester United, 3-2 at Portsmouth and 1-0 to Charlton at The

Hawthorns. Christmas was depressing. Albion lost 4-0 at Birmingham before shipping five goals against Liverpool. Robson was under pressure already. Horsfield, meanwhile, was not impressed to find himself out of the team. "That Blues game....I was on the bench," he said. "I was fuming. A bit of it was because it was my old club but also because we were 3-0 down in about half an hour. Robbie Savage was bullying us to death.

"At half-time, I didn't say a word. At full-time, I came in, having not got on, and booted some bottles across the dressing room. Then I just lost it. I got up and just said: 'You're all a f***ing disgrace. Some of you want to have a look at yourselves tonight. At least if I've played, I know, no matter how badly I've played, that I've put a shift in. That's the big difference. I could have done something in that game. You didn't.' Some of those players that day didn't deserve to wear a West Brom shirt.

"Oddly enough, I had an exchange with Dave (Matthews), the kitman. I took my shirt off and was going to give it to Matty Upson. It's just something you do. Dave came over and said: 'So you want to swap shirts when we've lost 4-0?' I was already fuming and just popped. There was me trying to show people I cared and I got that. In fairness, me and Dave made up after a week and everything was fine. At least it showed how much it meant to him and it showed him how much it meant to me.

"Bryan got us in on the Monday for a chat. I was the first one to speak and told everyone what I felt. Andy Johnson and Neil Clement had a set-to as well. A lot of people got things off their chest. Bryan told me later that he hadn't wanted to send me on from the bench because he didn't want to embarrass me. That wasn't the problem with me. I was just angry with how some players had performed that day. They didn't wear the shirt with pride."

While some Albion players lost their head, Swiss international Bernt Haas was feeling his on the Monday after the St Andrew's defeat. He spent the night in hospital after frivolities at the players' Christmas party got out of hand. The right-back, dressed as Robin Hood and in a blonde wig, ended in casualty after being blind-sided by alcohol. He never played for the club again. Horsfield laughs when he recalls the story, not least as he missed the festivities. "I had tickets for Britney Spears," he says. "I'd promised my daughter I would take her. But I do remember the lads were drinking all day, went out and Bernie tried to play catch-up. He drank a lot quickly and ended up making the papers.

It wasn't often I wasn't involved in a night out, least of all where someone got into trouble. Luckily, Britney Spears saved me that night."

Albion spent Christmas stuck at the bottom of the Premier League, which, according to Premier League tradition, would mean certain relegation come May.

On December 28, 2004, Albion made their first visit to Manchester City's new Eastlands home. Their own website charts the tale of the turf. Manchester City: Shots on target: four. Shots off target: seven. Albion: Zero shots on target. Zero shots off target. Result: Manchester City 1 Albion 1. The lasting image is that of Rob Earnshaw chasing Richard Dunne's back-pass into an empty net. The Albion striker never quite reached it to claim what would have been his sixth goal of the season. A Dunne OG, it was. The Baggies drew their next two games, at Bolton and at home to Newcastle. As the players left the field following the goalless deadlock against Graeme Souness's men, the theme from the Great Escape was played for the first time.

Off the field, Kevin Campbell was granted a free transfer from Everton to the Black Country. He was joined by Kieran Richardson, who signed on loan from Manchester United, and Richard Chaplow, who arrived from Burnley for £1.5m, having impressed Albion no 2 and ex-England under-20s coach Nigel Pearson. Albion took five points from five games from the middle of January to the end of February. Not brilliant, but progress. With 27 played, they remained bottom but only four points behind 17-th placed Crystal Palace. The survival battle was shaping up to be between four clubs, with Southampton and Norwich making up the quartet. After the 0-0 draw with Southampton, Albion tried to restore some sunshine into their season by jetting to Florida for five days. Eyebrows were raised. They were bottom of the table. What on earth could be gained from a jolly to the Disney attractions? Horsfield elaborated.

"We had an international week and Bryan said we could have four or five days with our families or go somewhere hot. What a choice!" he laughed. "I don't think anyone hesitated. We trained in Orlando, watched some baseball, went to theme parks, went for meals and got a lot out of it. Bryan was happy for us to go out but made it clear we were up for training the next day. We respected him in that way. It made a difference. It was that kind of team.

"There were no outcasts. Cams (Kevin Campbell) was key to that. He'd been in Turkey with Trabzonspor, he'd been at Arsenal and been at Everton so he had a good lifestyle. He opened his wallet to pay for a round at the airport and one of the lads noticed a card, like a black American Express card. None of us knew what it was. Cams said he could buy anything up to £1m on credit. We couldn't believe such a card existed."

Albion returned from the USA to beat Birmingham 2-0, with goals from Neil Clement and Campbell. They were no longer bottom. The Great Escape music, now piped over the sound system after every home game, was getting louder. Momentum was being generated. Two weeks later, Albion travelled to Charlton. More than 3,000 Baggies supporters made the journey on free transport laid on by the club. As the 50 or so coaches left, each fan was issued with a 'survival pack' consisting of food, armbands and inflatable hands. All were paid for or branded by T-Mobile, who were whole-heartedly backing the Great Escape project, the brainchild of Albion's commercial department.

Albion won 4-1 at The Valley thanks to a hat-trick by substitute Rob Earnshaw after Horsfield had opened the scoring. It was the biggest attendance at the stadium for some three decades. Robson's men beat Everton in their next match and drew at Villa and Spurs before suffering a disappointing 4-0 defeat at Middlesbrough, where the scoreline flattered the home side. They then drew with Blackburn before losing to Arsenal.

When Albion arrived at Old Trafford on May 7 for their penultimate game, they knew their fate could be sealed that night. Their match against Manchester United was a teatime kick-off. Southampton and Crystal Palace, two of the other protagonists scrambling for their lives, were meeting earlier that day. An injury-time Danny Higginbotham goal for Southampton against Palace meant Albion had to claim a point to take the battle to the final weekend. They fell behind to a Ryan Giggs goal in the 21st minute – a free-kick which deceived Russell Hoult and, in doing so, caused the Albion keeper to damage his back as he scrambled to keep it out. Whether the goal should have stood is debatable. Giggs took the kick before referee Mark Halsey had signalled. Albion players were still trying to form a wall but the goal was allowed and Hoult was forced off. Enter Tomasz Kuszczak for only his second Premier League appearance. Horsfield takes up the story.....

"We were up against it when Houltie did his back, though by then it could have been his back, knee, arm, shoulder, anything. He was struggling with injuries all the time. Tommy came on and was amazing. I honestly believe that performance got him his move to Man United. He pulled off so many great saves. And we did just enough. I remember the ball coming towards me from Ronnie Wallwork and John O'Shea nudged me. Over I went. Earnie scored the penalty and we clung on to draw. We knew we had a great chance in the final game." Albion were denied a second penalty when Kanu was impeded by Giggs. Yet there could be no complaints. United struck the frame of the goal and found Kuszczak invincible. It finished 1-1.

With Chelsea already crowned as Premier League champions, Sky Sports had their ideal scenario for the final day of the season. Survival Sunday was ready to roll.

Horsfield decided to prepare for Albion's biggest game for years in his unique manner. "The week before, everyone was around us," he said. "I've played in a Cup Final for Blues, in a play-off final too, yet there was more attention that week. The game was on a Sunday, so we had Saturday off. I'd bought a couple of houses in Sutton to do up and, in one of them, I had a big internal wall to knock down. I started at 9am and finished at 7pm. It was the biggest game of my career – and I mean that, it really was – and there I am knocking down an 8ft wall with a lump hammer," he added. "It's a good job I didn't drop anything on my feet but I did catch my finger. It got swollen. In the evening, I went for a Chinese. I just did it to take my mind off it."

Whether or not the oriental meal included fortune cookies wasn't made clear. But Fortune was to become key in Albion's progress. In every way. The maths were fairly simple. The Baggies had to better the outcome of all their three rivals. Norwich were 17th on 33 points, bottom-placed Albion had 31. Between them were Southampton and Crystal Palace on 32. Norwich were demolished 6-0 at Fulham and were swiftly out of the equation. Relegated. Southampton took the lead against Manchester United at St Mary's through a John O'Shea own goal. Darren Fletcher equalised and Ruud Van Nistelrooy was to score a second. Harry Redknapp's side were struggling. It was between Albion and Palace.

And Horsfield, named as a substitute that day, has vivid memories of the Sunday afternoon. "I was on the bench and really, really disappointed not to be starting. Oddly enough, I found out some time later that it was in my contract that, if I'd started, I would have got a fairly big bonus. Bryan Robson dropped me but only found out about that clause himself a few months later when he helped me renegotiate my contract.

"Rob Earnshaw took my place and I could understand that because he was prolific. But I was devastated. I always remember we knew Fulham were beating Norwich, so that game was decided. It got to half-time and I went to Bryan Robson and told him I would score if he put me on. I went on for Jono Greening (in the 58th minute). Zoltan threw the ball in, it came back and I saw it fly across the box, so I just volleyed it in. It was so surreal because the crowd were telling us what was going on. At that point, we were safe. Southampton were losing by then, out of the equation. So it was us or Palace. But then Andrew Johnson scored for Palace at Charlton to put them 2-1 up."

Across the West Midlands, Birmingham City were playing Arsenal. It was a meaningless game, with Blues fans seemingly more tuned into what was happening a few miles away. When Horsfield opened Albion's scoring, The Hawthorns echoed over and over to the chant: "Feed the Horse...and he will score." A large section of Birmingham fans, showing more interest in the progress of their neighbours than their own dead-rubber game, sang the same chorus in tribute to their former hero. But, while Albion were keeping their side of the bargain, results were not going well elsewhere.

"Kieran scored for us after I back-heeled it to him but we were still going down at that point because Palace were leading," added Horsfield. "We knew it wasn't going for us. The whole ground was flat. It was a very strange atmosphere. We'd look towards the crowd and, about five minutes before the end, Jonathan Fortune scored for Charlton. I remember the name like it was yesterday. So it was 2-2 in that game. Our game finished and no-one really knew what was happening. We were stood by the dug-out with Houltie and Johnno (Andy Johnson). All of a sudden, it came over that Palace had finished. They'd drawn. We were safe. It was chaos. The elation was amazing."

Albion's 1,000th top flight win was one of their most dramatic.

Excitement on the pitch was reflected in the general prosperity in performance off it. Turnover increased to £36.5m, with a profit of £5m generated. Dividends to shareholders increased to £3.65 per share. Evolution was prevalent in the shareholding fraternity. In January, 2005, Albion were delisted from the AIM and taken private. Shares not changing hands in large quantity was one of the reasons cited, as was the significant cost involved in being listed. A new company, West Bromwich Albion Holdings Ltd, rose. Shareholders in the existing company were offered the choice of transferring their shares or selling at £72.50 per share. There would now be no automatic trading facility for Albion shares; a return to the pre-1996 days at The Hawthorns.

The number of shares in circulation fell to 80,000 and, as a result, the number of shareholders was reduced from 2,500 to around 1,600. S4A prompted shareholders to act and preferably take up the new shares with West Bromwich Albion Holdings Ltd. Concern was expressed about the possible cost of up to £5.5m of purchasing shares from the old company and shareholders opting to sell. A loan facility of £10m was put in place with Barclays to more than cover this possibility. The club claimed the increased income, from hopefully an extended run in the top flight, would justify the expense. Albion believed the climate was ripe to be more progressive. Jeremy Peace's stake was now 54 per cent. The S4A AGM in November was not attended by anyone from the club – a sign of things to come...

Summer 2005.

Albion prepared to jet off on a trip to California that included a game against LA Galaxy. But David Beckham soon put paid to that. Or at least his club Real Madrid did by muscling in with a big-money friendly of their own over there. Albion were shunted off LA's itinerary and were forced to swap Los Angeles for the Algarve. Based in the Portuguese resort of Vilamoura, they were to play friendlies against Sevilla, Benfica and Sporting Lisbon. The first, against Sevilla, who were without injured ex-Albion man Enzo Maresca, would be played just across the border in the Spanish town of Cartaya. The final match, in Albufeira, was so hastily arranged that, until two days before, Robson was unsure it would go ahead. The tour promoters over-ruled Robson, who would have preferred not to play it. Horsfield recalls those 2005-06 preparations, which included plenty of work, occasional play and a VIP visit.

"The trip to Portugal was brilliant," he smiles. "We knew it would be a hard trip because we played three tough teams. The heat was intense. We were in a brilliant complex in Vilamoura. It was a good trip and a footballing lesson. We played Benfica, who were managed by Ronald Koeman. I played the first half.

I think I touched the ball three times in 45 minutes. We were three or four nil down at half-time (Albion lost 5-0) and Bryan just said: 'That's what you get in European football.'

"Richards Hawkins was our new fitness coach. He had come in from the FA and has since moved to Man United. Even now, I continue a lot of his sessions now I'm coaching at Vale. Off the pitch, we had a great time. We'd have triple sessions each day but Bryan honoured our rest time. When it came to our day off, Bryan said we had a choice. Those who wanted to play golf could do and those who didn't want to were told to meet by the harbour at 6am. I opted for the harbour.

"We all arrived to find Bryan had hired two massive boats – one for the players, one for the staff. We sailed off, had a couple of beers and stopped in this private bay, completely secluded. Daft as we are, Andy Johnson, Paul Robinson and I jumped off the boat and swam to this beach. Trouble is we'd forgotten we'd had a few beers. Jonno Greening followed us. He wouldn't jump in, so someone pushed him. The four of us were sat there chilling out on and looking out towards the boat, which was a few hundred yards away by now. From a distance, we saw someone with huge bags attached to his arms dive off the boat and swim towards us. This figure came out of the water and said: 'Here you are lads, I thought I'd bring you some beers.' It was Bryan Robson. Unbelievable. He must have been nearly 50 by then and he swam all that way with bags of beer strapped to him. Amazing. It sounds strange but, as young footballers, you relate to someone like that. That's why a lot of players would run through a brick wall for him. He's a phenomenal man.

"The only trouble we had, though, was swimming back after a few more beers. Bryan could sure drink. So could his son Ben, mind. He joined us on the trip. And then Paul Gascoigne turned up for a couple of days. He was about to start working for Algarve United. He was a great man. We were all in awe of him. He came to meet Bryan at the training camp and went to watch us in one of the games. He seemed like such a good bloke."

The Baggies floundered in 2005-06. They strengthened but the failure to bring back Kieran Richardson for another loan spell seriously derailed Robson's plans. Worse still, the Albion boss struggled to pick a settled side. While the previous season, his side played in a pretty regular 4-4-2 formation, he now chopped and changed and Horsfield was to leave before the campaign was completed.

"We had a good team there," he said. "We brought in Chris Kirkland, who was different class. We also got in Darren Carter, a good lad who I knew from Blues, and then also Watto (Steve Watson) from Everton. Curtis Davies and Nathan Ellington were good, young lads. Curtis came from Luton. Big things were made of him and, when we first saw him, he looked the business. He was agile, quick, strong, knew where the ball was and read the game. You could tell he was going to be a good player. It's a shame he has had back luck since.

"But we never got the results. It just didn't work. Fitness never changed, training didn't change. We just didn't click and maybe the Premier League got stronger. Did we spend enough? Maybe not. The gaffer changed the team a lot more, whether down to injuries or to try to stop any bad runs we had. The previous year, it had been pretty much an unchanged side from Christmas onwards. That year, it didn't work like that. We just weren't good enough."

Horsfield's final game for Albion was a dreadful 6-1 mauling at Fulham. He was soon bound for Sheffield United as part of an initial loan deal which became a binding £1.2m summer move. The Yorkshireman recalls his departure with unease and regret. "I didn't want to leave," he added. "I had just 18 months left on my contract. My daughter was living up north with my ex-wife and coming up to going to senior school. I wasn't seeing her enough and I'd heard a rumour Sheffield United wanted me. It was 20 minutes from my ex-wife and they were offering me a three year contract. At my age – I was 32 and a half – I couldn't turn it down.

"I'd come into football at 24, which is quite late, and I needed to look after myself and my family. I wanted to stay at Albion. I loved the club, the players, Bryan and Nigel. I had to think about it a long time but I thought it was the right decision for me at the time. Sadly, it didn't work out that way. My last game at Fulham was very hard to take. I'd been feeling my hamstring all week and I should have said no. I started the match and my hamstring went after about five minutes. I didn't want to let the gaffer down but I was being stupid. I told him I couldn't carry on and had to come off at half-time.

"It was my last game for West Brom and I was absolutely gutted to be part of a team who lost 6-1 in my final match. Really devastated. I apologised to the manager afterwards but I didn't want to let him down. He did try to keep me but they said no. At my age, it was a lot of money for the club. And they were getting £1.2m from Sheffield at the end of the loan deal, so I can't blame Jeremy Peace. It was good money for me, especially as I'd come for less.

"After that defeat at Fulham, we came back and I reluctantly told them I had to leave. Nigel Pearson walked up to me and said: 'Geoff, we really don't want you to go but we understand you have to.' I had to walk away because I was welling up. Sheffield offered me a better and longer contract and I would be nearer to my daughter by joining them. But West Brom had become a club I loved. I went up to Sheffield, played the first couple of games. Trouble is I can be outspoken. Nick Montgomery and Phil Jagielka, I'm mates with both, but I had a pop at them after one game. Neil Warnock took offence to that. They were his kids. He never forgave me and we didn't see eye-to-eye after that. Bryan Robson got back in touch and asked me if I wanted to go back to Albion. But it never happened. I wanted to come back permanently but Sheffield weren't interested."

Horsfield's final memories of the Hawthorns were disappointing, yet the Great Escape remains the highlight of his career. Speaking at The Bell, he pipes up with one final comment: "No-one expected us to stop up. It had never been done before. We had a collectiveness. It's my fondest memory. I've got pictures all over the walls, the photos which were mocked up by the local papers. They're all hanging there, including one I've put on a giant canvas from that period. It's the best period of my football career."

Perhaps the final word on the 2004-05 campaign belongs elsewhere. As Albion players, coaches, staff and fans celebrated the Great Escape, the club's fax machine whirred into action. A sheet of paper flopped into the tray. It was a handwritten fax from Sir Bobby Robson and read: "Bryan, I couldn't be prouder. You've always been like a son to me. To see what you've done at one of my clubs makes me so happy. All the best to you and your team, Bryan. Kind regards, Bobby."

Darren Carter

"What do you do or say to a guy who is stood here close to tears? In all my time in football, I've never known such an emotional moment within a dressing room."

A fan yells from near the Halfords Lane press box as Albion stumble along against Sunderland. "Carter, yow'm rubbish!" It's an isolated voice during a lull. Isolated for now, at least. Chances are Darren Carter won't have heard it. Only it gets worse. In the 72nd minute, he appears to be fouled by Liam Lawrence. Referee Phil Dowd waves play on, allowing Lawrence to play in Anthony Le Tallec. Paul Robinson slides in to tackle the Sunderland man but the ball ricochets. It hits Albion defender Steve Watson and the flight deceives Tomasz Kuszczak. Sunderland lead 1-0. It's all a little slapstick. Only nobody is laughing.

It's January 21, 2006. Sunderland, who have won just once all season, go on to win 1-0. It's classed as a Watson own goal. Kuszczak, Watson and Robinson escape criticism. Instead, the focus of anger falls on Carter. For the remainder of the game, he is booed every time he goes near the ball. Not just a trickle of boos but more a choral boom. The Express & Star is unimpressed with Albion fans. Their match report reads: "Shameful. That is the only way to describe events at The Hawthorns on Saturday. And I'm not referring to Albion's dreadful defeat but the victimisation of a player by a small group of his own fans. The Baggies should use the Hawthorns CCTV system to identify every single person who booed Darren Carter. Each one of these so-called supporters should then be ordered to write a letter of apology to the midfielder or told to not bother coming back again this season. It was a disgraceful, shameless spectacle – one which defied all logic. All they will have achieved is to shatter the confidence of a young man who is finding his way in the Premiership. It is a worrying development, one which is the toxic by-product of a game whose coverage in certain quarters has spiralled out of control."

Rewind 12 weeks. Albion are facing an Arsenal side who are FA Cup holders and still featuring most of the Invincibles; Ljungberg, Lehman, Pires, Bergkamp, Reyes, a young Fabregas. In the 76th minute, Carter takes a loose ball on his chest. He drives a left-footer past Jens Lehman. Albion win 2-1. Carter is lauded. Such are the extremes of his career. At 18, he scores the winning penalty which sends Birmingham to the Premier League following a shoot-out to decide the 2002 play-off final. Just a few weeks earlier, he was barely a squad player. More extremes.

I catch up with Carter on an overcast July Tuesday in 2011. Rupert Murdoch and Rebekah Brookes are being quizzed by MPs over the phone-hacking scandals. No need for phone tampering here. Carter is relaxed, happy and open. We're at the Arden Hotel, a few miles from his home town of Solihull. A few weeks ago, he was a Championship player for a Preston side about to be relegated. Now he's in limbo. With North End struggling to offer him decent terms, he faces an uncertain future. Unattached at the time of writing, he is to miss most of 2011-12 anyway through injury.

Such is Carter's career. He has almost bought into the 'boing boing' philosophy of Albion, albeit more by default than design. Highs and lows, all the way. Memories return as he takes a sip of latte. Back in 2005-06, he was a scapegoat. Booed and jeered for mistakes, derided as being overweight by small sections of the crowd. Carter, a midfielder who always posed an attacking threat, smiles when the subject of his weight is brought up. Questioning it now seems utterly inappropriate. The Carter sat in front of me is sun-tanned, has a boy-band haircut and is as lean as he claims to have ever been. There is more fat in his coffee.

He recalls that Sunderland game, a seminal moment in his career. "I know I didn't play well – I didn't feel myself, I hadn't done for a while," he says. "The goal came from a foul anyway but I took a bad touch, Liam Lawrence knocked me off balance and the ball fell away and broke. Until then, my career had been steadily going up. I'd never had criticism or adversity. Yet here I was getting abuse, booing. It was a new experience. As I came off the pitch, I could hear comments from individuals; abuse, hurtful words.

"I understand how fans are. You pay your money and it's frustrating if someone isn't having a good day. To get abuse from my own fans made me realise I needed to deal with boos and jeers and it made me stronger. It hardened me to everything else. I had family at the match. That part is never easy. As my career's gone on, I've been watched by my dad and my mum. They'd had fans around them being negative about me and people don't appreciate who it is they are sat by. But they hadn't seen me experience this. This was new to all of us. I'm on the pitch wondering what they are thinking. I've got the worst things going through my head; I'm rubbish, I'm not cut out to be a footballer, my own fans hate me. You want to hide. But that game was the other side of football. Yet in a strange way, I'm glad I experienced it. Eventually, you get this will to prove people wrong. You realise one fan can love you, another can hate you – not always for rational reasons."

Any weight or size issues he had were simply down to nature. In 2005-06, Carter was 21, turning 22. He was still growing. "People didn't know my body was changing in a way and I was filling out," he recalls. "I was a young adult and still growing and I was never, ever, at any point, overweight. I was doing more weights, more gym work and that's all there was to it. I'm 6ft 2in, I was skinny, so the rest of my body needed to catch up and it's something Steve Bruce (Carter's manager at Birmingham) had often mentioned. I was no longer a boy and I needed to develop. As I went to West Brom that year, I did change physically. People used to seeing me at Blues were noticing the change and thinking I wasn't looking after myself. Yet it was simply a case of a boy growing into a man."

The Arsenal game, in mid-October, brings happier recollections. It was the first time Albion had come from behind to win a Premier League game. The victory ended a run of three straight defeats. "I was on the bench for that game," he continued. "I went on as a substitute. Kanu had scored to make it 1-1. Diomansy Kamara came inside and the ball bounced to my side. I caught it on my chest and just launched my foot at it. It flew in. It was one of those which came at a good angle. To beat them was a big thing. Arsenal hate losing. I remember just before the final whistle they had a free-kick and I just got barged out of the way by Cesc Fabregas. He was riled. They were rattled. That was a big result for us and it got under their skin. It was a fantastic day for me."

Carter arrived at The Hawthorns on July 4, 2005. He was the first part of Bryan Robson's £11m spending spree. Leaving Birmingham was easier than he thought, despite the status as a fans' hero that came with the winning spot-kick against Norwich; one that propelled the teenager into the national limelight. He had lived the dream. And yet he was still a kid. But Birmingham's gain was to become Carter's loss. The inevitable strengthening of the side was at a detriment to Carter's career, with the likes of Robbie Savage, Stephen Clemence and Aliou Cisse arriving. Carter, who had made his Birmingham debut against Albion in January, 2002, remembers where he was when the call came. "I was away with my friends when Steve Bruce phoned," he added. "He'd had an approach from West Brom and had spoken to Bryan, who was a good mate of his. It never occurred to me that I might leave Birmingham for good.

"I'd been to Sunderland on loan and there was a possibility of me going back. But when someone like Bryan Robson wants you, it can obviously turn your head. I went to meet him with Cyrille (Regis), who was my agent at the time, and everything seemed right. I was getting vibes from Blues that I would never be considered a proper first-teamer. This was my chance to be regarded as a senior player, whereas at Blues I was only ever a kid who'd come up through the ranks.

"I was brought up a Blues fan and that penalty changed my life. But, in a strange way, it was counter-productive because money came in and more experienced players started arriving, like Christophe Dugarry and, in my position, the likes of Aliou Cisse and Robbie Savage. The play-off final at Cardiff was the best day of my life but it didn't help me in the long term. Mind you, I would never change it."

Carter continued: "Bryan came in and wanted me to better my career under him. I'd always known about him as a player. My dad used to drum it down my neck about what Bryan was like as a player. He'd tell me to watch how he played, how he timed his runs and got around the pitch. He was one of the best ever. A combination of him wanting me but also becoming the kind of midfielder he had been was a massive draw for me. I've been part of some good squads but nothing compared with that one at Albion. I had made the right decision and was happy. We had a great team spirit. I'd say it was even better than the Birmingham sides I played for. You make friends with players and, from that squad, I've got friends for life."

Much was expected. Carter was the first to check in that summer and was followed by Nathan Ellington (£3m), Curtis Davies (£3m), Diomansy Kamara

(£1.5m), Steve Watson (free) and Chris Kirkland (loan). Nigel Quashie arrived for £1.2m in January, along with Williams Martinez and Jan Kozak, both on loan. Albion tried to bring in Igor Tudor from Juventus, the club even considering help from former Wimbledon champion and the defender's fellow Croatian, Goran Ivansevic, who is a Baggies fan. The link was set up through Adrian Chiles' Croatian origins but the deal never materialised.

All wasn't well on the pitch. Albion were 16th in the table, three points above the drop zone, after that Sunderland game, with 15 to play. Four points from the next two matches masked a major problem. They had scored just six goals in ten games. The lack of strikers arriving was compounded by perhaps one of the more questionable managerial and boardroom decisions of the period – the sanctioning of Rob Earnshaw's exit to Norwich and Geoff Horsfield's no-recall loan to Sheffield United.

Carter sighs as he recalls the transfer window of January, 2006. "I'd known Earnie for a long time. He was a goalscorer and still is. He was similar to Kevin Phillips in so much as you knew he'd get chances and he'd find the right position at some point during the game. He wanted to start more games and he didn't get that opportunity as often as he thought he should have. Selling him was costly, as was losing Geoff Horsfield, who was such a big player for us. These were people who could score goals for us, yet we were hardly known for scoring goals and they were sold, but not replaced. It was a mad decision in many ways."

The departure of Diomansy Kamara and Kanu to Egypt for the African Cup of Nations in January, 2006, didn't help. They were representing Senegal and Nigeria respectively. Then there was the increasingly acrimonious stand-off between Nathan Ellington and Robson owing to a toe injury suffered by the striker. The manager implied his striker wasn't pulling his weight and was making hard work of a supposedly routine injury. Ellington argued that he was in immense pain and needing jabs to get through games. Carter reveals now there were other issues which were perhaps affecting the 'Duke,' who remains a close friend.

"It was around the time he was getting into his religion," he remembers. "He turned to Islam and used to bring the Qur'an and other literature on to the team bus. A lot of the lads weren't interested, so he'd try it with Curtis or myself. He'd start reading passages out and I guess I felt sorry for him because it was obviously very important to him yet not many were willing to talk to him about it. It's not exactly the kind of banter you get in dressing rooms.

"I used to sit with him and try and debate with him. It was difficult for him to get into that when it was still new and fresh to him. I think these days he would know how to deal with it but at the time it was tough for him to mix it with the demands of football. He never got any resistance as such. We didn't have anyone who would disrespect him in that way. But I think some people were dismissive of it all, maybe simply ignorant of what it involved.

"He was diving in head-first and I think the situation was often a bit tricky between him and Bryan. He had to try and adapt his lifestyle and how he did things. Perhaps the gaffer thought it was distracting him and was sceptical about how it was affecting his game. He changed his food habits, there were times he had to fast and that's not ideal in football, where diets, nutrition and refuelling after games are so important. There were things Bryan was unsure about, as regards the Duke himself and the team as a whole."

Losing Kanu, who was just coming into form, didn't help matters. The Nigerian was away when Albion needed him for top-flight duty. Undoubtedly skilful and stylish, the languid striker had a mixed spell at The Hawthorns, only sporadically showing his mastery and phenomenal ball manipulation. A bigger mystery was his age. A Guardian feature in 2010 revealed him to have been born nine years earlier than his official birthdate of August 1, 1976. Harry Redknapp went further, claiming in a Sunday Times interview in May, 2008 that the striker was then already in his late 40s. "I knew he still had something to offer," the manager said. "He was on a free, his wages were small, I wanted to give him a go. How old is he? About 47."

Whether Redknapp's comments were intended as a quip were never established, although there was certainly some credence to the comments. Carter laughs when asked about Kanu's age. "That's a good question," he replies. "No-one knew how old he was. He seemed to have won the Champions League when he was about 16. He would just laugh at us when we asked. But it didn't matter to us. He was a phenomenal talent, nobody could get near him. He had so much technique and natural skill. Mind you, he had his faults. That year, he contributed to about three quarters of our fine kitty. He was forever late, he'd forget things, leave clothes lying around. He just did his own thing, very laid-back. Didn't really have a care in the world. Yet we missed him when he went to Africa. He was a massive threat for us and he had just scored two goals against Tottenham (on December 28), so it was a blow to us when he went to Egypt."

The Baggies were heading south. On February 11, 2006, they travelled to Fulham. They lost 6-1 in a game that was notable as Geoff Horsfield's final outing for the club and Thomas Gaardsoe's last-ever match. A degenerative groin injury ruined the career of a popular and talented centre-half. Supporters were turning on the players and, more so, on the manager. The antagonism was heightened when it emerged that Albion were flying to Dubai the following morning for a mid-winter bonding session.

The squad had been to Florida the previous season on a trip cited as a key reason in them staying up. But it didn't have the desired effect this time, with Albion taking just four points from their final 12 games and finishing 19th. Dubai was to be remembered for another reason, as Carter recalls. "Yes, that was awkward for us. The gaffer had planned for us to go away, only for us to lose to Fulham. I was on the bench that day, cringing that we would be heading off after losing 6-1. The trip was never about football. The gaffer had organised one the previous year and it had worked. You couldn't blame him for trying it again.

"It was intended to bring the lads closer together. We had dinners together, played golf, went shopping, did bits of training and did things as a team. It wasn't all that simple, though. In Dubai, you have to be 21 to get into bars. Curt (Davies) was under age so we had to quickly forge an ID for him on a photo-copier. He was being turned away from places, so we snuck into this office in the hotel where all the photocopiers were and did a bit of improvisation. Duke fancied himself as a computer whizzkid and designed this fake ID for Curt. That was nothing. It was just a drink or two. But then it got worse. A fire extinguisher went off. To this day, I honestly don't know who did it. But it wasn't me, I know that.

"In the morning, people realised it was wrong and the damage was paid for and any mess was cleaned up. But it was too late. Someone on the hotel staff had tipped off a tabloid newspaper. Here we were....'Big Time Charlies, bottom of the League but living it up in Dubai and letting off fire extinguishers.' It wasn't like that at all. It was an isolated incident. I started getting texts and calls from people asking what was going on because the papers had printed this story about us trashing a hotel, which was simply taken out of context. The leak came from someone at the hotel. They were obviously annoyed and maybe even made a bit of money out of it by tipping the papers off. Who knows what their motive was but there was never any malice on our part. Yes, it was wrong but there was no intention to cause harm."

Albion's final two months were miserable. The Baggies slipped out of the Premier League. Jeremy Peace, on holiday when Albion's relegation was all but confirmed at Newcastle, considered sacking his manager. He resisted. But only just. Yet fingers remained pointed towards Robson. The Birmingham Mail commented: "Too many soft goals were conceded this season, too many chances were missed. Bryan Robson must take his share of the blame for not being able to settle on his best XI and for persisting with a clearly off-form Kevin Campbell when they needed goals and wins. Too many of his signings have yet to perform, which brings us on to the money men. The board, to their credit, handed Robson £11m to spend in the summer but Albion's wage ceiling means they were unlikely to attract the very top players."

The Baggies' return to the Championship was rubber-stamped before their Monday night game against West Ham on May 1. Portsmouth had won at Wigan on the Saturday. Jonathan Greening, meanwhile, headed for the supermarket. "I was shopping in Sainsbury's at the time and a fan came and told me the Portsmouth result had not gone our way," said Greening. "Then the texts started coming through from Robbo and Jonno. I almost stocked up the trolley with a load of chocolate to cheer myself up but, with two games left, I thought I'd better not mess with my nutrition. This is the first relegation in my career and when I found out we'd gone down, it felt sickening. We just weren't good enough in the end."

Albion fans talked of a white-flag protest to symbolise the team's Great Surrender. Few bothered, with apathy, slow-claps and Mexican Waves prevailing. Carter revealed the hurt of Albion's decline and eventual demotion. It was particularly felt by Robson, who, while fast losing the fans, still had most of the dressing room very much on his side. "Bryan and Nigel Pearson (assistant manager) are people I had a lot of respect for and still have," added Carter. "Losing hurt them. They were immensely proud, yet they never seemed to lose it with us.

"They knew how to channel any frustrations or anger properly. We stuck together for them. No-one was ultimately blaming anyone else. We shared the blame because we had respect for each other. The thing that was so endearing about Bryan is that he felt every defeat. You could see the pain within him. As a player, you felt a sense of failure. We could relate to that."

Debate about football matters was everywhere. Elsewhere, all was quiet. Albion recorded a turnover of £23.8m and a profit of £5.4m. The squad would find themselves decked out in Umbro kit for the first time in nearly two decades during the 2006-07 season. The announcement came just weeks after Albion had agreed to extend their partnership with T-Mobile.

Darren Carter's second season at Albion was to be his last. September 18, 2006 was one date he wasn't to forget. Albion players filed into the training ground ready to prepare for the following night's Carling Cup clash against Cheltenham. It was to be no normal Monday morning. Carter recalls the day's events. "I'll never ever forget the day Bryan came in to tell us he'd been sacked. We were shocked. We were in the dressing room and he was in a right state. It was hard to see this bloke who cared so much about the players and the club so upset.

"It was horrible and the feeling was just one of utter shock and disgust. What do you do or say to a guy who is there close to tears? I just stood up and applauded him and the others followed. In all my time in football, I've never known such an emotional moment within a dressing room. None of the players wanted him to leave. Nobody wanted him to be sacked, yet he was going. We were just powerless. It was a shocking thing to see. If he'd stayed, we might well have won automatic promotion. Looking back now, I think we would have.

"We hadn't started the season well, we accept that, but we were starting to show improvement and form. After he left, we beat Leeds 4-2, scored five at Ipswich and beat Palace. Kevin Phillips started scoring regularly. Joe Kamara returned from injury and was scoring. These results weren't because Bryan had gone. They were simply the course of results because of the team he built. We should have got automatic promotion with that squad and we didn't. When Nigel (Pearson) took over, he had to lift everyone and he did a good job. The

Jonathan Greening at work, rest and play.....the skipper is lined up with his colleagues and ready to go (below) in this picture from a 2008 Albion tour date in Germany.

The eyes have it. Robert Koren, happy and restored to full health after a major scare over his sight

Koren again (right).....a neat contributor to the Baggies cause over his three and a half years at the club. Below: Roberto Di Matteo, or at least the version portrayed by the thriving Mask-arade company run by Albion fanatic Dean Walton, is joined by In Pastures Green author Chris Lepkowski (right) and Shareholders for Albion chairman Neil Reynolds.

Hardly your archetypal English-based professional footballer. Paul Scharner, looking more professor or film star than tough Premier League campaigner, cuts a sharp image for the camera. The former Wigan player was a journalist's dream at Albion - and very much an individual.

No latter-day publication about Albion favourites is complete without healthy reference to the highly popular and respected Darren Moore. 'Big Dave' is now back on the club's staff in a coaching role and was only too willing to step forward and write one of the forewords for this book. In the background in the picture on the left is the Baggies' former assistant manager Frank Burrows.

Above: Curtis Davies on tour with Albion in Scotland in the summer of 2006. The talented defender was one of those to see his future elsewhere after the club missed out on promotion at Wembley the following spring. Right: Striker John Hartson detected happier times ahead on the trip north of the border but admits Baggies fans didn't see the best of him.

Left: Ishmael Miller, the ex-Manchester City forward who helped fire Albion to a place in the FA Cup semi-finals in 2008 after impressing during a goal-filled spell on loan. In the end, injury blighted his career at The Hawthorns. Below: Albion on tour, this time in the United States. The formalities captured here are before the match against San Jose Earthquakes in 2011.

It's not only on the pitch that the club have made such advances. Hand in hand with the rise fr
a place among the also-rans in English football's second grade, Albion have been impressive
developing their training HQ and the techniques, especially in sports science, that go with it.

An image that, happily, captures the essence of life as an Albion supporter in the opening deca
or so of the 21st century........ fans celebrating yet another successful outcome to a season. Th
green pastures have been a very fertile place for the dreams of a legion of followers......

lads would have been delighted with him staying on but obviously Tony Mowbray came in and brought his own style."

Much of the speculation following Robson's departure pointed to his potential demons with alcohol. Carter believes the innuendo was unfair. "Bryan would support you, he understood his players and would protect us from abuse or flak. He would rather take it himself than expose us to it. That's why players loved him. As for the drink, the gaffer was 'old school'. It's no secret that when he was a player, everyone was more relaxed. These days, it's more taboo but not once did it ever get in the way. What he did away from the lads never came into his job. If it was a drink a night before the game, he would wait until everyone had gone to bed. After that, it was the staff's time. It's the same at all clubs. The players go to bed before the game, then the staff have a few drinks and have their own time. Drink was never an issue."

Carter is more uneasy when talk turns to Mowbray. Although he clearly has a respect for the incoming Albion boss, it's clear he was never comfortable with his methods. And he wasn't the only one. "Tony was weird in the sense that he was set in his own ways," states Carter. "I admired his principled stance in many respects. He got his points across and he wasn't a conventional manager who would shout or bawl. I enjoyed working for him because he wanted to play the ball in the right way but what that team needed was someone who could help us find that extra few per cent to dig us out of trouble.

"Southend was one game which sprang to mind. We lost 3-1 on New Year's Day and were battered. It needed someone to come in and tear down the dressing room walls at half-time and full-time. That's where we needed a Nigel Pearson or Bryan Robson to get a reaction. That softer side of Tony Mowbray perhaps explained some of the sub-par performances we had. The reaction in the dressing room wasn't great either. He was different in every way to Nigel. We'd just do passing drills all the time. He was right in one respect as we needed to get those fundamentals right and it was all basics. But a few players were frustrated that it was just pass, pass, pass.

"In some games, especially in the Championship, you needed to be direct, bully people a bit and just battle. That Southend game was a perfect example. We had Joe Kamara, Jason Koumas, Kev Phillips, myself, Jonno Greening, Zoltan Gera, John Hartson and we got bullied. No disrespect to Southend but they were bottom and got relegated – yet they bossed us. That was a warning which was never taken on board. Bryan and Nigel were proud, in your face. Tony was quiet and reserved. Too many people became comfortable during his first few months at the club."

Carter's luck dipped as Mowbray watched Albion beat Ipswich 5-1 just before his official unveiling. With Albion leading 4-1, Carter struck what he assumed to be the fifth goal. In fact the linesman had flagged and referee Andy Woolmer had blown his whistle. Carter didn't hear the whistle due to the noise of the crowd and was duly booked for unsporting behaviour – a ridiculous decision given Albion were cruising (Phillips scored the fifth during injury time). It was Carter's fifth yellow card and triggered a one-game ban, which left him sitting out Mowbray's first proper game in charge, a 3-0 win against Wolves. Not the ideal way for him to make an impression.

One player who found the new regime particularly damaging to his career was Chris Perry. The experienced former Charlton defender was dropped early on in the Mowbray regime, only to return later in the season when all available centre-halves were ruled out through injury. It even prompted a quip on Perry's part when Sky Sports came to film the 'crossbar challenge' at the Albion training ground during that campaign. Each player is required to say to camera his name and position as he prepares to launch his kick from the half-way line towards the goal frame. Perry ran up to the camera and said: "Hi, I'm Chris Perry....I used to play for West Bromwich Albion."

Carter gave an insight into his team-mate's exile and why the mood was not what it should have been within the inner sanctum. "There were people who weren't on board with what he (Mowbray) wanted to do," recalled Carter. "The problem was that there was still a lot of resentment and animosity, not so much about Tony but more that Bryan and Nigel had gone. We were still angry with that decision from the top. The team spirit we had that year was disrupted. People didn't buy into what Tony wanted to do. We went from a player's manager to one who was reserved.

"Some of us tried to buy into that – I did myself – but even I accepted that we were guilty of not adapting our style when we should have. It was a crying shame because we should have been a top-two side that year. And then there was the Sheffield Wednesday game when we lost 3-1. There was a bust-up between Chris Perry and Mark Venus (assistant manager). Pezza was a good professional and we all respected him. He'd played at the highest level but we were struggling against Wednesday. It was a combination of things that blew up.

"He felt disrespected to be being dragged off at half-time as he thought he was made out to be the scapegoat. Nobody wants to be changed at half-time. He was a senior player and he lost it. We were coming out for the second half and it all kicked off. It escalated and became a shouting match. Chris had to be held back because he and Veno were really going for each other. That was the last we saw of Chris in the first team until the very end of the season and, again, that didn't go down well. It was like he was being made a scapegoat, yet he was someone so respected by the other players."

Carter nevertheless has fond memories of this time at B71. He eventually moved to Preston, with a loan spell at Millwall. The Brummie describes the period from 2005 to 2007 as the happiest of his career. Albion's sacristy was not for the shy, reclusive types. With Geoff Horsfield, Andy Johnson, Paul Robinson, Russell Hoult and Jonathan Greening running the dressing room, there were few places to hide. Carter, who made 67 appearances for Albion and scored six goals, recalls with fondness the camaraderie, not least that of Greening.

"We had the likes of Horse, Johnno (Andy Johnson), Jono Greening, Robbo and Houltie," he said. "Andy Johnson and the Horse were a team – they were beasts to be honest. You had to have your wits about you. Horse knew me from Blues, so he looked after me a bit. Jono Greening was the whipping boy. Any banter tended to involve him and be at his expense. His boxer shorts would go walk-about or he'd go home with dead mice attached to his car. Seriously, he had no idea.

"He'd come out with these stupid comments. There was one time where we were sat down after training and everyone was talking about the Christmas do, which was coming up. It's my girlfriend Sally's birthday on December 5 and that year the party fell on the same date as her 21st birthday. I told the lads I couldn't go and had to go with her. Andy Johnson and Horse were crucifying me, really laying into me, so Jonathan Greening stood up and said: 'Come on lads, you can't have a go at Carts. It's his girlfriend's twenty-oneth [sic] birthday.' Only he could get it so wrong and invent a new word. As soon as he said that, I was off the hook and everyone turned their attention to him. I thanked him for deflecting it away from me and went out for her birthday instead. Cheers for that, Jono."

It wasn't just players who were the butt of jokes. Shooting practice during training was to provide a red-faced moment for goalkeeping coach Joe Corrigan. "We'd been shooting and one of the balls flew into a tree in the woodland by the pitch," recalls Carter. "We look over and Joe had climbed up...and didn't come down. Turns out he was stuck, calling out for Luke Daniels. How Luke kept a straight face, I'll never know but Joe was somebody you didn't want to upset so we didn't make a big deal out of it."

Carter retains an affinity for the club he called home for two years. He added: "The first season was more of a learning curve, having to deal with lack of form, criticism. In the second season, I felt happier. I contributed more. But, over two years, I enjoyed it. It was probably the best time I've had within a squad of players. I'm still good mates with Curtis and Duke. Martin Albrechtsen is another player I see. Paul Robinson, Horse, Jono Greening – I'm still in touch and see them every now and again. I have no regrets. It's where I grew up. And, for that, I will be grateful. Blues gave me a chance to play but Albion taught me how to be a footballer."

John Hartson

"My cancer had spread to my lungs and my brain. I had to have eight operations and 77 sessions of chemotherapy."

IT'S summer, 2007. Albion's players are undergoing intense pre-season drills in Murska Sobota, Slovenia. It's touching 35c in the shade, the humidity is sheer and the squad are stripped down to shorts. No shirts, occasionally bibs. "Do me a favour lads...no pictures of Big John please." Mark Venus, the club's assistant manager, asks the Birmingham Mail and the Express & Star photographers to point their cameras away from John Hartson as they click away during a training session. They respect the coach's request. Pre-season is not the time to be upsetting managers, coaches or players.

Like most of his team-mates, Hartson has removed his shirt. He could be a normal 32-year-old who has stripped off because of the heat. But he isn't. Next to the ripped, finely-toned torsos, Hartson's look is less flattering. This is not usually a problem. He has always been powerfully-built and blessed with great strength. Yet he is toiling badly here. He chases the ball, he's struggling. Training in high temperatures in the former Yugoslav Republic is doing him few favours.

He has always found pre-season tough and he has always carried more bulk than others. But, unusually, Hartson is way behind his team-mates. Something isn't right. Within him, a hidden front is moving in, one which threatens to wreak devastation. Cancer has infested him. He doesn't know it but he's seriously ill. Or, at least, he will be soon. What started off as a few testicular lumps during his time at Coventry, some six or seven years earlier, are now a more sinister animal. They are making their own journey. The cancer's eventual destination is Hartson's brain and lungs.

In 2007, the Slovenian climate isn't kind. Nor are the training sessions. Struggling with his weight and fitness, Hartson is making little impression on the coaching staff. And what impact he is making can't be good. He struggles with a bike ride, he labours during a running session when accompanied by goalkeeping coach Joe Corrigan. It's no good. Hartson is six months away from retirement. And he probably already knows it.

Two years later, almost to the day, Albion are heading back to Slovenia as part of their preparations, this time under Roberto Di Matteo. On the day Albion players head out of the UK, news breaks about Hartson's illness. The squad, this time based in Ptuj, are shocked when told of his plight as they settle into the Primus Hotel. Speaking to the Birmingham Mail, skipper Jonathan Greening said: "It's absolutely devastating news. The lads are totally shocked. Harts is a fighter. All we can now do is keep everything crossed as he begins his treatment. His family are also in our thoughts at this difficult time. We're praying for them all."

Hartson's cancer almost kills him. To use a football analogy, he scrambles the ball off the line. But only just. The linesman's flag remains down. He is that close to losing this particular game. Looking back now, he refuses to shed responsibility for his fitness or form. And he regrets the dereliction of duty regarding his own health. "I found the lump a few years before," he recalls. "I was a Coventry player then. I'd had it six or seven years to be honest and I didn't tell anyone. I certainly didn't tell any of the lads around me. You just don't, do you? I'm a footballer, I've fathered children, so why should I have testicular cancer?

"By the time I got to West Brom, I was struggling with my fitness and it was worrying me. I remember that trip to Slovenia very well. That was a struggle more than most. I was carrying cancer around with me and not realising. Maybe that's not right. Maybe I was realising but I wasn't accepting it. I had the fears. I can't make excuses. I take full responsibility for my career, for my life and everything I do. I wasn't going to run away from challenges. That's the way I am."

Hartson expressed his worst fears over his health to his wife during his time at Albion. She instructed him to speak to Kevin Conod, Albion's doctor. After an examination, Hartson was booked into a clinic. He didn't attend. He recalls the story with unease and regret. "I showed Kevin the lumps on my testicles," he sighs. "He was absolutely fantastic and got me an appointment straightaway to see a specialist in the urology department but I ignored it. Let me make it clear that Kevin did everything in his power to help me. I'm still friends with him to this day. But the doctors aren't going to hold your hand and take you to a specialist. You have to take on the responsibility yourself. My fault, my responsibility. I told a white lie to my wife. I told her I would follow Kevin's advice and do as he told me. I didn't. I regret that."

Hartson left Albion in February, 2008, effectively retiring in the process. His health was in decline. Cancer doesn't disappear. It chips away. It nags, it tugs, it hurts, it eats away. Hartson was in trouble. This was not going to be a quick fix. "I started to get headaches and, from there, it all happened quite fast," he added. "I was in a bad way. It was as close as you can get to dying. I believe I did die. I touched the other side. You feel it happen. I went, I was going. I slipped into a coma and it was causing a lot of worry. I wasn't in a good place.

"Blokes survive testicular cancer because they get it diagnosed early. They get the testicle removed and, in some cases, don't even need chemotherapy. My cancer had spread to my lungs and my brain. I had to have eight operations and 77 sessions of chemotherapy. People will never appreciate how ill I was. Am I clear now? You're never clear. It could come back tomorrow, it could come back in 20 years but, for now, I'm ok. I would hope my body, my lungs, my brain have been flushed out. Six years ago, I was in denial almost. And it pretty much killed me."

Hartson's problems underline the ambiguities of medicals in football. Players are subjected to rigorous examinations and fitness tests. Core areas are scanned. But Hartson feels that isn't enough. He insists football needs to do more. He believes the absence of neurological and haematological examinations is baffling, not least in an era in which eight-figure fees are being paid.

"Medicals these days are intensive but not enough," he claims. "They scan your knees, they scan your ankles, they scan your hips, they scan your back and that's about it. That's the medical. You don't even get a blood test. It's obscene when you think about the investment that clubs make in players. You're paying £50m for a player who might have a brain tumour. It's madness. I was carrying cancer for the best part of six or seven years from what I know. If they'd given me a CT scan, they'd have picked up on it. The unbelievable thing is they scan your body but you don't get a brain scan. If you don't do that, how do you detect brain illnesses? But it was my responsibility – that, I accept."

John Hartson arrived at The Hawthorns in summer, 2006. Bryan Robson lauded his new signing just before the club's trip to Scotland in the July. "John Hartson is a good, battling player," he said. "Even around the West Bromwich area, you get vibes from the fans that they are very happy with the signing."

Away from the press conference hyperbole, all wasn't well between chairman Jeremy Peace and his manager. Robson was coming under increasing pressure from Albion fans following a shambolic 2005-06 campaign. Rightly praised for keeping Albion up in 2005, the Baggies boss was losing his way. Not once did he pick an unchanged team during 2005-06. This was in contrast to the Great Escape campaign, in which the basis of the side's success was a relatively constant team moulded around a core of players, notably the talismanic Kieran Richardson – on loan from Manchester United.

Albion were bracing themselves for a return to the Championship. The relationship between Peace and the first manager he appointed was disintegrating.Ugo Ehiogu's move from Middlesbrough in January, 2006 was shelved, despite the player being given a guided tour of the training ground. Albion's power-brokers believed Ehiogu's wage demands did not represent value for money; even less so if the club were relegated. At various points in that campaign, Robson wanted Stephane Henchoz, Matt Holland, Andrew Johnson and Jimmy-Floyd Hasselbaink. Not one signed. He was effectively told to brace himself for a survival fight. The battle was lost.

Come summer, 2006, Robson welcomed Hartson and Chris Perry and was to add Kevin Phillips, Paul McShane and Luke Steele, the latter two arriving as part of the deal which took Tomasz Kuszczak to Manchester United. Robson briefly broke away from Albion's tour of Scotland to fly back to England. His aim was to sign Danny Shittu and David Thompson. The latter was struggling with his fitness and wouldn't accept a pay-as-you-play deal. Shittu, meanwhile, was close to signing, only for the dynamics of the deal to change late on. He ended up at Watford following lengthy talks at The Hawthorns.

Eduardo, who was to pitch up at Arsenal in an £8m deal some 12 months later, was targeted, too. Dinamo Zagreb wanted more than £6m for the

Brazilian-born Croatian. Albion had no chance. Yet it was the controversial signing of Pascal Zuberbuhler which was to signal the beginning of the end for Robson. The Swiss international was brought in after keeping a clean sheet in every game he played at the World Cup. Even so, Peace was unconvinced.

With Kuszczak bound for Manchester United, Albion were seeking a resilient goalkeeper. And the Baggies chairman, by now reasonably well connected within the game, was getting conflicting reports about the credentials of the 35-year-old. Such was the lack of confidence in the Basel keeper that Peace left it to fellow director Joe Brandrick to complete the transfer formalities. A cosmetic gesture it might have been but it was another display of no confidence in his manager. Peace's hunch was to prove justified. Zuberbuhler's sloppiness cost Albion early on in the campaign.

Robson, meanwhile, was feeling the pressure. By the end of his Albion tenure, the toxicity around The Hawthorns was overwhelming. His fate wasn't helped by a very public falling-out with Jason Koumas, who was still highly regarded by supporters. In an interview in the summer of 2006, Robson insisted Koumas would never play for the club again after effectively failing to show for pre-season training. Whatever the ins and outs – and plenty of vitriol had been served up by both parties – there was always a feeling that Koumas's eventual return was forced on the Albion boss. The Baggies board showed little will to move Koumas on.

Robson's end was to come with a 1-1 draw against Southend in the eighth game, on September 16, 2006. Off the field, he had long since lost the battle. The fans never took to him on the whole. Rightly or wrongly, he was perceived as damaged goods by the time he pitched up at B71, not least as he had struggled during his final years as manager at Middlesbrough and made little impression with a troubled Bradford City team. Older fans had struggled to forgive his departure to Manchester United in 1981, although after nearly 250 Baggies games and eight years, his stay as an outstanding player at The Hawthorns would be considered 'long-term' these days.

The Old Trafford shadow followed him back to the West Midlands as manager. One of his weaknesses was a tendency to answer most questions honestly and accommodate any topic brought to the table. He would willingly address matters put to him by TV reporters or national newspaper writers about issues at United. His views on, say, Sir Alex Ferguson, David Beckham, Roy

Keane or England still carried weight. Albion quotes were shredded, never to be broadcast, never to be printed. Supporters, often unaware of the brutal editing of his comments, were unimpressed.

The soon-to-be-former Albion boss did little to help his cause within 24 hours of the Southend draw when he was shown laughing and joking with Kuszczak ahead of the Pole's United debut in their 1-0 home defeat against Arsenal. The following morning, September 18, Robson was summoned to the training ground, where he was relieved of his duties. Albion were ninth in the table. John Hartson was stunned. "I had no idea Bryan was in trouble," he continues. "Jeremy Peace wouldn't have allowed him to sign me or Kevin Phillips if that was the case, surely?

"Yet, after a few games, the board and Mr Peace got together and said: 'Now is the time to make a change.' That surprised me. But Bryan was successful. He gave the club that great day of survival and he was always a hero. It can't have been an easy decision to sack him. I was very excited when I joined. Here I was playing for Bryan Robson – a big idol, a player I looked up to. He signed me for £500,000 and I was so proud to be playing for him. Like Graeme Souness, he was that kind of personality, that leader you aspire to work with; a brilliant man.

"I remember him telling me just after the season started: 'John, I'm going to have you and Kev up front, Greening on one wing, Gera on the other. We'll rip this League apart.' In Scotland, I had won the League title the season before. I scored 20 goals along with 'Magic' Zurawski for Celtic. I played and scored in Albion's pre-season game against Kilmarnock. I played against Motherwell and Dunfermline and then scored both goals against Hull in the first League game. I was on fire but then Bryan got the sack and it started to go wrong for me."

So Robson left and we waited for West Bromwich Albion manager number 34. The Birmingham Mail chewed the fat over potential candidates. "Mick Wadsworth was mentioned as a possible candidate in a two-tier managerial system, although it's plausible he may be wanted to work as a coach," said the Mail comment piece. "You get the feeling Alan Curbishley is beyond Albion's reach but, then, who thought Martin O'Neill would end up at Villa Park? Tony Mowbray at Hibs must also be considered a serious option given his record at

Easter Road. Mike Newell is a decent shout while Lawrie Sanchez cannot be ruled out. Albion considered Mark Hughes while he was still manager of Wales, so wouldn't necessarily be put off by Sanchez's international, rather than club, pedigree."

Steve Cotterill was spoken to but didn't impress during his interview. Nigel Pearson was successful as caretaker manager but clearly wasn't comfortable with the post-Robson landscape. He didn't apply for the job. Newell and Micky Adams were swiftly ruled out, the latter being denied an interview by Coventry. Steve Round, deemed to be among a new breed of 'super coaches' and a protege of Steve McClaren's at Middlesbrough, was also given some consideration.

Jeremy Peace, meanwhile, spoke to the press about his plans to bring in a sporting and technical director, thus installing a continental style of management whereby a traditional manager would work in tandem with a member of staff whose responsibilities would include overseeing the football infrastructure of the club, looking after the welfare of overseas and youth players, helping identify transfer targets and developing the club's academy. News of such an appointment raised inevitable fears that managerial candidates would be put off. This wasn't how we did things in England.

Yet Peace insisted that the Albion model would be very much based on a continental structure which had been adopted by many smaller to mid-sized European clubs, such as FC Basel and Bayer Leverkusen. Speaking to the Birmingham Post at the time, Peace said: "Everything we are asking the sporting and technical director to do is non-threatening to whoever takes over as manager and is in fact designed to help the manager do his job as effectively as possible. The feedback we have had has been entirely positive and in no way do I see it as a barrier to an appointment. I've been in the job for four and a half years and we're back in the Championship, so clearly something has to change. There are some things we can do better. This is a model which has worked very successfully in Europe, where a lot of clubs of our size or even smaller have enjoyed a lot of success. There is a culture of resistance to it in this country but I see it as a progressive way forward and it's time for us to embrace it."

On the managerial front, it was to be a battle between three. Ex-Rangers boss Alex McLeish, Cardiff manager Dave Jones and Tony Mowbray of

Hibernian were spoken to. Gordon Strachan was also considered – very strongly. Jones apparently wasn't keen on the system Albion were wishing to implement. In any case, Albion had already made their choice. Mowbray, who promised a willingness to embrace Albion's new continental-style management structure, was to get the nod. The 42-year-old watched the side's 5-1 win at Ipswich, where Kevin Phillips scored a hat-trick, before being unveiled to the media on October 18, 2006.

Hartson, an used substitute at Portman Road, recalls his thoughts at the appointment of 'Mogga': "I knew Tony well from Scotland. He was, and is, one of the nicest people I've ever known in football. I played against his Hibernian sides a few times when I was at Celtic and generally did well against them. He was well aware of my attributes but I don't think he realised how little impact I was to make. Perhaps he expected more from me. I think he preferred his strikers to be more mobile."

Mowbray and his assistant Mark Venus were all smiles as they sat in front of the cameras and reporters in the East Stand's Richardson Suite. Surrounded by memorabilia from different eras, including photographs of many heroes, Mowbray was absorbed by his new surroundings. Albion were not just acquiring a football coach, but also a deep thinker. "I like to think of myself as a 'philosopher-coach' because I believe in thinking," he said. "I believe in how you treat people, how you organise the team, how you play. My job is to facilitate the players, make sure they enjoy their work and are motivated and know their jobs.

"For me, young players need psychological help along the way, so you give them pictures to help them, little sayings which you explain to them. (At Hibs) I had them displayed on the walls of the tunnel and in the dressing room. Some were thoughtful sayings, others were funny ones. We had one from Muhammad Ali saying how he won fights. It wasn't him dancing under the lights, it was him on the road doing his running and getting in the miles. It means you need to practice good habits every day to transfer those on to the pitch in matches. The way you train is what you achieve on the match day.

"They weren't just sporting ones either. We had one: 'If you're going to cut down a tree and you know it's going to take you eight hours, spend seven hours sharpening the axe' – that was Abraham Lincoln. There are already one or two things which I've tried to bring in at Albion – just fine detail, which can make a big difference. All I will do is ease my way into the club without making too many disruptions. I bring with me a bag of humility. I'd like to think I'm an educator, a facilitator and a teacher. Footballers have to want to learn whether it's physically or mentally."

Away from the philosophy came a potentially brutal baptism. Mowbray's opening fixture was a home game against Black Country rivals Wolves. The Baggies won 3-0 thanks to goals by Jonathan Greening, Diomansy Kamara and Hartson, the latter with a penalty late on. For Mowbray, aesthetics were just as vital as the result. He continued: "I try to be educated on football. I study football and have a passion for it. You can certainly throw in West Bromwich Albion with other clubs like Tottenham, West Ham and the clubs I played for, Celtic and Ipswich. There is an expectation to not just win but play a certain style. If you're winning by playing a different way, I think supporters accept that but, if you're not winning and playing that certain style, it can become difficult.

"I'm very conscious of the great Albion team of the late 1970s, the one including Cunningham, Regis and Batson, all players of great flair and excitement. I'm aware of the culture and the history of this club. It falls into the philosophy I believe in. I said a similar thing at Hibs and a lot of (press) gentlemen around the table said: 'Talking is easy.' But I'd like to think we achieved that objective and gave the fans an attacking brand of football and brought the supporters back to Easter Road in their thousands. Although I know there is a huge fan base at West Brom, I want to bring back the people who are on the periphery with a brand of football which will create excitement. For me, it's an entertainment business as well as a winning business."

Never mind appeasing the fans, Mowbray was to face different challenges off the field.

"Football, football, football." So said Tony Mowbray in that deadpan kind of way when asked to explain his philosophies on the game. He was true to his word. Albion scored 60 goals in the 35 League games they played that season following his appointment, including seven against Barnsley and five when Coventry came to town. But they also conceded 44. And there was Mowbray's biggest problem; shoring up a porous defence.

Behind the scenes, he was having problems. One player was reading a newspaper at the training ground when he noticed that a rival for his position was a major doubt for the forthcoming game. "He better be fit because I won't be playing," he remarked. His card was marked by staff. Two more players were to give Mowbray headaches. Martin Albrechtsen and Diomansy Kamara told him they intended to leave at the end of the season, regardless of whether Albion went up. Their timing couldn't have been worse. Both statements of intent came in the week leading up to the play-off final against Derby. The culture of self-indulgence was troubling Mowbray. On the eve of Albion's Wembley showpiece, he made it clear there would be changes during the summer, promotion or not. Speaking to the media, he released his frustrations.

He said: "I'd love someone to sit on my shoulders for a year and deal with the issues that come along. If only every club was about having 24 robots, picking your fast one there, your big centre-half there......but it doesn't work like that. There are personalities who react differently to decisions you make but what matters is how you manage them and how they react to those decisions and whether they fit in with your philosophies and beliefs, and what you expect from your team. If somebody rebels and is me, me, me, I'm not interested. He can go as far as I'm concerned because I know that spirit and togetherness are more crucial than any individual talent.

"I have my own ideas and thoughts but we have to remember that this club were relegated from the Premier League less than a year ago and we've kept a lot of those players. I wasn't here then, so I don't know who wanted to leave or who wanted to stay, or whether there's a frustration among them but it's something I have to deal with. If we go up, fantastic, but our problems still don't change and they will still need to be addressed. There will be decisions which people outside may not understand but I will give them an inkling as to why I'm getting rid of someone they might perceive to be one of our best players. There may be a situation where someone may leave for the benefit of the team.

"I hope I'm given the time to implement the changes to get this club going in the right direction, whether it's this year, next year or the year after. We need the right personalities and I won't change things for the sake of it. I want to be successful and take this team up but I know there's a big job to be done. That makes this summer all the bigger, regardless of what happens."

Hartson is bemused when this notion of trouble behind the scenes is put to him, despite Darren Carter's comments in the previous chapter. Hartson feels the spirit within the camp was high, with any dips in form more down to the competitive nature of the League. "I didn't detect any problems," the striker continued. "Tony maybe expected our quality to be better. We always had good passers of the ball. We had Ronnie Wallwork, Jonathan Greening, Zoltan Gera, Nigel Quashie – players who could pass the ball. But we weren't consistent enough.

"Should we have gone up automatically? Maybe. But there are six or seven teams who think they should go up. Nobody has that right, no matter who they are. It's a ridiculously tough and intense league where you have to dig in. People can argue we had the ability but we got to the play-offs and lost to Derby. Better clubs than West Brom have missed out and done worse than we did. One thing we did was score a lot of goals.

"We had Kamara, Kev, myself, (Nathan) Ellington, then (Craig) Beattie came along. Tony liked his sides to be offensive, he liked us to play. Maybe now he accepts they needed more experience at the back, which perhaps we didn't have. But again we were good to watch and I don't remember too many complaints at the time. We were similar to Kevin Keegan's Newcastle side at times and people remember that team for the quality of football."

Mowbray and his predecessor were different when it came to recruitment. Experience and know-how were key for Bryan Robson. The arrival of Chris Perry, Nigel Quashie, Steve Watson, Kevin Phillips and Hartson bore the hallmarks of his philosophy. Mowbray, meanwhile, eased in a policy of younger, 'hungry' players. Hartson has fond memories of his team-mates. Looking back, he feels there was enough quality for Albion to have prospered and several players left a lasting impression on him, notably Paul Robinson and Kevin Phillips, the latter being described as one of the best of his kind.

"We had a good set of players, some good professionals," he recalls. "Paul Robinson was probably one of the best professionals I'd worked with. A good trainer, a good, hard man. He was a proper little tough nut and I'm not surprised to see him going on to have a good career in the Premier League. He was my type of player, my kind of person, fearless in the tackle, committed and the kind of player you want throughout the team.

"Kevin Phillips was another great professional. I was amazed how good a player he was. I knew he scored goals, I'd followed his career. But it's only when you play with someone that you realise how good he is. He had this ability to always find himself in space on the pitch. He always looked like he had time on the ball because he was so clever on the pitch. Kev was a great finisher who could score anywhere. I'm not surprised he has continued playing nearly into his 40s. He was incredibly fit. I'd have to say that not only is he one of the best professionals I've known but probably one of the best players I've ever played with and I've played with some greats in my career."

Every club has someone who is the butt of all jokes. At Albion, back then, one candidate stood out. "Richard Chaplow used to get it from everyone," Hartson chuckles. "Chris Perry, Steve Watson, myself, Kev – we were in our early 30s and there was Chappy, who was still a kid, hanging around and trying to sit with us. He was the brunt of a lot of jokes as a result. He's gone on to have a good career and in many ways he reminds me of what I was like. I wanted to mix with the older lads when I was young. He got slaughtered by us at times but he was a good lad, a nice lad. I saw him and his missus on holiday some time ago. I'm glad to see him doing well elsewhere. We had a good bunch of lads at West Brom. It's just a shame it never worked out for us."

Away from the pitch, Albion acquired academy status, which meant the club would have greater potential in attracting and grooming young players. Dan Ashworth was instrumental in this development and his influence would increase over the years. A new indoor training facility was built on the Tom Silk site, the club investing £1.7m in developing a state-of-the-art facility including a full-size pitch. The Sandwell Academy was opened in September, 2006. Turnover increased to £35.5m but with a £2.7m loss. This was due to the write-down of player registrations, as the club actually made a trading profit for the year. No dividends were paid to shareholders. During the latter stages of the 2005-06 season, Albion also unveiled their new crest. It would be worn for the first time the following season – a campaign which also saw the Baggies sign a kit deal with umbro.

Albion's erratic form continued into the last two months of the 2006-07 campaign. Six defeats in the final 11 games, four of those coming at The Hawthorns, ended any hopes of a top-two finish, with Sunderland and

Birmingham City gaining automatic promotion. Derby were third, eight points ahead of Albion, who finished level on points with surprise side Wolves. Mick McCarthy had transformed the Baggies' neighbours beyond all recognition, Glenn Hoddle having found a unique way of burying bad news (Wolves supporters might argue it was 'good' news) when he quit Molineux one summer weekend as the nation prepared for England's World Cup quarter-final against Portugal.

Wolves were to meet Albion in the play-offs while Derby diced with sixth-placed Southampton. The Baggies, who had already impressed at Molineux that season with a 3-0 FA Cup fourth-round win, returned from there this time with a slender lead. Kevin Phillips scored twice, with Diomansy Kamara grabbing the other. In the return, Albion's advantage was rarely threatened, Mowbray's side claiming a 1-0 win under the Hawthorns floodlights, Phillips scoring his sixth goal in just three games. Hartson, by then, was playing little part.

The Baggies would face Derby, who had beaten Southampton on penalties following a 3-3 draw, in their first visit to the new Wembley. It wasn't to be for them. Stephen Pearson's second-half goal beat them on a sodden pitch. Out-of-favour, lacking fitness, Hartson watched the game on television. "I didn't go to Wembley," he concedes. "It's very difficult. I supported the lads, they were in my thoughts but what's the point in being there? I was a big-name player. I couldn't hide. The cameras would have been on me and I didn't want to be there when I wasn't playing. It was about the lads who played. It's for someone to become a hero. When you don't play, you're not part of it. I watched the game and was supporting us. I remember Stephen Pearson, my mate from Celtic, scored but people forget it was Tony's first season – not even a full season. To get to Wembley was a good achievement for us."

Hartson was to last just a few more months as a footballer. He spent a month at Norwich City in October, playing four games and scoring none. On February 7, 2008, he announced his retirement, citing his long-term struggles with weight and fitness as major reasons. The striker, who began his career at Luton and also played at Arsenal, West Ham, Wimbledon, Coventry, Celtic and Albion, was not prepared to end at a low level.

At the time, Hartson gave a somewhat crude analogy to his weight problems. "I'm going to miss that competitive edge," he said. "That was my weekend, letting off steam and terrorising centre-halves. But I'm not going to miss training. To be honest, I'd lost my desire to get back into the West Brom side. They say you should go down the leagues and just play for enjoyment because it will be easier. It's not. I have been fighting my weight for 12 years. I can't have a burger without putting on half a stone."

These days, Hartson is more reflective. His life has changed, priorities have altered. The landscape was to change forever when he almost died. The one complaint from his career remains his time at Albion, not least as he still feels a pang of regret. "My West Brom career came to an end under Tony and if anyone would have any reason to be unhappy with Tony, it would be me," he went on. "But my feelings are totally the opposite. Tony was very gracious and honest with me.

"I want people to know how positive I was about this period. I was so happy to be at a club like West Brom. It really does make me sad that they were probably the only club, with the only set of fans, who never got to see the best of John Hartson. Every single one of my other clubs – you look through the record books – I was liked. I scored more than 100 goals for Celtic in five years. I played Champions League football, I was considered a legend for my country. I started well at West Brom and then it all went wrong. I went from Champions League football to reserve games at Kidderminster in the space of 18 months.

"Without wishing to make excuses, I was struggling mentally. I was really missing my children. I was going through a divorce and the kids were in Wales. Let's face it, I was probably already ill. These things take their toll. For 31 years, football was everything I knew. I had a beautiful house in Hockley Heath, in Solihull. I still have it. But I had personal issues. My divorce was horrendous.

"I wasn't at my best at West Brom. The fans must have been delighted to hear John Hartson was coming to their club, this player who has scored in the Champions League and World Cup qualifiers, won trophies. But I was disappointing. That's not Tony Mowbray's fault. It's mine. He remains a good friend of mine. He'd lost his first wife through cancer and he was supportive when he found out about me. But, on the pitch at West Brom, I can have no excuses. The fans, players, staff......everyone was absolutely brilliant. I'm not apologising but I want to use this [interview] to explain why I wasn't my best.

"I'm now back in Swansea and busy with media work. I have several contracts, columns in newspapers. I also take a couple of kids' teams and I'm involved with my children's school and with a testicular cancer foundation. I have all my badges and will coach one day. The timing isn't great. But that's what I want to do. Maybe it will be sooner rather than later. I should have so many bad things to say about West Brom because it's where things went wrong. But I haven't. I still love Baggies fans and am very fond of everyone there – the office staff, the girl on reception, the lads who I knew from my time there, the ladies who do the laundry, the kit man, everyone. They were all great to me. It was my own doing that it never worked."

Kevin Phillips

"I was confident in my own body. Tony Mowbray knew that and the club knew that. I would love to have seen my career out at West Brom."

KEVIN Phillips doesn't do much travelling these days. He doesn't need to. Speaking from his home on the outskirts of Lichfield – a stunning residence as it happens – Phillips has an arrangement of convenience with his current employers Blackpool. He trains, and trains hard, on his own from Sunday to Wednesday. On Thursday and Friday, he works with the team. On Saturday, he plays. And when he plays, there's a decent chance he might score a goal or two. His manager Ian Holloway is happy with the arrangement.

It's the third week of January, 2012. Phillips has already opened his account in the calendar year, against Ipswich. Before the month is out, the 38-year-old scored twice more – in the FA Cup against Sheffield Wednesday and then against Coventry. Blackpool would miss out by a stroke on returning to the Premier League. West Ham United beat them 2-1 at Wembley in the Championship play-off final. His knee, he assures me, is in fine working order. More of that later.

Goal-scoring comes easily for Phillips. At the time of writing, he has 276 from nearly 620 appearances. Of those, 46 were accrued in 81 outings for Albion. If not the greatest goals-to-game ratio of any post-war Albion player, it's certainly well up there. His Hawthorns career was all too short and the very fact he was still scoring in his late 30s – he netted 17 times in the 2011-12 season – is a reminder that Super Kev should have had longer.

Two years is obviously enough time to create a Baggies hero. Laurie Cunningham managed it from 1977 to 1979. Phillips did so three decades later after moving across the West Midlands in August, 2006. The switch ended his underwhelming 14-month spell at Aston Villa, where just five goals in 27 games drew comments that Phillips – injury-hit during that spell – was past his best. Think again. Sunderland, where he scored 143 goals in 239 games, were keen. Albion were lucky to secure his signature. For that, they have Bryan Robson to thank.

"I was told I could leave Villa and I'd actually made contact with Niall Quinn, who was in charge at Sunderland at the time," recalls Phillips. "I'd agreed to go and speak with Niall but, the day before, I and my agent had a call from Bryan Robson, who said West Brom would be interested. It made sense. A part of me wanted to go back to Sunderland but a part of me wondered whether going back was the right thing. Could I still make an impact? So when West Brom came in for me at the last minute, obviously I was interested. I was due to go to Sunderland the next day, so I'm pretty sure I would have signed for them – almost certainly – just because of the pressure clubs put on you when you go for talks.

"West Brom had just been relegated but kept most of their players and looked a strong outfit to me. And Bryan was a legend in my book. I agreed to talk to him and, as you get with a lot of clubs, once they've got you inside their training ground, they're not going to let you go. Basically, they matched my Villa contract, they sorted a fee out, gave me the quickest medical I've ever had and asked: 'Are you prepared to sign now?' I got in touch with Martin O'Neill, who had not long been appointed as Villa boss. He was surprised it was happening as he wanted me to stay. But I was happy, I signed. It probably didn't go down well with Quinny but I think he understood deep down. I was living in Lichfield. The kids were settled in school and I didn't want to uproot my family for a year or two. You also look at players who go back to old clubs and it doesn't always work out. I feel I made the right decision and the two years proved that. It was a good move. Had Bryan not called, I probably would have signed for Sunderland."

Phillips' journey under Robson was brief. Just four League games, to be exact. A 1-1 draw with Southend drew the Albion manager's era to a sudden end. Phillips, whose 81st minute shot in that game struck the post, was unimpressed. 'Premature and harsh' seemed to be the over-riding memory as he looks back to September, 2006.

"The day he got sacked, I remember going to training and it just filtered through to the dressing room what was going on," he adds. "Yet Bryan was still at the training ground. A few of us senior players said: 'Is there anything we can do?' It was too late. There was a lot of anger in that changing room. I was extremely disappointed. Bryan was a good man. To keep West Brom in the Premier League when they were bottom at Christmas was incredible. His standing in the game and the mere fact he wanted me to join him was a big pull, yet in a few weeks [of the 2006-07 season] he gets the sack. I was absolutely gutted because he was one of the reasons I signed. What was frustrating is we'd kept a lot of the players, we had some great experience and I think people were expecting us to be top of the league. But it's never that easy. Yet, equally, we weren't exactly struggling."

Albion players were happy for assistant manager Nigel Pearson to take over. Chairman Jeremy Peace had other ideas. Tony Mowbray was appointed in the middle of October, watching his first game from the stands at Portman Road, where Albion won 5-1, aided by Phillips' hat-trick. "We were very, very surprised to see Tony get the job," continued Phillips. "I'd played against him in the early days of my career. I knew who he was but, in terms of managerial experience, we'd just lost a household name in Bryan Robson. So it was a surprise to see that we replaced him with Tony.

"We'd heard rumours that this manager from Hibernian was going to get the job. I suppose deep down we felt there was someone established who could have done it. My own thoughts were: 'Why have they got rid of Nigel to bring someone in who had done well in the Scottish League – with all due respect to the SPL – but was unproven?' I had total respect for him as a player but we were pretty sure Nigel could have done it. We'd had some great results during his period in charge.

"In Nigel's final game, we all knew Tony was taking over and Nige gave this very powerful and emotional speech in the hotel. It was fantastic and passionate. He told us to carry on, go out and win promotion. It was like his farewell speech. We knew that. I think all of the players at the time would have said the same about Nigel. He was a great fella, a terrier, very honest and I've learned that there aren't many of those around. That 5-1 win was dedicated to Nigel. Obviously we knew Tony was in the stand, so people want to show him what they can do but we won that game for Nigel. It was his speech which helped us hammer Ipswich."

The issue of whether Pearson was a candidate or, indeed, even wanted the job remains a mystery for Phillips. Shrugging his shoulders, he answers: "In an ideal world, he would have wanted the job but perhaps he felt a sense of loyalty towards Bryan, too. Yet this didn't change anything towards Tony. Once we knew he was getting the job, then you, as players, have a responsibility to that man. And history shows he was a very good appointment.

"His philosophy was a total and utter surprise to me, personally. He was a big strong, powerful centre-half who would put his head on the line – he was an old-fashioned defender. But when he came in and said he wanted us to play from the back and along the ground, we were all a bit surprised. It was fantastic. A really nice fella who loved his football and knew so much about the game. He was completely absorbed by it. We were concerned that our next manager would be route one but Tony stuck to it and we carried on where Bryan and Nigel had left off."

The Phillips home is an evident, albeit subtle, nod to his playing career. Awards and match balls are displayed in a room as you walk through the front door. Yet his achievements include a statistic which is difficult to quantify in terms of trophies or pots; derby goals. He scored heavily for each of his teams in games against local rivals. He grabbed two for Watford against Luton in as many games, four in six for Sunderland against Newcastle, one against Portsmouth in his spell at Southampton and one against Birmingham City in a St Andrew's derby for Villa. And then we come to the big Black Country derby.....

In 2006-07, Albion were to meet Wolves five times – twice in the League, twice in the play-offs and once in the FA Cup. Wolves fans best look away now. All told, Phillips has scored seven goals in competitive games at Molineux. As an Albion player, his tally was four in five fixtures. That included one in a 3-0 demolition in the FA Cup fourth round tie and a further two in the thrilling 3-2 play-off semi-final win. He netted one more in the return fixture at The Hawthorns a few days later – Albion's 100th goal of the 2006-07 campaign.

"I have some great memories," says Phillips, who also won eight caps for England. "The Wolves fans always make their feelings known. Before I signed, I didn't even realise West Brom and Wolves was such a big derby. Now I live here, I am bordering the Black Country and I get people driving past yelling things! It means a lot to the people. The play-off games were just incredible. To beat them there and then score the only goal in the second leg was great. They were fantastic games."

That particular story didn't have a happy ending, though, for Albion. After the 4-2 aggregate victory against Wolves, Phillips' achievements and all, the footnote to the season was the inglorious 1-0 defeat against Derby at Wembley in the final. Sighing, he adds: "We just couldn't get the breakthrough. It was one of my quietest games and it was just a horrible feeling when they scored. You knew it was going to be one of those days. It was heartbreaking because it was the second play-off final I had lost. I'd gone through it at Sunderland and it kicks you where it hurts.

"You work hard, we had a change of management and it was devastating. You wonder about the players who will leave. A lot of players stick around for one season but, if you don't go up, they tend to leave. So we knew it was going to be very tough for us during that summer. I felt so sorry for the supporters. I think at times we didn't win games we should have won. We had a few injuries. We lost Curtis Davies for a while and lacked consistency. Perhaps the transition between the three men who had been in charge was too much. It was new for Tony. We were trying to know him, he was trying to get to know us as players. I think to get into the play-offs was a decent achievement. It was a relatively successful season for the club even though we didn't quite make it. It was a great learning curve for the manager, for the players and a taste of things to come in the following year."

Summer, 2007 was one of transition. Club captain Curtis Davies left on loan to Aston Villa with a binding permanent transfer worth just over £10m tied in. His move went through just before the end of the transfer window. On a July day dubbed 'Black Monday,' Albion agreed a fee of around £6m for Diomansy Kamara with Fulham and accepted Wigan's £5.3m bid for Jason Koumas. In hindsight, the departures were anything but disastrous. Neither Kamara nor Koumas reached the same levels of performance again.

Paul McShane (£2.5m) went to Sunderland, Nathan Ellington switched to Watford for £3.25m and Darren Carter (£1.25m) departed for Preston. Steve Watson and Chris Perry were released. Paul Robinson was close to joining

Sunderland and Wigan but neither move materialised. Robert Koren, who had joined from Lillestrom the previous January, was to miss the first few weeks of the season after being caught on the eye by a stray ball during training. Although he made a full recovery, the injury caused temporary blindness.

Albion shopped around to fill the voids. Before the August transfer deadline, 12 new signings arrived. Seven were handed debuts in the opening game of 2007-08 at Burnley – five from the start, two as substitutes. Arriving were Chris Brunt, a £3m recruit from Sheffield Wednesday, Leon Barnett (£2.5m from Luton), James Morrison (£1.5m from Middlesbrough), Craig Beattie (£1.2m from Celtic), Pele (£1m from Southampton), Carl Hoefkens (£750,000 from Stoke), Bartosz Slusarski (£680,000 from Dyskobolia Grodzisk), Filipe Teixeira (£600,000 from Academica Coimbra) and Tininho (£230,000 from Beira Mar).

Signing on loan-to-permanent deals were Manchester City striker Ishmael Miller, whose eventual move cost about £1.7m, and Heart of Midlothian forward Roman Bednar. His fee was £2.3m. Slovenian Bostjan Cesar arrived on loan from Marseille. The newcomers on show at Turf Moor were Hoefkens, Barnett, Tininho, Teixeira and Beattie, supplemented by Morrison and Pele appearing off the bench.

Behind the scenes, Albion had appointed Simon Hunt as their first sporting and technical director. He had previously worked with George Burley at Hearts as assistant manager and chief scout, before taking on an administrative role at Southampton. Tony Mowbray, speaking at the time, gave an insight into the role. "I think Simon, first and foremost, brings his knowledge of players and football," said. "He has worked in the industry for a long time and has a lot of good contacts. The chairman and Simon should be recognised for the amount of work and effort they put in to try to make these signings happen. All the staff behind the scenes should be congratulated. I've been at home with my family late at night and taken calls from people, yet they're still in the office working."

Regarding those who had left, Mowbray continued: "I said to the players after Wembley that if you don't want to be here, we'll try and facilitate your departure. We have to congratulate the chairman for the price he got for some of the players." Phillips was one of the few to stick around during this period. He was not surprised by the farewells. "I expected players to leave," he added.

"Once we lost to Derby, I knew we'd lose Koumi because he was quality. Kammy had scored goals, Curtis was highly rated, too – they were our top players basically.

"It became a worry because we feared the squad would break up but when you've got a manager like Tony, he identified some great players. Robert Koren, for instance, was tremendous. I remember.....this little guy with bad hair turned up for his first day's training and we had no idea who he was. He started playing and 'topped' one of the lads, dragging his studs down the shin. I can't remember who it was but one of the other lads said: 'What the hell are you doing?' He just said: 'I'm on trial, I want to make an impact' and I thought: 'Fair play.' From then on, he was accepted. I didn't think he'd be as good as he was. He was excellent.

"Ishmael came in and Tony got the best out of him. Brunty, Mozza, Filipe Teixeira – all good technical players. Brunty from Sheffield Wednesday was a great signing, Mozza was brilliant and Filipe had great ability. We just seemed to gel and the football we played was some of the best I've ever played in my career. I was happy to stay. I was excited about the following season. I knew that with Tony in charge and with the football we played, we would have a good chance of promotion."

Phillips was pleased to see Mowbray and assistant manager Mark Venus finally settling in. Their bedding-in had not been the most comfortable, especially for the no 2. "Tony came in and changed things gradually," continued Phillips. "I've been at clubs where a manager comes in and changes everything quickly. That can piss people off. But Tony didn't want to change too much and he said he was lucky to get a job with so many good players. We had a strong squad and a great chance of promotion. He instilled more discipline and changed things to how he wanted the club to be run. Everyone was fairly happy, he was approachable.

"With Mark Venus, it was more difficult. It took the lads a while to take to him. He had a few problems at first. Some of the lads said things which were out of order and they had no right to say. I like Veno because he's a bubbly character. You find some players don't like that but he made me laugh. He was a perfect foil for Tony. Tony was quiet, whereas Veno was a lively bloke and a joker. It was a good combination. Some of the senior players didn't take too well to a coach coming in who was relatively unknown in a football sense.

Some things were said in the heat of football that were regrettable. But Veno and Tony were a good team."

Some time in the future, 2007-08 will be regarded as a vintage campaign for Albion. For now, it remains perhaps too recent. That it came during such a seminal decade for the club perhaps doesn't do this particular season justice. Mowbray's side won the title with 81 points, scoring 88 League goals and reaching the FA Cup semi-final.

Following the opening-day defeat at Burnley, Albion took 13 points from six games. They finished 2007 as leaders, three points ahead of Watford. A meeting between the two clubs at Vicarage Road in November provided a fascinating backdrop. Watford, managed by Aidy Boothroyd, could not be more alien to Mowbray's Albion. The Hornets were robust, physical and played the ball from one end of the pitch to the other with the minimum of passes. It was route one. They started the game nine points ahead of third-placed Albion. By the final whistle, the Baggies had destroyed them through incisive, passing, expansive football, built on movement and technique. Phillips, Ishmael Miller and Martin Albrechtsen were the scorers.

Mowbray was in no mood to abandon his principles. "I will never manage a football team that plays long ball. It goes against my grain and what I want to do," he told the Birmingham Post. "I know you can win playing football. Manchester United and Arsenal are at the top of the Premiership every year. Yes, you may argue that they have the best players but I would argue that they play the best style of football. And I've seen the proof that you can play football at this level without the need to batter your way out. Some teams can but I believe if we express ourselves, we will become consistent year in year out and we'll always be striving to get out of the division.

"I also think it's important to play this way to allow your players to showcase their talents. The top clubs want players who do that. Manchester United only sign players who can express themselves. It's the same with your Arsenals, your Tottenhams and your Chelseas. They don't buy players who knock it 50 yards down the channels, who can do no more than flick-ons. Some managers want to play percentage football and I think some players are lost to that kind of football. We follow a similar belief and philosophy here as we did at Hibs, where there are a lot of players who clubs are coveting. Maybe half a dozen could move on to bigger things. That's because they've been allowed to showcase their talent.

"I follow a philosophy with life and football and while I'm only dipping my toes into the first team, the ideas and philosophy will hopefully filter down and I want players to express what they can do. We've got enough footballers at this club who can achieve the demands that are put on them by manipulating the ball, by passing the ball, by playing in tight areas, by spreading the pitch out, by getting it wide and by getting it into the box as opposed to going direct with the long ball and through percentage football.

"We might be playing well and not winning games or we might be playing rubbish, getting a 1-0 win and I might be wondering when the wheels are going to fall off, not knowing what I'm going to get next week. That's the society we're in, it's results-driven and I know I'll be hammered down for being an idealist. When I walked into Hibs. I was the bookmakers' favourite to be the first manager to be sacked. But I won't compromise and start playing a big centre-forward who can't play because, one day, I may get the sack and end up thinking: 'What am I doing, why am I compromising my own principles?' If I'm going to fail, I'll fail doing it my way."

Phillips enjoyed Mowbray's philosophy. He fed off the chances being played into his feet. He found Mowbray, as a man-manager, easy to deal with. "Tony was always very focused," he said. "If you went to see him about something you weren't happy with, he would explain things to you, explain why he'd done it. You wouldn't always agree but he was very composed and very relaxed. Problem is, at times we had to score two or three goals to win or draw a game. We knew as players what the problem was. We couldn't keep clean sheets. He never lost it and that was one of the problems maybe. We had experienced players and at times you'd want him to come in and give the defence a rollicking, really lose it. But he never did. He would talk calmly. I saw him raise his voice a few times but never really lose it."

Crucially, Super Kev was still scoring at a tremendous rate. His return of 22 League goals in 2007-08 was even better than the previous season, when he netted 19 times. Yet he had every right to feel frustrated. As a whole in his Baggies career, he started 60 matches and was substituted in 23 of those. He bagged two hat-tricks during his stay – at Ipswich and home to Barnsley – yet he could have had more. The manager's 'hook' did not rest easily on his shoulders. Phillips reckons his goals-per-game ratio could have been even better.

"I certainly would have preferred more minutes on the pitch at times," he confirms. "If you come off after 75 minutes, you know you've missed the time when the game opens up. I probably could have got a couple in that time. That was frustrating. I think I probably missed out on some hat-tricks as a result but the problem is when you get to 33 or 34, people assume you can't last 90 minutes. So, yes, I did speak to Tony about it. I still believe I can play 90 minutes now for Blackpool, yet I [supposedly] couldn't then. But I can see why he did it. It's never easy to accept because if you're a goalscorer, you glide through games. I'm happy I started a lot but it was certainly frustrating because I reckon I could have scored many, many more goals for West Brom. Scoring 20 two seasons on the bounce was good. I got 24 in all competitions in my second season but didn't score for the final six, which was pretty gutting. I should have ended that season with 30 goals."

Albion won the title, finishing four points clear of second-placed Stoke and six ahead of Hull. Mowbray's class of 2008 could score goals. But they also conceded 55 – ten more than relegated Leicester. The Baggies clinched the title on the final day, Chris Brunt and Do-Heon Kim scoring at Queens Park Rangers. It was the club's first championship triumph since 1920. It was to be Neil Clement's 300th Albion game – his final professional match, with the long-serving defender suffering a final knee injury during a pre-season friendly against Real Mallorca a few months later.

Loftus Road was also special for Phillips. Supporters saluted his efforts by dressing as super heroes, as a nod to his 'Super Kev' monicker. Little did he know it would be his last game for the club. The striker was coming towards the end of his contract and wanted a two-year deal. Albion had a 12-month contract in mind, with a one-year option dependent on him fulfilling a certain number of games. Phillips had suffered a partial tear of his cruciate in the 1-1 draw against Sheffield Wednesday on November 6, the injury keeping him out for just over five weeks. The seeds of doubt were already planted, certainly in the corridors of power......

Phillips recalls the period and gives his personal insight into the contractual negotiations. Looking back, he feels he could have done with more support from the coaching staff. "I had no idea QPR would be my last game," he said.

"I didn't want to leave and we'd been chatting for a while. They wanted to offer me a year but I wanted more security for my family and was looking for a two-year deal. I'm a fit person, look after myself, never caused problems and I was confident West Brom could get two good years out of me.

"Because I'd ruptured part of my cruciate that season, I think they felt that if I went down in the first few weeks of my contract, they would lose me for a year. So I can understand the club's situation. But I knew I could play for two years and, by the end, it became messy. Initially, they said I could have the extra year but I'd have to play 20 games. Then that went down to 12 and, by the time I was about to sign for Birmingham, Tony rang me and said: 'We will get it down to about eight.' But it was the principle of it. What's eight games? Just give me the two years and I'll sign now. But they wouldn't do it, so I signed for Birmingham. I had Jonno (Greening) calling me, Robbo (Paul Robinson) calling me trying to convince me to stay. I was gutted because I didn't want to leave. I felt Tony could have pushed it more, too. Deep down, did he really want me to stay? I don't know. That's not for me to answer."

Albion's response lacked class. A statement on the club's official website made reference to Phillips turning 35 'later this month.' It also referred to his 'four goals in 23 appearances' for Villa when he had last played in the top flight. It was hardly a glowing tribute to a player who had helped Albion to promotion. Albion were to score just 36 Premier League goals in 2008-09. They finished bottom, three points from safety but with a worse goal difference than those above them. Would Phillips have made a difference? Maybe. Perhaps not. But, given that Zoltan Gera also left that summer, Albion were left depleted for goals.

Phillips, meanwhile, helped Birmingham to promotion in 2009, scoring 23 goals in a three-year spell for the club before his move to Blackpool. At the time of writing, he has had over 130 outings since his Hawthorns release. He has suffered no significant cruciate problems since November, 2007. "It's clear the two-year option was a problem," he added. "I knew I wouldn't start many games but I knew I could come on for the last 20 minutes and do something, make a nuisance of myself and get a few goals. We'll never know. I ended up promoted with Blues and it was a good season. But you're always jealous when you're watching your old club and ex-colleagues in the Premier League. It's where you want to be. These things happen in football."

Phillips added: "Whether the injury prompted the club to not commit, I don't know. I felt occasional pain when I first came back but in those four years or so, I've never, ever had a problem with that knee. I've passed medicals with other clubs, so that frustrates me. I can understand it from a club point of view yet I was confident in my own body. Tony knew that and the club knew that. I would love to have seen my career out at West Brom. Would I have made a difference? I don't know. I'd like to think I would have done. The two years were fantastic and I never got a chance to thank the fans. I would have loved to have played at The Hawthorns again but when they saw me warming up for Blues at St Andrew's, they were singing 'Super Kev', which for away fans in a derby game is pretty impressive. I can't speak highly enough of the club. I only wish I'd stayed there. It's a fantastic stadium, great training ground. Hopefully, our paths will cross there again."

Success on the field brought promotion. The balance sheets brought smiles within the boardroom. Turnover was £27.2m and profit was £11.3m but no dividend was paid out. Jeremy Peace made a cash offer to shareholders of £80 per share. There were just over 90,000 shares at the time, so effectively placed a value of £7.26m on the club. The accounts appeared to show a value of around £24m. The independent directors stated that the offer was at 70 per cent discount to the tangible net asset value per share.

S4A took up the cause, strongly advising shareholders not to sell. For the first time, S4A directly opposed the chairman by arranging access to purchasers who would pay £100 per share to those who either needed to sell, or decided they no longer wished to retain their stake. The rationale behind that was to try to encourage a healthy level of independent shareholding in the club and provide a better financial deal to those wishing to sell. Inevitably, this gave rise to the impression that there may be ill-feeling between the two parties. From S4A's perspective at least, this was not the case. The committee consistently stood behind the chairman in his running of the club, through good times and bad, but always felt compelled to show responsibility towards the small shareholder.

The Baggies remain the only club to win promotion and the FA Cup in the same season. That was in 1931. They went close in 2008 to repeating this unique feat. In the FA Cup third round, Charlton Athletic were overcome 4-3 on penalties after a replay. The Baggies then faced three successive away games, beating Peterborough 3-0, Coventry 5-0 and Bristol Rovers 5-1. Manchester United, Arsenal, Tottenham Hotspur, Chelsea and Liverpool had all been knocked out. The final four comprised three Championship clubs – Barnsley, Cardiff and Albion. Portsmouth were the sole Premier League club.

The Baggies were drawn against Pompey in a Saturday lunchtime game at Wembley. They lost 1-0. Robert Koren's shot went closest for Albion when it hit the bar. Portsmouth scored through ex-Baggies man Kanu. Milan Baros collected a Glen Johnson ball on his bicep and, having already pulled clear of Martin Albrechtsen, squeezed in a shot. Dean Kiely saved but was unable to keep out Kanu's follow-up.

"That cup run was brilliant," Phillips continues. "When we got Bristol in the quarter-finals, we couldn't believe our luck. We had to be professional but we knew it was a great chance to reach Wembley. I don't agree with playing the semis there because it spoils the final but, as a player, you want to be there. We were a bit lucky with the teams we drew but we also got some great results and scored five at Coventry and Bristol. Sadly, our luck ran out against Portsmouth. It was sod's law. Barnsley, Cardiff and Portsmouth are the final three teams...and we draw bloody Portsmouth. Typical.

"The way we were playing, we knew we'd give them a good game. Harry Redknapp (Portsmouth boss) said on the day that we were the better side and deserved to win. It was bad luck. Milan Baros handled the ball, Kanu scored and we were gutted. Playing the semi-final at Wembley was amazing. My little boy Toby was mascot but it was another appearance at Wembley tainted by half luck. We hit the bar but couldn't score. The most frustrating thing was knowing we'd have had Cardiff or Barnsley in the final. We'd have fancied that."

Phillips remains close friends with several of his former Albion team-mates. It's clear there are some he'd sooner share a lift with than others. "There was one day my car wouldn't start," he recalls. "I knew Jono Greening lived in Mere Green and was aware it was about 20 minutes from his door to mine. Tony had come in and instilled more discipline, which included a fine system if you were late. You'd get a straight fine and then be fined on top of that for every minute. The way the West Brom training ground is laid out, you have to pretty much drive past the manager's office, so he was always going to notice. And, if he didn't, big Joe Corrigan (Albion's goalkeeper coach) would clock you. Even if you were a minute late.

"Anyway, my car won't start and I've phoned Jono. Training started at 10am and I knew he would have left his house at 8.30 to get to mine for about quarter to. It got to 9.15 and he hadn't arrived, so I call him. 'Yeah Kev, I'm on my way,' he said. At 9.30, I ring him again. 'Yes Kev, don't panic. I'm on my way.' At 9.45, I know we're going to be late, so I called him and said: 'Jono, where the hell are you?' He replied: 'Uttoxeter.' He'd only gone and typed in Uttoxeter instead of Uttoxeter Road on his satnav. To get to Uttoxeter, which was about 15 minutes from me, he would have had to drive past my front door and yet he kept driving, heading to Uttoxeter. When I explained, I just heard him say: 'Ah, oh shit.' So he turned round and we ended up getting to training about 10.45. The lads slaughtered us and we got fined. Cheers for that, Jono.

"Robbo is a good mate. I'm godfather to one of his kids, I still speak to him every week. He was one of the big reasons we did so well. Never shirked a challenge, he had drive, gave rollickings if necessary and was a winner. RoKo (Robert Koren) was a lovely fella and we had some other good characters in the team. One of the daftest was Zoltan. He was such a nice bloke but we'd give him so much stick. Whenever training had finished, we'd be walking around saying: 'Where's Zoltan today...did he not train?' when he'd be stood next to us. He would bite for fun on that.

"Pascal Zuberbuhler was a giant. He was a great shot-stopper but struggled with low shots at times. He wasn't really commanding either but, on his day, he could be brilliant. He was a lovely fella and a good-looking six-footer. The women must have loved him. Deano brought experience and a calming influence. He's a top pro and I'm not surprised he has gone into coaching because he carries that authority. Filipe was a quiet lad. Technically, there was no-one better at the club but his physique let him down sometimes. He wasn't the kind of guy to work in the gym on his strength. He'd rather be out there practicising his technique. In the Championship, you need to be strong. He couldn't always cope with that but he was so talented on the ball; a fantastic player."

Some players never quite fulfilled their potential at The Hawthorns. Bryan

Robson signed Phillips to dovetail with John Hartson in the same way Phillips had with Niall Quinn at Sunderland. For reasons which were to become clear when Hartson was diagnosed with cancer, it was a union which never materialised. "John was a cracking fella but obviously we weren't aware what was happening with him at the time," Phillips laments. "He would have been ideal for me up front. He was the strongest man ever. You'd play the ball up to him and defenders would not get it off him. That would have been a great foil for me. And he could score goals. He was a quality player over the years and it's great to see him doing so well in the media.

"We had other players who were talented. Koumi was fantastic. I am very surprised he didn't make more of his career. Funnily enough, he won Player of the Year for the Championship. At the time, my wife Julie was doing a TV programme in London, so I was spending a fair bit of time down there. I happened to be in London when these awards were on at the Grosvenor. I was there having a few jars because Julie was working until 4pm. I noticed a call come through and it was John Simpson, the club press officer, basically saying he needed a favour.

"He explained that Koumi couldn't make it for his award, so he asked me to go. I didn't have a suit, I'd had a few drinks and the awards weren't until late that night. He told me to make sure I could walk and talk and not to worry about anything else. I turned up at 7pm, everyone's in dinner jackets and dicky bows while I'm wearing my jeans and a Great Ormond Street charity hoodie, which was part of the show Julie was working on. I didn't realise these things were like gold dust.

"I collected the award from Jeff Stelling, put my professional head on, did an interview and, as I'm walking back to the table, a bloke stopped me and offered me £100 for the hoodie. He then raised that to £150, which I passed on to the charity. Luckily, I had a t-shirt on underneath. I ended up phoning sick the next day as I wasn't feeling too healthy. On the Tuesday, all the lads told me I didn't look too sick on the Sunday night. Tony knew but he was fine with me. It was the only time I missed training."

Phillips won the Championship Player of the Year, as voted by the FourFourTwo magazine, in his own right in 2008, having just missed out on the top award the previous year to Koumas. He was also declared Albion's and the Supporters Club's best performer for the title-winning season. Leaving with a championship medal gave some comfort to the reluctant departee. "I've been promoted three times now and the way we played that season, with new players joining the club, trying to adapt to our style of play but also conceding goals, we did wonder sometimes whether it would be one of those years," he concluded. "We played such good football that it was a pleasure to play in the side. We always sensed we could get promoted and wanted to do it as champions. It was a well deserved title for all of us."

Jonathan Greening

"I had to drive to Sutton Coldfield with these dead mice stuck to my wife's pink Mini and people looking at me every time I stopped at traffic lights."

JONATHAN Greening has a sense of humour. And, let's face it, he needs one. There can't be many English outfield players who have been involved in two major European club finals...and featured for a sum total of one minute in them. Greening, an unused substitute for Manchester United in 1999 when he was the main beneficiary of suspensions to Roy Keane and Paul Scholes, did at least claim a winners' medal following the 2-1 victory over Bayern Munich. Eleven years later, he went on in the 119th minute for Danny Murphy, his Fulham side having conceded a second goal just three minutes earlier. Atletico Madrid secured the 2-1 win within seconds of Greening's introduction. It's just as well he had a little more to show for his time at West Bromwich Albion.

Nobody played for more Baggies gaffers during the first decade of the new century than 'Jono.' He was signed by Gary Megson, nurtured by Bryan Robson, transformed into captain material by Tony Mowbray and then waved on by Roberto Di Matteo. Even when he left Albion for Fulham, it was to link up with a man who would eventually replace Di Matteo at B71, Roy Hodgson.

In many respects, Greening is the seminal player of the era. Only two others, Neil Clement and Paul Robinson, bettered his 225 appearances for the club in the opening 12 years of the 21st century. He was only the second Baggies captain to lift a trophy after Graham Williams climbed the Wembley steps to raise the FA Cup in 1968, Darren Bradley having collected a trophy for Albion's 3-0 play-off win in 1993. From 2004 to 2009, those were the Greening years. And more of this 'sense of humour' later......

Albion claimed promotion in 2004. Gary Megson, growing increasingly nervy ahead of the club's second bite of Premier League football, wanted new players. He sought out Greening. Long-haired, usually bearded (a rare exception being his clean-shaven look during Albion's title-winning afternoon at Queens Park Rangers) and, most importantly, a midfielder capable of playing on the flanks or through the middle. Greening was an established figure at Middlesbrough. Starting his career at York, he moved on to Manchester United and made ten starts and 17 substitute appearances for them before heading to Teesside in 2001. He was to play 109 games before Albion paid £1.2m for him in July, 2004.

Megson's abrasive reputation had registered with him but did not deter him. On the contrary, the Albion boss was instrumental in him joining. "I'd had a bit of interest before West Brom," he recalls. "When I was at Boro, I was very close to joining Leeds when they got relegated. I'd gone back to pre-season at Middlesbrough in 2004 and Steve McClaren called me into his office to tell me West Brom were interested in me. People like Mendieta and Zenden had not long since joined and I wanted to play. I knew I wouldn't play, so I told him I'd be interested in speaking to them. I travelled down with my brother. Kanu and Zoltan (Gera) signed around the same time, so it was an exciting time for the club. Gary was top class. He really sold the club to me. He took me to the stadium, showed me the plans for the training ground and, to this day, I still get on really well with him. Had it not been for him, I wouldn't have signed."

Megson was to last just ten Premier League games before Jeremy Peace's patience snapped. Bryan Robson was named as his successor. Greening was not complaining about the new man's arrival, although sad to see Megson depart. "I'd heard a lot of opinions about Gary but I always got on really well with him," he continued. "As long as you were honest with him on and off the pitch – especially in games and training – he'd be fine with you. If you took your foot off in training or a game, you would be left in no doubt what he thought. That's what he was like. He wasn't there for long with me but I liked him. And then Bryan came in. I just loved him. With him being a former Manchester United player, I was going to have an affinity for him anyway. He was my dad's hero when I was growing up. He was always talking about him, so I was very proud when he took over."

The differences between the two managers were stark. Robson was keen to shoulder the blame when results took a dip. "Players could relate to Bryan," recalls Greening. "He protected us if we had a bad game. He'd take criticism from us and on to himself. Sometimes, you appreciate that as a player. We were all devastated when he left a couple of years later. Where Gary showed his emotions in a raw way, Bryan would keep things away from the players. If he was angry, he wouldn't always tell us, although, when he did lose it, you knew about it. He made us relaxed, comfortable in our work. Gary was happy to do the same but he would be on to you all the time to show that energy. Both demanded it but Gary would bollock you publicly. Bryan wouldn't."

Summer, 2007. Tony Mowbray's Albion have been defeated by Derby County in the play-off final. Derby players head for the Premier League. A succession of Albion stars look for the nearest exit. Paul Robinson declared his intention to leave within minutes of the final whistle at Wembley. He was to stay for two more seasons. But Diomansy Kamara, Jason Koumas, Curtis Davies and Nathan Ellington didn't hang around. Greening had a chance to leave but Mowbray had different ideas. Not only did he want him to stay, he presented him with the captain's armband. The 2007-08 season was to be the best of Greening's career. And it wasn't too shabby from the club's point of view either. Alhough the player needed some convincing about assuming the responsibility, he needed little time to think about his future. He signed a new three-year deal.

"I had a chance to go back to Middlesbrough," he remembers. "Gareth Southgate had enquired but I wasn't guaranteed to play. Tony was good to me. I enjoyed playing for West Brom and he told me he wanted me to stay and be captain. I had no intention of going. I loved the football and stuck with it. I'm glad I did because it was the best year of my career in many respects. To win the title that year was incredible. When he said he'd be making me captain, I just looked at him and said: 'Seriously? Are you having a laugh?' He accepted that I wasn't the most vocal on the pitch but felt I was a good trainer, a good example, willing to take responsibility on the ball. He wanted people to follow my example.

"His words were: 'I want you to be my captain this year'. When a manager tells you that, you can't fail to be inspired. I told my mum and dad, phoned my missus – I was proud beyond words. It turned out to be my best season. But the manager was one of the reasons I wanted to commit my future to the club. He wanted to build a team to play the way I like to play. You can't ask for anything better than that as a player."

Greening continued: "I've never been one for responsibility. I felt lads like Robbo (Paul Robinson) were better suited for it, certainly vocally. But Tony felt it would improve my game. It gave me more responsibility. He felt I could bridge any gaps between the English lads and foreign lads and believed I was the right man to do that. It gave an edge to my game. I felt I could encourage others, gee them up when I did so. The way we played, the amount of goals we scored and a trophy at the end of it.....it was just amazing. Again, we had a Wembley disappointment. We played well against Portsmouth and could have drawn one of the Championship clubs in the semi-final but we were still confident. It wasn't to be that day. And given what we know now about Portsmouth, it still grates with me."

As Greening speaks, he looks at one of the favourite photos displayed in his house. It shows him lifting the Championship title; Albion's first for 88 years. His grin as he holds aloft the magnificent trophy in front of the away fans at Lotfus Road will be familiar to all. "It's fantastic. I'm stood here now still looking at it," he smiles. "It was one of the greatest days of my life. To be the man who lifted the trophy.......I was working for a man who had great belief in my ability as a player and showed great faith in making me captain. I remember that day fondly.

"We'd all had a lot of beers on the coach heading home. Tony Mowbray was really laid-back and then Valerie, the Amy Winehouse song, came on. Robbo and Super Kevin Phillips started singing at the top of their voices: 'Mowbray...why don't you cheer up...Mowbray.' I think he saw the funny side of it. That was the day we had the Championship trophy at the front of the bus. We passed it around and kissed it a few times. It's still my greatest season as a player. And that was probably my greatest single day."

At the time, Mowbray explained why Greening had been handed the honour of leading his side. "He brings just about everything I like in a footballer," he said. "In his own way, he shows great responsibility. Captains don't always need to be charging around the pitch, clattering into people, shouting or shaking their fist. Jono shows his leadership qualities with his ability to want the ball, his ability to be brave enough to play for the team. I was a captain most of my life but I also understood the players around me in the team. There were people who were more vocal but there are certain qualities a coach looks for in his captain. Jonathan has the respect of the rest of the players, not only because of his ability but because of the way he is. He is not hot-headed. He is very calm and a good footballer. He's someone I can talk to on a level."

Albion prepared for 2008-09 without Kevin Phillips and Zoltan Gera, who left the club on Bosman free transfers. Phillips joined Birmingham after they handed him a two-year deal. Gera simply wanted a new challenge. He was to join Roy Hodgson's Fulham. Arriving at The Hawthorns were defenders Gianni Zuiverloon and Abdoulaye Meite for more than £3m and £2m respectively. They were joined by Marek Cech from Porto (£1.4m) and Jonas Olsson, who pitched up from Dutch club NEC for a remarkably low fee of £800,000. Scott Carson chose Albion over Stoke for £3.25m – a club record fee for a goalkeeper at the time. The loan deals of Luke Moore and Roman Bednar had already been formalised into £3m and £2.5m permanent transfers.

With just a few days of the window remaining, Albion paid a record £4.7m to Real Mallorca for Borja Valero. A similar move for his Mallorca team-mate Oscar Trejo failed. Mowbray said of Borja at the time: "He has great technical ability and weight of pass, has an excellent work-rate and an eye for a goal. He can link up the play from back to front and he will enhance the excellent midfield options we already possess." The 23-year-old former Real Madrid midfielder was an intriguing addition, regarded as a deep-sitting play-maker, occupying the territory just in front of the back four.

Borja was confident of being successful in the Black Country. "The coach has a more Spanish style than others, so that is better for me because it is more physical here," he said. "We play in a more Spanish way. Maybe I couldn't play in another team in England. Bolton and Stoke probably wouldn't suit me."

Yet the Spaniard never got to grips with English football. He was unsettled by unforgiving bruising midfield encounters and had a new language to learn. Although Mowbray's passing football had the potential to suit him, the failure to bring in a more physical player to compliment him didn't help his cause in his 12 months here. There was nobody to do the scurrying and harrying at his side. It was all a bit too cosmetic where perhaps more attrition was called for.

Albion's passing play opened itself up to accusations of profligacy during 2008-09; a lot of ball retention but little end product, the critics said. Furthermore, at times it seemed that the art of ball-winning was regarded as some form of larceny within the Baggies camp. By January, 2009, Mowbray knew the Borja project was still not fully firing. The midfielder was struggling.

"I think it is always something that is going to take time," he said. "It almost took his breath away how intense and physical this league can be. I saw him come off the pitch and he has looked shocked because he has never played in football which is so hurly-burly and hectic. I think he has always played in matches where they pass it and he can wander around in midfield and he can have a few passes and link a few balls, to come in behind the play, and it is nice and easy. He can come off with his jacket still on. It is 'Welcome to the Premier League' and you either sink or swim really. Yet there are signs he is growing into it."

Speaking about Borja's physicality, Mowbray continued: "If you are 9st 7lb, you have to use every ounce of that in a confrontation against someone who is 15st. You have to put your body on the line and be strong. He can be outmuscled in midfield as long as he uses what he has got for the benefit of the team. I think sometimes you can see that he can hold people off when he has the ball. He shields it and uses his body weight to spin away from them. He is a clever footballer and I am more than happy with his contribution."

Reflecting on that period, Greening accepts Borja never really settled. "It's hard moving within your own country, let alone coming from a league which has different demands and styles," he said. "He had come from Spain, he didn't speak much English, he had no friends or family here. If he'd given it a longer go, it might have worked for him. He was restricted but we knew he had it in him. We could see glimpses and we've seen it since during European nights. So much so that clubs like Barcelona and Madrid have been linked with him. Yet it never worked for him at West Brom.

"The Premier League was fast and strong and it caught him by surprise. It was maybe just the wrong time for him. It's a shame as he was a lovely guy, a brilliant trainer and so obviously a great player." Borja returned to Real Mallorca on loan in 2009. He joined Villarreal a year later, moving for a similar fee to what Albion had paid for him two years previously. He has since been capped by Spain.

Meanwhile, back in 2008-09, Albion were labouring. Steve Bruce, Rafa Benitez, Jamie Carragher and Harry Redknapp were among those who came out to praise Tony Mowbray's side for their football principles. But 'principles' alone were not about to help their survival cause. Albion were unable to score goals, although Marc-Antoine Fortuné's arrival from Nancy in January helped. Jay Simpson, on loan from Arsenal, made less of an impact. Playing as a lone striker, Fortuné helped bring Albion's midfielders into play. James Morrison, Chris Brunt and Greening all prospered. As did a young Graham Dorrans, who had joined from Livingston, and Argentinian loanee Juan Carlos Menseguez.

At the back, Albion were lacking quality. Jonas Olsson missed two months' football after the turn of the year with tendonitis. During that period, Albion played seven games and took just four points, three of those coming against Middlesbrough, who would join the Baggies in the bottom three come May. They conceded 17 goals in those seven games. Defenders Leon Barnett, Shelton Martis and Ryan Donk were willing but, equally, limited and lacking experience. The Match of the Day pundits were unimpressed.

Gary Lineker, Alan Hansen, Mark Lawrenson and Alan Shearer were all critical of Albion during that campaign, describing Mowbray's side as a soft touch, too expansive or simply not good enough. Mowbray insisted he was giving a wide berth to the 'experts who sit on sofas.' He had no intention of abandoning his principles. "What do I do after a defeat? Well I made a snowman with my kids last time and I eat chocolate," he told the Sunday Mercury. "My kids are one and four. They are pretty lively and don't care if you win or lose. They go to bed and my wife makes me watch something or another but I don't want Match of the Day.

"I like to stay single-minded and focused on my team, yet I've got the world telling me I'm doing this wrong, that wrong, that my team is playing like that but should be doing this instead. It doesn't interest me. If you start listening to this influence or that influence, you can lose track of what you believe in. I pick the team I want, I pick the players I want. Managers get enough people telling you what you're doing wrong, even if you've won ten on the bounce. Jose Mourinho, for instance, won leagues but was told his Chelsea team didn't play entertaining football. We did okay, playing open, attacking football last season.

"It isn't about whether you're playing 4-5-1, 4-4-2, whether you're rotating the midfield or pushing the full-backs on. It's about what happens in the box. If your strikers take their chances and your defenders head the ball out of the box at set-plays, you've got a good chance of winning. If we stay in this League for five years and do okay, the expectation will change and neither the fans nor myself would accept us being bottom. Yet we have only five or six players who have played in the Premier League. I'm feeling our inexperience, especially in defence. The best defenders are relaxed and so in control because they have been there and done it. They don't foul as much, whereas ours are often uptight because they're learning."

Albion finished bottom on 32 points. It was the only time during that decade they would finish 20th. They were just three points behind 17th-placed Hull City. They scored only 36 goals. Between them, Phillips (22) and Gera (eight) had scored 30 League goals the previous campaign. Greening accepts the duo were never replaced adequately.

"Kev wanted to stay but the chairman didn't feel he should get a two-year contract as he had injury problems and because of his age," he claimed. "It was a gamble and I think Kev has proven him wrong since. Eventually, he left and was a big miss for us. He was so important to us, scoring goals but also helping the midfield because he linked up play and it opened up chances for people like myself, Zoltan, James Morrison and Chris Brunt. We never replaced that. Zoltan was slightly different. He'd made it clear he wouldn't be staying or signing a new contract. He wanted a new challenge. They were big losses for us and we never got over it."

Greening looks back with regret on that campaign, his last full season for Albion. And he feels Mowbray should have been given greater scope to strengthen in January. "I remember we would play really good stuff and lose," he added. "We battered some sides but couldn't score. The game that best sums us up was Liverpool the day we were relegated. We were dominant, couldn't score and Shelton Martis made a mistake and they scored. We lost Ishmael Miller to a cruciate midway through the season, Roman had his problems and even I ended up out with ligament problems.

"We had people telling us how well we were playing and how we couldn't go down but we did. We just weren't good enough in terms of goals. We made mistakes at one end and didn't score at the other. Tony needed more backing. We didn't do much in January and we suffered for that. Tony did what he could.

He coached us well and I think he appreciated we couldn't spend millions but he gave us the impression he wanted more quality, especially in January when things were going a little stale. We only really brought two or three in and it wasn't enough. It was dispiriting at times. It was the same story every week. As players, we enjoyed playing for him but we were losing games we should have drawn or won. And to go down by three points shows how close we were."

Off the field, the Albion Foundation was launched, with work in the community and sport for the disabled among their remit. The academy was showing signs of bearing fruit, with Chris Wood making his first-team debut at Portsmouth and becoming the first home-grown player to come through the ranks for several years. The 17-year-old arrived at Fratton Park without a shirt number and Portsmouth staff had to hastily add a number and letters to his shirt before the game. Another relegation, but a record turnover of £47m – albeit with a loss of £13.3m – was posted. Some of the shortfall was attributable to adjustments in player valuations and was largely an accounting issue. There was an underlying trading loss of £7.8m, with net debt standing at £6.6m.

In autumn, 2008, the long-anticipated share consolidation proposal was launched by Jeremy Peace. This had originally been suggested a year earlier but, following opposition from S4A and other shareholders, was deferred. The consolidation meant all shareholders had to increase their shareholding to ten shares, in order to receive one new share valued at ten times the value of the old shares. In the case of a shareholder with one share, valued notionally at £80 for the exercise, it would involve a further investment of £720 to meet the requirement of the proposal, with the new shares taking on a value of £800, which still meant the club were valued at well below what the accounts appeared to suggest.

S4A called an EGM to discuss the implications with shareholders and to offer ways of navigating a course that suited them individually. It was accepted that the consolidation would take place due to Peace's dominant position held with voting rights. At the time, there were 1,674 shareholders, of which 1,353 held fewer than the required ten shares. Of the latter number, 568 held just one share and were most vulnerable in being forced to sell if they could not afford the cost of the additional shares.

Again, a market of willing purchasers at above the £80 was organised. Advice was also provided to enable groups of shareholders to get together to fund the purchase of the necessary minimum holding. Ultimately, the shares in issue were reduced to just under 10,000, notionally at a value of £800. The number of shareholders reduced from 1,674 to 758. The sad fall-out of this meant many life-long Albion fans were no longer able to afford, or did not wish to afford, the outlay needed to remain a part owner of their club. Peace now held about 57 per cent of the shares. Of the 758 shareholders remaining, 712 owned fewer than ten of the new shares.

Albion saw out the campaign at Blackburn, with supporters paying tribute to Tony Mowbray. Just weeks before, in the 2-2 draw at Portsmouth, the manager hinted he was introducing a new wave of players. Youngster Youssouf Mulumbu, who had been injured following a move from Paris Saint-Germain, loanee Juan Carlos Menseguez and Wood were included on the bench. Graham Dorrans was recalled to the starting line-up while Luke Moore, Filipe Teixeira, Do-heon Kim, Marek Cech and, notably, Borja Valero were either left out or unused as substitutes. Yet Mowbray never did fulfil a second 'revolution.' A few weeks later, he was gone. Celtic needed a new manager and Albion had no intention of standing in his way.

The Baggies gaffer's relationship with chairman Jeremy Peace was weakening and the eventual parting was unfortunate for Greening. But he wasn't overly surprised. Celtic were Mowbray's former club – more so, a club he was with and had taken to his heart during his wife Bernadette's battle with cancer. She died on January 1, 1995. Mowbray's dignity during her illness and subsequent passing had made him a big hero to a generation of Celtic fans. It was a mutual affinity which remained long after he left Parkhead to conclude his playing career.

Ultimately, his time as Celtic boss was unsuccessful but Greening understands why his boss took the leap. "I wasn't really surprised Tony left," he said. "Tony had his frustrations at the time but we must remember what Celtic meant to him. It was the club he played for, his wife had died of cancer when he was up there and I can imagine it was an emotional decision for him as much as anything else. He'd had words with the chairman, knew there was a chance of European football and trophies and it seemed like the right move.

Does he regret it? I guess only Tony knows but I'd be amazed if a part of him doesn't wish he'd stuck around.

"I was gutted when he told me. I was in Cyprus with the family, I'd seen rumours and then he called to tell me, thank me for being captain and wish me all the best. He made the biggest impression on me. He put trust in me to play in central midfield, he made me captain when no-one else would have thought of doing so and he gave us confidence to play. People say we were too weak in midfield. Maybe we were a bit but Tony wanted footballers and wanted us to play a certain way. It can be good to have a physical presence but Tony didn't want to compromise the way we played.

"I'm glad I had the experience of playing for him. He was the best boss I had. I'm so old now that I remember playing against Tony. Before he joined us, I had some mates playing in Scotland and they said how well he'd been doing at Hibernian but more so how good the football was. I was really impressed after a few days' working. He was a quiet guy, he would sit back and watch you. But he wanted to play football the way it should be played. Those were good times. I'd played in central midfield once or twice for Bryan but Tony saw something in me to move me inside into that position as a regular central midfielder. You would enjoy playing under Tony if you were a player who liked being on the ball."

Greening retains a wicked sense of humour. Former team-mates speak of a player who was the butt of jokes and the perpetrator of pranks. He can only nod his head and chuckle at some of the memories of his time at The Hawthorns. Some of the stories fail to make these pages. They are simply inappropriate. One thing's for sure: If you're ever in the company of Greening and his former Baggies room-mate Andy Johnson, you need to stay on your guard.

"Johnno is a weirdo," laughs Greening. "I'd roomed with him for a few years and he was terrified of cotton wool. If it's in the room, he has to walk out. So I stuffed his boots full of cotton wool and when he tried to put his foot in, he obviously had to pull out what was in there and he just went mental. He started running around, screaming. He was almost crying. He was like: 'Jono, I'm going to f***ing kill you.' A few days later, my car had gone in for a service and I had to drive my wife's bright pink Mini into training. I came out of training and he'd tied loads of dead mice to it. They were attached to the windscreen, the back of the car, the aerial, everywhere.

"The problem was that I was coming out of training late and, because I had the only car, I had to go and pick my little one up from school, so I didn't have time to remove them. I had no way of getting them all off. I had to drive to Sutton Coldfield with these dead mice stuck to my wife's Mini and people looking at me every time I stopped at traffic lights. My missus Anna saw it and went mad."

Andy Johnson wasn't by any means the only team-mate to keep an eye on. Greening added: "Scotty Carson was a wrong 'un. He used to keep cutting up Marek Cech's socks. Marek was really into his designer underwear and designer socks. He'd pay loads for clothes that no-one could even see – and Scott used to take it upon himself cut them up. Marek would go mental. A lot of people got wound up by Scott. There's a perception that he was quiet but in the dressing room he was ruthless. He would slaughter some of the lads. Scotty was a real test for some of the weaker ones. Robbo was just mad. I still watch that tackle of his on YouTube, the one where he tackled Moritz Volz when we were playing Fulham. I tell my little lad: 'That's how you tackle, son.' Robbo would tackle a moving bus if he had to. I think Volz ended up with a punctured lung."

Mowbray was replaced by Roberto Di Matteo in July, 2009. By then, Greening wanted out. A return to the Championship, under a new boss, didn't appeal. Fulham made their move during late July. A 'derisory' undisclosed offer from the Londoners was turned down. Greening eventually moved in late August, signing a season-long loan deal with a permanent switch guaranteed at the end of the campaign. He played just twice for Di Matteo. The midfielder made 50 appearances during his two-year Craven Cottage spell before moving to Nottingham Forest in July, 2011. Although he made fleeting appearances in the Europa League, he accepts he was hasty.

"I regret leaving," Greening states. "Definitely. I wish I could turn the clock back but my mind was different then. I wanted to play in Europe, I was offered a great deal by Fulham and felt I'd reached my comfort zone with West Brom after five years. I needed a fresh challenge and Fulham was a great move at the time. Had I stayed and signed a new contract, it might have been better.

I'd have played for Robbie Di Matteo more. I was only there for his first two games. He seemed a lovely guy and I enjoyed his and Eddie Newton's training sessions but we'd been relegated twice, Fulham were in the Europa League and Premier League and there is always that nagging fear that the club might not get promoted again.

"I was wrong about that but you always worry about it. And if a club offer you Premier League football at 30, you take it. I got to the final of the Europa League and played for the final few minutes – still more than the Champions League final – but had I stayed at West Brom, I might have stayed captain and won promotion again. I still regard Albion as 'my' club. I had my best seasons there, lots of ups like the Great Escape, reaching a cup semi-final, and a few lows. Every club I've worked at has been amazing but there is something special about West Brom."

Robert Koren

"The doctor brought me into a room, switched off the lights and asked me to cover my other eye. When I did, I was blind. I couldn't see anything."

HAVE you heard the one about the Slovenian, the Englishman and a badly-timed challenge? Robert Koren, with West Bromwich Albion and in his first training session, crashes into Curtis Davies. 'RoKo,' as he is to become known in the dressing room, has barely introduced himself to his new team-mates. But his captain's shin is on first-name terms already. That'll be the Baggies skipper, who is rated at £11million by the club. It's not quite the welcome Davies, or the other Albion players, had in mind. But Koren has his own agenda, albeit one executed with over-enthusiasm. The first Slovenian to play for the club was officially checking in for duty. It was his: 'Hi, I'm Robbie...how do you do?' moment.

Koren, far from aggressive, was simply trying to impress manager Tony Mowbray. It was January, 2007. The midfielder had arrived at The Hawthorns from Norwegian club Lillestrom. Having started his career at Slovenian club Dravograd in the late 1990s, Koren popped up at Celje in 2001 before moving to Scandinavia three years later. He joined Albion on a Bosman free transfer at the end of the Norwegian season.

Koren refuses a bottle of water as he joins me at the Village Hotel in Watford. Hull City, his current club, are playing at Vicarage Road tomorrow afternoon. We're into the closing stages of the 2011-12 season. His team-mates see him being interviewed. They respectfully keep their distance. Hull will eventually fail to make the play-offs. They missed Koren when he was injured. The Tigers depended on him. Ten goals spelled a good return. But an enforced three-week absence, including four games during March, was costly. Nick Barmby was sacked within a fortnight of Hull's failed challenge ending.

Back in 2007, few knew Robert Koren. His opening training session in England still raises a smile. "I remember it well," he says. "I know who it was, and which player. I'm sure Curtis Davies remembers it. He was one of the best players and worth a lot of money. But let me explain: I didn't really tackle him. We played a small game, four versus four, and just before I had a shot, I slipped and still managed to kick the ball. I scored as it happens but, as I did so, Curtis came in and we clashed. I caught him with my studs. His shin was bleeding...but it was an accident."

The badly-tuned singing and sporadic chanting is a strain on our ears. Noise surrounds us. The hotel bar is starting to fill up. Everton fans are forced to spill into the foyer, where Koren sits. They either don't recognise him or are too drunk to care. Possibly both. Tomorrow, Everton face a lunchtime kick-off against Liverpool in the FA Cup semi-final. Albion's most recent FA Cup semi lingers in his memory. Koren's shot bounces against that Portsmouth crossbar every time. Albion went on to lose at Wembley and Pompey won the Cup. Koren's shot never did go in. The heartbreak comes a year after the Baggies are defeated by Derby in the 2007 play-off final. Koren is fed up of Wembley. While Everton fans top up the bar till on the eve of a defeat to their Merseyside neighbours, Koren speaks of his angst; a feeling Everton fans will know only too well themselves a few hours later.

"I was very close against Portsmouth," he reiterates. "We had a great run, a great spirit and we did well in the Cup. That game at Wembley was a great occasion. Everyone fancied Portsmouth but we had a belief. They struggled even though they won. I hit the crossbar and it wasn't to be our day. The 2007 play-offs were even worse. That was my first half of a season in England. I was here just four months and I didn't really realise how big the disappointment was. It was massive. That was hard. We lost a lot of players then but that's football. It was a big change but the main players were still there. Yes, we lost Koumas. And we lost Kamara. But we knew we had a great squad. James Morrison joined, Chris Brunt. They had great skills. Roman Bednar, Ishmael Miller – they could score goals. The club were building with a family atmosphere. We felt part of it. That's what Tony Mowbray was about."

By summer, 2009, Albion are readjusting to life in the Championship. It's becoming a regular process. Only this time there is a shuffling of personnel backstage. Mowbray was gone. The pull of Celtic was too strong. He hadn't been happy for a while. Albion received compensation in the region of £2m. Mowbray spoke of his dissatisfaction with Albion to the Express & Star following his appointment in Scotland. "I fully endorse the way he (Jeremy Peace) runs the club, as the protector of it, because he keeps it running in a straight line," he said. "But there were just a few instances this year where I think things could have been handled a bit differently.

"He knows it, I'm not talking out of school. We have had conversations about it. I don't think the working environment would have been right for me. Who is to say, even if we had stayed up, I might not have made the same decision? A man has to enjoy going into work every day and to be able to do his job to the best of his ability. That probably wouldn't have been the case this season for me at Albion."

One of the biggest criticisms levelled at Mowbray after his departure was comments he made to the media following relegation just a few weeks earlier. He informed the players they owed it to the club to stay at the club and fight for promotion. Within weeks, he was Scotland-bound. In the same interview, he said: "I balance it with a very clear conscience. I think footballers' and managers' contracts are hugely different and football is all about relationships. When you look back to my first summer there, when we sold everybody, that only happened because the relationships were broken.

"If the players were using that as an excuse on a match-day, there was no point preserving things. You have to separate and move on and that's how I felt. We had come to that point. Whether I could have given the same commitment and desire to win every game next season, after the events of this campaign, was questionable. The players have to look at themselves now but I don't think they've got anybody to have a broken relationship with. The new manager will have to talk to the players now and they will see what he thinks. I would suggest that the players now, like the ones when I first went there, have to get their heads down and get on with the job – if that's what the new manager wants."

To quote the job description, the Baggies needed a new 'head coach' – one who could work in tandem with sporting and technical director Dan Ashworth. Former captain Derek McInnes, then St Johnstone boss, was deemed too inexperienced. Dave Jones didn't seem keen on the structure Albion were expecting their next 'gaffer' to operate within. Swede Hans Backe, Sven-Goran Eriksson's no 2 at Manchester City and Mexico, was also spoken to. No go on that front. Alan Irvine emerged as the favourite. But something went wrong. The Scotsman, then managing Preston North End, claimed he turned the job down. Albion counter-claimed that no offer was made. The truth lies in between or, perhaps, in how one interprets an 'offer.'

Roberto Di Matteo swiftly emerged as a candidate. He was a bright, young coach, who had led the Dons of Milton Keynes to a play-off semi-final the previous year. Spectacular and outspoken, he wasn't. Ambitious, calm and fashionable, certainly. With charm and intelligence in abundance, he fitted the off-field profile well. Crucially, he was more than willing to work in Albion's tiered system.

He also liked a cigarette or two. Supporters and media, searching for a much-needed drink during the 3-0 friendly win against Slovenian side NK Nafta, were a little surprised to see the new Baggies boss enjoying a swift smoke during half-time outside Lendava's Mestni Stadium. Indeed, a post-match cigarette just outside stadia boundaries, accompanied by the club's press officer (who would bring a packet as part of his match-day duties), became a regular occurrence during Di Matteo's spell at the club. Often, the biggest challenge was finding a restricted part of an away stadium where the Italian could indulge. At The Hawthorns, he simply frequented the gap between the East Stand and Smethwick End Stand while the media patiently (or not) awaited his after-game reaction.

Joining Di Matteo was his former Chelsea team-mate and MK Dons no 2 Eddie Newton, who would be his assistant. One-time Olympic sprinter Ade Mafe, who represented Great Britain at Los Angeles in 1984, pitched up as fitness coach. Koren was sorry to see Mowbray depart. "When you're in football, you think you're on the same page but you never know what lies ahead," he admits. People move on. I didn't really know if Tony would go or not. It was a disappointing season. We were thinking about what would happen.

"Some players wanted to stay in the Premier League, some were happy to stay. It was very disappointing that Tony was leaving. We all liked him – or at least most of us did. Even those outside the 11 generally liked him. Most of the players enjoyed working under him. I can only be positive about him. He allowed me to come to England and he wanted us to play football. That suited me. We tried to enjoy our games and play to his football style but it was disappointing we went down. Our big problem was that we couldn't score goals. Most of the games we played well in but struggled where it mattered – in front of goal. When Tony left, I was back home in Slovenia. You get speculation, you read it, you hear it. It was not good news for me or for most of the people at the club. He did such a good job. But life moves on."

The previous campaign had been a source of major regret for Koren. Albion were relegated – but not by much. Three points, four if you count goal difference, separated them from survival. They scored just 36 goals. The previous season, they had scored 88 in the Championship, Kevin Phillips netting 22 of those. Koren sighs as he reflects on the paucity of post-Phillips firepower.

Grimacing, he adds: "Was it (letting the striker go) a mistake? That's difficult to say. There are political aspects to this. There are people in charge of West Brom who make these decisions. They control the money. They give the manager money to spend. But, from my point of view, he was a big, big miss for us. Perhaps the other problem was not replacing him. He could have offered us something. He is still playing now. In my view, it was the wrong decision. It's easy now to say this but those of us who knew him, knew he was good enough for us."

Relegation was a strange experience for Koren. Albion's purist approach to football was commendable but relegation always seemed a formality. Koren was shocked by the reaction of supporters. It made a huge impression on a player who was used to an altogether different reaction where failure was concerned. "It was a really disappointing season," he continued. "We put a lot of effort into staying in the Premier League. It was an amazing experience for me in my career, just to be in it. We played Liverpool at home right at the end of the season. We lost the game and that was the day we knew we were going down.

"We got back into the dressing room and we had a message telling us to go back out on the pitch. I was expecting something negative. All I heard was: 'The fans are waiting for you.' You have to remember I am from Slovenia, former Yugoslavia. People over there support their teams differently. If the team is not successful, the fans show you and it can get nasty. We had a full house, we got relegated and everyone is there to clap us as we walk around the pitch. I don't think fans realise how amazing this is for a player. Everyone waited for us yet we had lost and been relegated. To see our manager walking 20 yards behind us and getting applauded says a lot about the support. It was something very special to experience that."

Roberto Di Matteo clocked in for the first time on July 1, 2009. Wearing a grey, fitted suit, the Italian waited at the training ground doors as the media filed in for his unveiling. Each journalist was greeted with a smile and a 'good morning.' The 2009-10 season was to be his adventure. Three years on, it is April 2012. Koren is remembering that campaign. Di Matteo, meanwhile, is preparing for a Champions League semi-final against Barcelona as interim manager of Chelsea. It's a semi-final his side win, reaching the Champions League final. Didier Drogba ensures Di Matteo's place in Stamford Bridge folklore by securing victory against Bayern Munich with a successful kick in the 4-3 shoot-out win after the game ends 1-1. Di Matteo duly earns himself a two-year contract. Koren, meanwhile, is in a state of flux.

A lot happened in the 33 months in between. Koren and Di Matteo never quite struck a mutual chord. The midfielder noted a shift in dynamics at the club. Gone was the warmth he felt epitomised Mowbray's regime. Now he sensed a cold front. "When somebody else comes in, you try to be professional, do your job and fit in," he said. "I was not too concerned about the next manager. I was used to Tony's style and I was used to the Championship. I knew I was good enough to carry on playing at that level. And then Di Matteo took over.

"I knew he was a good player, with a lot of playing experience. He was still a young coach. He did a good job at Milton Keynes. I knew I had the belief to be in the team. Robbie was very different to Tony; a different mentality. Things changed a lot. Tony was a really nice person. I'm not saying Robbie wasn't but Di Matteo kept his distance. He didn't like to get close to his players. Tony wanted to know about you, your family, how you were. All managers are concerned about style, winning games, philosophies, how they wanted you to play. But Tony wanted you to be comfortable in his company. He would engage you in conversation. We were his 'family.'

"Di Matteo was professional and no more. Eddie Newton did most of the talking, gave us all the information during meetings. It was a different way of working. He was a different kind of manager and it works for him. Everything was all right at first." A 'but' looms in our conversation.......sure enough, Koren continues: "Suddenly, I was out of the team. There was no good reason. You accept that from a manager. We won a lot of games but the information I got from Di Matteo was that I was not scoring enough goals. He wanted me to be scoring more from the area I played. That's fair enough. I always think you share this responsibility with your team-mates. I am not an individual player. I am a team player. I wanted to look after the players around me. I am not that kind of player to do individual things. But we were winning games and I was pleased with my game. I thought I was doing my job correctly."

Apart from the resignation of a manager, the summer of 2009 brought other problems. In May, on the morning of that relegation-rubberstamping exercise against Liverpool, Roman Bednar was the subject of a News of the World story alleging he had bought drugs. He was suspended without pay by the club and received a three-month ban from the Football Association. While Albion players prepared for the new season at their training ground, Bednar pounded around Sutton Park on his own. He was re-introduced to the squad by Di Matteo in August and was to become crucial, scoring 11 times.

Koren was friendly with the Czech Republic international but felt a pang of disappointment at his team-mate's activities. He said: "I had a good relationship with him but only as a footballer. I was not that close to him to know what happened in his private life. I only knew what everyone else knew. When this happened, I was surprised. But I was disappointed, too. We know now why Tony Mowbray dropped him in the games before that. We don't judge each other. When he came back, everyone helped him. We thought it was one mistake. Only he can know what went on. Something happened in his life. Everyone has a past. I understand that. And I sympathise with that."

Albion, meanwhile, had started well despite drawing the opening game against Newcastle (also just relegated) on the day Sir Bobby Robson's death was marked with a poignant tribute. The Baggies then clicked. Di Matteo didn't taste League defeat until September – at home to Crystal Palace. A 3-1 loss at Barnsley followed but five victories punctuated the next eight games, including a 5-0 home success over Watford and back-to-back four-goal hauls against

Bristol City and Sheffield Wednesday. Di Matteo's side had already beaten Middlesbrough 5-0 away in September. All was well.

Yet the club's early-season prospects had been harmed by the departures of Paul Robinson and Jonathan Greening. Club captain Greening, the only man to play for four Albion managers during the first decade of the new century, joined future Hawthorns gaffer Roy Hodgson at Fulham. Robinson went to Bolton. Both left on loans which became permanent. Koren had his concerns about Albion's campaign.

"I wasn't happy when Jono and Robbo left," he continued. "They were big players for us. I learned a lot from them. They were experienced and looked after me when I joined. We missed them a lot. I wasn't sure where the club were going. We were strong enough to fight and get back but, when you're losing Jonathan Greening and Paul Robinson, that's not good. They were big off the pitch, too. They were best friends but different characters. They were very important for us as captain and vice-captain."

On the pitch, Koren's appearances were becoming more and more sporadic. The blossoming partnership between Youssouf Mulumbu and Graham Dorrans was restricting his progress. Albion began to labour around Christmas. In seven League games from early December to mid-January, they won just twice, drawing three times and losing twice. Koren was unimpressed to find himself drifting out of the picture. Not least as he had an extra goal in mind – World Cup qualification with Slovenia. "When Jono and Robbo left, I was the most experienced player, yet he (Di Matteo) didn't want to know," Koren reflected. "This was a problem because I was captain of the national team and we were doing very strongly in the qualification group for the World Cup in South Africa. I needed to play games. We were fighting for first or second place in the group.

"I knew that if I wasn't getting games for my club, I would struggle to get into the national team. It was frustrating, more so because there was no proper reason to take me out of the team. I was on the bench at times. A player is never happy on the bench but I knew I would be the first or second substitute. I would work harder but knew there was no proper reason for me to be dropped. And then I got injured. I started feeling my hernia. With a hernia, it's never a problem at first but, because I went through the early stage of my injury, helped my country to the World Cup and then wasn't playing much for West Brom, I took the decision to have the operation in December. I could have carried on but it wasn't right."

Koren considered leaving. And then along came the club's game with Nottingham Forest on January 8. It was to define the season for both clubs. They were vying for automatic promotion. Billy Davies' side were emphatic, winning 3-1 at The Hawthorns. And, from there, Koren found himself in demand. Albion were to claim 46 points in their final 22 games. Forest, meanwhile, took just 34.

He added: "You think about other options when you're not happy. My agents considered preparing a move where I could play games. The World Cup was a big issue for me. I was national captain, so it was a big pressure for me. Questions were being asked why I wasn't playing. But I made a decision. I wanted to show I was good enough. I felt a strong connection with West Brom, with the club, with the fans, so I didn't want to leave. Then I got lucky because the team started to struggle. When a team are fighting to go up, you're part of 13 players, even if you're on the bench. You know there is a chance.

"Yet, after the injury, I was strong and fit. Then we played Nottingham Forest. It was a big game for us and a bad result because they were another of the teams wanting to go up. It was bad for the players, the fans, everyone. Even if you're not playing, you have to stay positive. The manager suddenly turned towards the experienced players some more. I was on the bench against Forest. After that game, Di Matteo came to me and said: 'Are you ready to play?' Yes, of course I was. I never had any fights with the manager. We passed information to each other in a different way. It was strange because I didn't get any reasons why I wasn't playing in the first place. If you get reasons why, you can use those and react. I was dropped and I didn't know why. I knocked on his door and asked. Then everything changed against Newcastle. We had dropped points but that game at Newcastle was important. We put in a good performance, we drew 2-2 and we should really have won. We showed what we could do."

Koren was starting to enjoy his football again. Perhaps his future did lie at The Hawthorns. But he had reservations. "One of the things I didn't like was that he knew the team at the start of the week," he said. "He knew who would play on the following Saturday when we came in on the Monday or Tuesday. I know this because it happened to me and I saw it all the time. I came in after

Forest on the Monday and was told I would play against Newcastle, no matter how bad I was during the week in training. That wasn't fair in my opinion. And it cannot be right. How can you know on Monday that you will play on the following Saturday? You could be poor or not playing well in training yet still play. It's madness. I didn't agree with that."

Albion tripped up in February. Dignity remained. But only just. Defender Gabriel Tamas had arrived on loan from Auxerre. Another, Steven Reid, a loanee from Blackburn Rovers, followed. A 3-1 defeat in the opening weekend of March at Queens Park Rangers in Neil Warnock's first game in charge there did not bode well. Albion were third, on 63 points, with Forest on 64. Newcastle were on 72. Out of sight. Yet the Baggies did not flinch over the final throes of the season.

Di Matteo's side won eight of the last 12 games and drew four for an impressive haul of 28 points out of 36. They finished second with 91 points, a club record. Newcastle were champions with 101. Forest were third, 12 points behind Albion. It should have been a happy time for Koren but it wasn't. In a 2-0 victory over Scunthorpe in February, he was substituted after 65 minutes. He reacted angrily. Di Matteo held his hand out, Koren snubbed it. Or so it seemed.

The Italian described his player's actions as 'selfish.' Koren had a different take on the matter. And he wasn't impressed that his manager had used the media to air his grievances. "I should not have done what I did," Koren accepts, looking back. "You should always think of the team. But Di Matteo was wrong. I am not a selfish player. I'm not saying he picked me out but that's how it felt. I didn't take it well when I was taken off. He surprised me when he tried to shake my hand. It seemed a little bit false. I was experienced, I was a big player.

"It wasn't my best performance and, yes, I was wrong. Did he shake hands with everyone? Maybe. I don't remember whether he did or not. He was the boss. And afterwards I regretted that I reacted like that. It was in the media but, for me, he was being false. We weren't fighting. I didn't apologise to him because I felt I'd done nothing wrong. I had maybe done wrong to the club, the fans. For that, I was sorry. The media put it out and it became a story. I didn't give him my hand and I thought that was fair. There was no sincerity about him doing it. After that, we didn't talk about it, ever. There was no meeting as he claimed there was. He simply went to the press and called me a 'selfish player.' That's wrong. I did think about going to the press myself but my agents spoke to me and gave some information out about my feelings. My only focus was doing well for West Brom and going back to the Premier League. How is that selfish? This issue remained in the media for a few days and then went."

Truce or not, no notion of harmony was forthcoming. Koren was released at the end of 2009-10. He had a 12-month option remaining on his contract. Albion opted against taking it up. The midfielder, heading into a World Cup in South Africa with Slovenia and with Albion elevated back into the Premier League, was no longer wanted. He wasn't shocked.

"My agents were telling me long before the season that it would be difficult for me to be part of this club because of where I was with my contract," he added. "West Brom had not made a decision. This is never a good sign. When you have a year's option and the club don't make a decision by April, you know you won't be staying. I knew if the club were to ask the manager, his response would be that he would not be bothered if I stayed or not. It doesn't matter what I had done. So I knew what would happen.

"We agreed it was time for me to move on. I had a good relationship with the club, the fans were brilliant. I was in Slovenia. We hadn't yet met up for the World Cup. My agent rang and told me West Brom had made the decision. They would not take up the option. It wasn't easy because the relationship with the fans was really good. I was a free transfer. We had a chat about what to do, where I could play, what was important. I told my agents I would concentrate on my country. I changed my phone numbers, both my Slovenian and English numbers. I knew if I kept the numbers, somebody would call to find out what was happening. I didn't want to think about that during the World Cup. We agreed we would only talk after the tournament. All of it was unfortunate. It was a shame. I loved West Brom and it was very sad."

Not surprisingly, Koren has fonder memories of Albion's title-winning promotion in 2008 than he did two years later. He said: "For me, it was much better when we first went up. Paul Robinson, Kevin Phillips, Jonathan Greening, Tony Mowbray – it was like a family. We were part of a big group. When Tony was manager, the experienced players helped everyone else. That wasn't the case when Di Matteo was manager. It was all about groups. It was very professional, very cold. We had a good team spirit but it wasn't the same. It was the players who generated that, not the manager. The first time was very good. It was amazing. We felt strong. It was a good bond in the team. The second time was not so good."

Promotion came with another share offer. The initiative was the creation of a new company, West Bromwich Albion Group Ltd, who would buy the shares of the existing company. Shareholders were offered £1,200 in cash for each share if they wished to sell, or a one-for-one swap in the new company plus a £100 per share 'dividend.' The cash offer was a 50 per cent increase on the value a year before but still valued the club at just £12m. Recent dealings at Wolverhampton Wanderers and Birmingham City had been at valuations of £30m and £80m respectively. Not surprisingly, S4A's stance was very much that shareholders should keep their share if at all possible, their argument being the new shares were seemingly no lesser value than the old ones and so were worth transferring into. Purchasers were arranged for shareholders to sell to if they wished, with values up to the £1,500 range. Again, this offered better value for the individual shareholder in monetary terms while maintaining the independence of those shares that changed hands. Ultimately, shareholders in the new group totalled 603. Shares were changing hands at around £2,000 and, by January, 2012, were touching £2,500.

Meanwhile, the AGM of West Bromwich Albion Holdings in January, 2010 was a perfunctory affair. The extreme weather deterred all but a few diehards, with the formal business concluded in 15 minutes. Turnover had fallen to £28.1m, on which a profit of £0.7m was recorded. There were no dividends. As a nod to Albion's global recruitment policy, the club had four representatives at the World Cup for the first time since 1958, when they had one Welshman and three Englishmen. In South Africa, there were Slovenian Koren, albeit in the throes of finding a new club, Chris Wood (New Zealand), Marek Cech (Slovakia) and Gonzalo Jara (Chile).

Having worn unsponsored shirts in 2008-09, with increased sales return, Albion exploited a non-Premier League ruling which allowed them to tender out their shirts on a game-by-game basis in 2009-10. Eleven different brands or slogans were displayed during the campaign – some more than once – as the most diverse markets were tapped into. A well-known local brewery, a nearby coach company, three different bookmakers, two charities raising money for disasters in Chile (as a nod to Gonzalo Jara), an automotive component firm, a shop-fitting marque, a pump manufacturer and a campaign backing England's ultimately unsuccessful 2018 World Cup bid were all showcased at some stage. The shirt displaying Black Country brewery Bathams is, by all accounts, a collectors' item, having been one of the only branded shirts to be sold in the season.

Koren generally looks back on his time at B71 with fondness. The notion that he is able to 'look' at anything is a result of good fortune and quick-thinking medical assistance. He shakes his head when reminded of a freak incident during pre-season training in 2007. He was on good form and had bedded in well after his move earlier that year. Then the ball hit him. Not just in the face, but in the eye. What follows was, and remains, unpleasant. Koren's sight is now restored but he had his fears. He explained: "We trained in Slovenia that summer with West Brom. All was going well. I was really strong and feeling very good about myself. It was a good period for me. We had about a week to go to the start of the season and then, in a training session back in England, we played a practice game.

"I hit a shot and it was blocked by Shelton Martis. The ball bounced on to the ground and bounced up into my eye. It sliced across my eye. Straightaway, the bleeding started. I fell to the floor and the physio came over. I just said to him: 'Give me some ice'. I remember it like it was yesterday. I couldn't see anything. We went in and realised something was bad. The doctor was there and what I didn't realise is my eye lid had flipped over. He flipped it back and it was a massive relief. I thought I was ok. I was very happy but then I realised it wasn't right. I quickly realised it was wrong.

"Ok, I'll be honest...I was shitting my pants. The doctor took me into a room, switched off the lights and asked me to cover my other eye. When I did, I was blind. I couldn't see anything. I was terrified. I got showered, changed and he took me to hospital. Here I am, being told by the doctor and physio that I need to go to a specialist eye unit. I was in front of the mirror. I could look through one eye thinking all was good. Then I looked through the other eye and I couldn't see anything. Although the doctor was positive, it was not easy. I went into the waiting room, sat down and the bleeding went down. I kept covering my normal eye. I wanted to see something. Suddenly, I started to see something. It was only a little bit but I could see.

"I had two weeks' recovery after that and I couldn't carry bags or anything heavy. I couldn't do anything that would or could affect my eye balance. I wasn't allowed to sleep normally. I was just sitting up, even at night. After a few days, things improved. My vision is okay now. I have to test my eye pressure every year. The first two weeks were shocking but, after that, it got better. But that was a bad day. One I won't forget."

It was Arsene Wenger who once said that an overseas player should be given a minimum period of six months to settle in. Koren didn't need as long. The influx of foreigners has meant a shift in how clubs deal with players. Where once an import would be expected to fall into line with his British colleagues, often with little help, these days there is more assistance available. Clubs employ personnel to sort out logistics – British bank accounts, houses, schools if necessary, cars, insurance, medical cover, English lessons where required. Footballers are left to the football. Mundane off-the-field chores are handled by the club. It's especially invaluable for players who speak no English. Albion were, and still are, on the ball in this respect.

"The club helped me. I don't know about other players but our manager Tony (Mowbray) and the staff were very close to the players," Koren explained. "We would be asked about our families, asked if we needed anything. It was all very friendly. It was a positive surprise how kind people were. There are people who work there specifically to help with such matters. Many are basically fans who help you with practical arrangements, like opening bank accounts, sorting schools out, getting settled in.

"A secretary, Jill, helped me open a bank account. She didn't leave me on my own. She went with me. It's a small detail which helps you. Just having someone there to help you. There were small things; things you can maybe do yourself but which bother you. The fans have to know this. The fans don't know if your wife or girlfriend is ok. Is the house sorted out for the child and family? Is the car sorted out? Are we insured? What happens with tax? So many things need sorting out. You cannot always deal with them. Training finishes and you need to sort yourself out. It's not easy if you don't speak very much English or you don't understand how the country works."

Koren thoroughly enjoyed his adventure at The Hawthorns. The first cycle of team-mates he had were a particularly close-knit set. High jinks among players are especially prevalent in football. Like, for example, Scott Carson arriving back at his car after training to find a snowman had been built and placed in the passenger seat of his Audi. Funny at the time, although the damage to the electrics within the frame of the seat was probably less amusing to the goalkeeper. Koren chuckles when reminded.

"You always have people who mix well. That side were like that," he continued. "Zoltan Gera helped me a lot. When I was looking for a house, he took me to the Sutton Coldfield area. His nickname was Mr Bean. The day Scott Carson's car ended up with snowman in it.....I knew what was going on but I wasn't involved. Honestly. There was another time when Jonathan Greening and Paul Robinson were sharing a room. We knew they were watching movies together, so about six of us decided to burst into their room with a bottle of water.

"I went down to reception, told reception I was in this room (so I could get a key) and we covered our heads in t-shirts and underwear. There was myself, Roman Bednar, Zoltan Gera, Bostjan Cesar and Sherjill MacDonald. We burst in and squirted water everywhere. Jono was screaming like a girl, hiding from us, but Robbo was so angry he chased us out. He could be quite scary when he wasn't happy. We had a great team spirit. We were generally a happy bunch of players."

Paul Scharner

"One or two players took exception to me saying we were lazy. That wasn't a problem. My main problem was keeping West Brom in the League."

PAUL Scharner walks from photograph to photograph. He studies each carefully. He asks his guide a question about every one. The Austrian could be in an art gallery. And, let's face it, he wouldn't look out of place. With his dark-rim glasses, sculpted hair and well-dressed look (as opposed to merely wearing something expensive), Scharner doesn't have the appearance of a stereotypical footballer. He is, in fact, stood in front of a photograph of a West Bromwich Albion hero, checking out the club's impressive memorabilia collection. Scharner examines one picture before moving on to the next. Each time, he wants to know more. Why The Baggies? Where did The Hawthorns name come from? His guide, Official Supporters Club chairman John Homer, fills in the blanks.

It's early autumn, 2010. Scharner wants to absorb himself in his surroundings. This isn't just a place of work for him. He appreciates he is in a footballing place of worship. Ten years ago, in the very place where Scharner stands, was the ramshackle Rainbow Stand, ready and primed for demolition. It was primitive, outdated and no place for a display of the club's finest iconography. Albion were losing £30,000 a week and scrapping for survival in the second tier. Gary Megson was yet to grab the club by the lapels and shake them back to life. Time has moved on.

Where to next? Scharner is in the Radisson Hotel in Birmingham's Mailbox, contemplating his future. It's April, 2012. His Baggies days are numbered. Tomorrow, Albion play Aston Villa. Scharner is playing out time. He needs to end the season with 25 or more appearances (of 20 minutes and over) to activate a clause that will earn him another one-year contract at The Hawthorns.

With four games left, he has played only 20 times. He is philosophical about his future – likewise his past.

The midfielder reveals what prompted him to leave Wigan for Albion in the final days of August, 2010 and become the club's highest-ever earner. "It was actually the commitment the club showed and the big interest shown by Roberto Di Matteo and Dan Ashworth," he said. "They wanted players who could keep them in the League. I had experience of it with Wigan. Never being relegated is something I am very proud of actually. And they were also looking for a defensive midfielder. I wanted to settle down in that role. That's why I chose to come here. I was also respectful of the philosophy of the club and the fans. By philosophy, I mean the playing style, wanting to play football along the ground; possession football. In the first few years at Wigan, we played direct football. Martinez changed it but he was only just starting to put his own philosophy into place, so it was a transitional period."

First impressions are everything. Scharner expands on his perception of the club. His passion for Albion's history was fuelled by his move. "It's a well-run club," he added. "The only thing I didn't like was the yo-yo reputation. But the history of the club was something I was very interested in. The fact they were founder members of the Football League, the cups they won, the trophies they won. I researched the background. They were successful in the 1920, 1930s, 1960s, late 1970s and early 1980s. It's different to Wigan. The Premier League was new to them but it's a rugby town. West Bromwich have all of this tradition and respect in football. They should be in the Premier League. That's why I was very pleased to sign for them.

"I don't just get up at 9am, go training, then come home and forget about football. I want to educate myself, learn about my club's history. In modern football, this isn't thought of as important. That isn't me. I am interested in travelling round and seeing new things. It's part of my personality to get as much information as possible. Modern footballers have a certain lifestyle and big money but it's not just about that. In Vienna, there is big rivalry between Rapid and Austria. I played for Austria and you cannot move from one to another. For me, it's not money or lifestyle. It's about wanting to feel part of a club's culture, being committed to that club, showing passion for that club."

Scharner is a journalist's dream; always willing to speak, forever shouldering the responsibility. Defeat, draw or victory – he is always available. Not long after he joined Albion, Scharner invited a group of select media representatives to a Birmingham hotel where he laid on a spread of Austrian delicacies and showed a power-point of his greatest football moments. His is an agile mind. Not one to bow to the conformists. Here was a player willing to bypass the media-controlled practices deployed by clubs and come straight to the journalists. He speaks from the heart. It doesn't always make him popular in the dressing room. But the supporters took to him.

Two moments in Scharner's first season stand out. The first was Albion's game at Arsenal in September, 2010. With the score at 0-0 at half-time, the onus was on the home side. Think on. Peter Odemwingie and Gonzalo Jara scored twice within the space of 180 seconds in the opening five minutes of the second half. Ex-Gunners youngster Jerome Thomas added a third in the 73rd minute to make it Arsenal 0, Albion 3. Improbable stuff. Samir Nasri restored some decency for the home side with two goals but Albion claimed a victory. Scharner feels confidence was the side's virtue.

"I went into the dressing room and said: 'Come on, let's take the three points,'" he recalled. "Just because it's Arsenal doesn't mean anything. We have a saying in Austria that all the ingredients are still just cooked in water. There's no difference. You might have more money but money doesn't always bring success. This is why I always like to play against big clubs. There is this feeling they should be better. Why? Even if you are deemed as underdogs, you need to stop respecting big teams. That's what you need to get rid of when you play the big clubs – forget the respect. Sunderland away, Everton away, Manchester United.....we had a few results like that."

Scharner has a point. Albion beat Sunderland 3-2, Everton 4-1 and picked up a 2-2 draw at Old Trafford. Yet their form slipped badly from November. In the final ten games of 2010, Roberto Di Matteo's men lost seven and drew at West Ham. They won at Everton and at home to Newcastle. The slide prompted Scharner's second contribution. Before the home game against Blackpool, he spoke out. He traced the club's slump to the closure of the dressing-room fines system and reckoned the move had helped breed complacency and laziness in the squad. As part of the code, the players policed themselves, punishing any lapses of discipline. Fines were collected and put towards the squad's Christmas party. Yet Scharner feels the absence of a players' pool after that had created a culture of apathy. And he was determined to express his concerns via the media, hoping his outspoken words would have maximum impact in the first-team camp.

Speaking in January, 2011, he said: "I think it was going well until the last game before Christmas, against Aston Villa. We stopped the fines at that point. Since then, we have got lazy and you can see it on the pitch. I have chosen to say this to the media because it will maybe get some more attention. I haven't told the manager. I am 30 years old, have spent 11 years as a professional player and I know what is needed. I'm one of the oldest in the squad and I feel a responsibility. My main focus is to wake up not only myself but the whole team. It has been bad the last few weeks and I am hoping the fines will return. I tried to bring them back on January 2 but it's difficult to set back up again because it can be an easier life to not do so. When I first came to the club, I got called Moanivator. Now my question is: Do my colleagues want to get relegated with a nice Paul Scharner or stay in the league and put up with the 'Moanivator?' I am very passionate about this because, at the end of the season, it will say on my CV that I've either survived or been relegated.

"At the moment, there is no relegation on there and I want to keep it like that. My main focus and intention is to keep West Bromwich in the Premier League. I've made mistakes in the last few games and it's not good enough for me, or my levels. And now it's time to change this, get focused and fight for the team. When we won a couple of games, we started to relax. We beat Everton and Newcastle, won six points, relaxed and had fun. It's not that easy in the Premier League."

Scharner's words helped to some degree. Albion beat Blackpool 3-2 the next day. Off the field, though, panic had started to ripple through the corridors of power. Had the Baggies been defeated by Ian Holloway's side in that January fixture, Di Matteo would have been sacked. The Italian's stay of execution was short-lived. Albion lost at Blackburn in their next game, salvaged a draw against Wigan at The Hawthorns in his final home game and then lost 3-0 at Manchester City.

The despondency of Albion players was obvious. They were lucky to only lose by three. On Sunday, March 6, just after midday, a text message filtered through to club players, staff, media and fans. Di Matteo was placed on gardening leave with immediate effect. The head coach left. As did his no 2

Eddie Newton and fitness coach Ade Mafe. Michael Appleton survived the cull. Scharner remembers it well. "I was on an international break," he recalls. "I was sat at Frankfurt airport when I got a text message from Dan Ashworth saying Robbie had gone. It was a surprise on one hand but I think it was an easy decision for the club. He did a great job, he brought them back to the Premier League but it was his first proper coaching job at this level. He was still learning. We started to lose our way and he couldn't stop it. As guys, they (Di Matteo, Newton and Mafe) were good people. But the club had learned from the past. When Tony Mowbray was manager, they were relegated and didn't make a change before that happened. Maybe that played on the club's mind."

Albion's search for a new gaffer would need to be concise. Sam Allardyce was spoken to – not because he was an obvious candidate, more because he was available and out of work. It would have been a dereliction of Albion's duty not to. Appleton was interviewed but was deemed too inexperienced, although he came across very well by all accounts. It would be between Chris Hughton and Roy Hodgson. Both were out of work.

Hughton wanted to bring in his former Newcastle assistant Colin Calderwood and ex-Baggies man Paul Barron as a goalkeeping coach. With Appleton very much regarded as an Albion 'project,' this was going to be an issue. More so given that Calderwood was boss at Hibernian during this period – a situation which would have necessitated not only compensation to the SPL club but a major and costly reshuffle of staff, especially with Keith Downing and Dean Kiely still employed at The Hawthorns.

Hodgson, impressive during his interviews, was a handy option. He came alone and was determined to rebuild a reputation that had been somewhat unfairly tarnished by a six-month period at Liverpool. He signed a contract until the end of June, 2012 – ideal if he was to be a contender for the England or Team GB (Olympics) jobs. The impact was immediate. His first game was a 1-1 draw against Wolves thanks to Carlos Vela's late equaliser. The Arsenal loanee repeated his trick a week later at Stoke, going close to a winner just moments after his 87th minute leveller. From that point, Albion played ten games, winning five, drawing two and losing three. They finished in 11th place on 47 points.

Hodgson's impact was noted. Scharner also nodded at Di Matteo's contribution. He feels his own strongly-worded comments earlier in the season also aided survival. "When we stopped up, we did so in his honour," added Scharner. "It was 50 per cent Di Matteo, 50 per cent Hodgson. A combination of the two made us such a good team. We were one of the best seven or eight scorers in the League. The problem was we conceded too many goals. When Hodgson came in, he made us more organised, gave us more shape in defence. We needed that. Roy and I had a past because I believe he tried to sign me for Fulham. Although I never knew him, he made contact with Wigan. We started to concentrate on not conceding, on defensive shape. Hodgson liked us to repeat, repeat, repeat stuff. But it made us better. It was a culture shock because Di Matteo liked to attack. But it worked out. Yet it is very unfair to Di Matteo that we stayed up in Hodgson's honour. It was a joint effort.

"The main problem with any promoted club, certainly the most dangerous thing, is when you have a good start to the season. That happened with us. If you remember the Blackpool away game.......we had Pablo Ibanez and Gonzalo Jara sent off and lost 2-1. That was where we started to lose our focus. People thought we had enough points already and I knew this was a problem. It was dangerous, especially as it came before Christmas. My job was to keep West Brom in the League. I needed to speak out. We were in danger of going down and I didn't want that against me. The main problem, I think, was that Di Matteo had a big fear about tiring players. Our intensity started to drop in training. We started to lose points and the training changed. We started to rest more than we trained because of the Christmas period. We weren't training properly and we got an unbalanced squad."

Scharner wasn't Mr Popular following his comments. He admits now that some team-mates were less than impressed. "A few weren't happy with what I said," he continued. "One or two took exception to me saying we were lazy. That wasn't a problem. My main problem was keeping West Brom in the League. I would like to think it worked. Nobody ever said so because it's very hard to find humans to say: 'You were right'. But I think if you ask them now, they might realise there was something in it. There was no problem with me and those players. It was what happened then and we carried on."

Season 2011-12 didn't start well. Back-to-back defeats against Manchester United, Chelsea and Stoke were not healthy. All three owed a little to Albion's misfortune. United's decider in their 2-1 win came from an own goal. Albion were dominant at Stamford Bridge but lost. And Stoke clinched a late victory through Ryan Shotton following a mix-up between Ben Foster and Gabriel Tamas. A victory at Norwich followed before a 3-0 hammering at Swansea set everyone back again. But Hodgson's side gradually improved. Goalkeeper Foster, Shane Long, Billy Jones, Gareth McAuley and Zoltan Gera had arrived during pre-season. All played a significant part, although Gera's input was cut short. He missed the second half of the season after his knee crumpled against Tottenham. Victories over Wolves, at The Hawthorns, and away to Aston Villa followed. Scharner scored the winner in the latter game.

Come January, 2012, Albion were 12th. Far from convincing but by no means looking like relegation cast-offs. On January 21, they travelled to Stoke. Hodgson made four changes. Gone was the 4-4-2 formation. In came Tamas at right-back, outcast Marc-Antoine Fortuné up front and Graham Dorrans in midfield. Fit-again Jonas Olsson returned, too. Dorrans was to score the decider in a 2-1 victory (James Morrison netted the first) that secured the club's first win on Stoke territory since 1982. Three weeks later came a highlight of Albion's season. They beat Wolves 5-1 at Molineux, Peter Odemwingie's treble being supplemented by Olsson's strike and Keith Andrews' first goal for the Baggies. Mick McCarthy was sacked the next day.

Yet Albion effectively lost their manager around the same time. On February 8, Fabio Capello waved goodbye to his job as England boss. Within ten days, the Football Association had identified Hodgson as the successor. This information was not disclosed until after Albion had drawn 0-0 with Villa on April 28, when the FA revealed they had sought permission to speak to Hodgson. He was to be the only candidate. On May 1, he was appointed as the new England boss.

Hodgson remained in charge for Albion's final two games – a 2-2 draw with Bolton and a 3-2 loss against Arsenal, the latter a match in which Marton Fulop conceded three times despite facing only one shot throughout. Albion finished in the top half of the table, in tenth. Former Chelsea boss Claudio Ranieri was considered a potential successor, as was ex-Malmo and Copenhagen coach Roland Nilsson. German Ralf Rangnick was also strongly linked and claims he rejected the job. Albion insist he wasn't offered it. Ultimately, Steve Clarke, a former Chelsea no 2 and ex-Liverpool coach, was chosen.

From Scharner's personal point of view, 2011-12 was not successful. He failed to earn an extra year's option that would have come with playing a set number of games. Initially, a stay of execution, on new terms, was mentioned. But Scharner was informed in late June that he would not be offered the chance to stay on. The Austrian was reflective.

"It's was a stop-start season for me," he continued. "I damaged my knee ligaments, got back, scored the winner against Aston Villa and then, after the international break, got injured against Wolves. Then I had an ankle problem. Hodgson decided to go another way – without me, rather than with me. That's frustrating because I'm not experienced in sitting on the bench but that's football. I had a chat with Hodgson and Dan Ashworth and I got the feeling they were counting my days. The option was on my side and I needed 25 games of more than 20 minutes. Before the Villa game, I had been involved in 27 games...but just 20 of those were of 20 minutes or more. So I knew I wouldn't be staying. The future was going to be somewhere else. That's very sad because I love the club, especially the supporters."

The Albion who began 2000 were unrecognisable to the club who ended Scharner's final season there. Apart from the natural turnover of players, the backroom staff increased by several members. Sports science was now a key area. Among the club's staff are a head of medical services, a performance physio, a rehab physio, a fitness coach and a lead sports scientist. The training ground boasts a hydro-facility and state-of-the-art equipment to aid recovery. Such amenities have opened a new sector of the market for the club – that raft of talented players who have had injury problems and who may be nervous about moving somewhere they may not receive appropriate supervision and expert attention. Such are Albion's facilities now that the club are confident such targets would no longer shun them.

Steven Reid arrived towards the end of the 2009-10, having played just four times for Blackburn during the previous campaign. He was to play 23 times in 2010-11, his first full season in the West Midlands. Jerome Thomas joined at the start of 2009-10 and made 29 outings that season. He had appeared in just three League games for Portsmouth in 2008-09. Giles Barnes was another gamble after he, too, had just three games under his belt in 2008-09. He made nine League appearances for Albion in the promotion season, with an inability to break into Roberto Di Matteo's first team on merit, rather than through any injury problems, accounting for that low figure. In the summer of 2011, Albion attempted to sign Owen Hargreaves. He eventually moved to Manchester City.

The club's scouting network had expanded to South and Central America. Albion have a presence throughout Europe and representatives in Africa. Players of 16 different nationalities represented them during 2011-12. Youth recruitment was expanded. This summer, Albion succeeded with flying colours when they applied for 'Category One' Academy' status under the new Elite Player Performance Plan (EPPP). Twelve years ago, Albion managers were seemingly putting out fires. The Baggies began the 2012-13 campaign with Steve Clarke in charge, having lost their previous boss to take over England for the European Championships and beyond. In the early weeks at least, the transition was seamless. By taking seven points from their first three games – and beating Liverpool and Everton at The Hawthorns and drawing at Tottenham in the process – they achieved their best start to a top-flight campaign since 1978-79 and the first Ron Atkinson era.

Scharner feels evolution is important. Mere survival should not be the extent of Albion's remit. "This chairman, Jeremy Peace, has done a great job," he continued. "The training ground is on the level of any club you would expect in the Premier League. Where can this club be in ten years? It depends how far they want to go. If they stick with a philosophy of just stopping in the League.....probably not too far. I get very frustrated when I hear clubs talk about staying up. Why do clubs only aim to survive? What is the point? If you have a relegation fight in your mind, you will fight relegation and possibly not more. We have managed to do more but not many do. Newcastle showed mental ambition. The potential is there. I hope this club do it."

And Finally.....

SO there it is, the dramatic 2000-12 period in West Bromwich Albion's history; arguably one of the most astonishing decades (and a bit) the club have ever known, with all its promotions, relegations, Great Escapes and cup runs. Someone needed to commit the whole story to print for the current generation of fans and those who follow in the future.

The idea for this book came in December, 2009, when the Birmingham Mail, with a special feature in mind, asked me to pick my best Albion XI from the opening ten years of the 21st century. As I started scribbling down names on a piece of A4, it struck me that we were dealing with a special era. No other club had experienced such jumps, bumps and jolts during those same years. I felt this urge to find out more, not least where, and how, it had all unfolded and how, at the time of writing in the autumn of 2012, it had ultimately gone so brilliantly right.

I wanted the story to be told through the eyes of players – not necessarily Albion heroes (although such status would undoubtedly help) but those with great tales to tell. Weeks turned to months, though, and months turned to over a year. And my project remained no more than an idea. Then, some time in early 2011, Shareholders for Albion (S4A) approached me about penning a chronological compendium about their role at the club over such a momentous period. So it was decided we would marry the two concepts. The 'idea' became a welcome and enjoyable obsession. Details of the club's financial structure would be topped and tailed by accounts of those who hallmarked a decade and beyond. Sounded like a dream job to me!

The name of the publication and the design of the front cover were pored over during meetings of the book sub-committee in West Bromwich. We were keen to avoid any mention of the cliched Boing Boing. Some titles were dismissed as being too wordy, some were inappropriate, some we just couldn't agree on or they simply didn't capture the imagination. We eventually opted for something a little more understated, although it's a line that is sung every match day. Well, thousands and thousands of fans can't be wrong, can they?

The cover also needed to stand out. We talked about crowd shots. But other books had already gone down this route. We wanted something the fans would instantly spot as being 'West Bromwich Albion.' I'd like to think that, following a lot of debate and head-scratching, we've achieved something which works.

The journey has been exhilarating, fun, annoying, hard-going at times and, occasionally, a sore test of my patience (thank you Jonathan 'Mr Elusive' Greening!). And I am already desperately missing the buzz I enjoyed from revisiting such an incredible period.

I am grateful to each and every one of the players who gave up time and made the effort to take calls, meet for interviews and generally be hassled by my demand for more knowledge or information. They really did succeed in providing me with an illuminating insight into their lives behind the headlines.

To those in our inner sanctum who went over every word of copy with their red pens and sharp eyes, I thank you. To David Instone, who advised and then 'managed' the operation – my first book – I say a big thanks. Neil Reynolds' and Dave Bassett's contributions and support were immense and most valuable. And to the other committee members – Peter Burford, Fred Carter, Martin Grange, Chris Saunders and Colin Wills – who were involved in the production of the book and in helping finance it, as well as in giving their input on various logistical matters, I again say thank-you. Without them, this new addition to the realms of Albion-related literature simply would not have been possible.

I would like to raise a glass to the good folks at the Hilton Hotel in Bromsgrove, the Ramada and Radisson Hotels in the Mailbox, the Holiday Inn at Great Barr, the Three Hammers Golf Complex near Wolverhampton, and even the Everton supporters who kept a respectful lid on their exuberance during my interview with Robert Koren at Watford's Village Hotel. And a quick nod also to the bartenders at the Old Hop Pole pub deep in West Bromwich Albion heartland, where I and S4A members would chew over the book's progress. I'll miss our quarterly meetings.

Elsewhere, I would happily buy some treats for Kevin Phillips' dogs, mainly for not exploiting my slight unease of larger animals as they greeted me at their master's home. Good dogs.

Much less dangerously, I was delighted to welcome on board TV presenter Adrian Chiles and club legend Darren Moore as writers of forewords. I shudder to think what some of the more cautious past Baggies managers might think but, in keeping with the club's traditional attacking ethos, we opted to go with four forewords on this occasion......Dave Bassett and Neil Reynolds linking up expertly with the ITV anchorman and Big Dave.

Others warrant a mention. I am indebted to the following for their help, guidance and advice over the last two years. In no particular order, they are Mark Ashton, Scott Field, legendary Baggies kit-man Dave Matthews (who also has a book on the way), Stuart Curtis, Sam Stapleton, John Homer, David Law, Lisa Marshall, Andy Walker of Birmingham City, Tony Vass and Christiaan Wallett from West Bromwich Albion Supporters Club London branch, Amanda Hume from the Sutton Coldfield branch, Tom Ross of Free Radio and the presenter of The Goalzone, talkSPORT's Ian Danter and Nigel Pearson, journalist colleague and friend Colin Tattum, Ken Montgomery of the Birmingham Mail, BBC WM's Mike Taylor, author and Daily Star journalist Dave Armitage and employees at Nottingham Forest, Notts County and in the ever-helpful Albion media office. There were other contributors who didn't wish to be named. You know who you are – cheers to you all.

To those friends who offered me discreet encouragement and support, yes, you, too, are included in this list. Whether it was a 140-character direct message on Twitter, a quick text 'to see how it's going' or a call to find out when 'the book' is out....nice one! Much appreciated. We were also all blown away by the leap of faith from those who ordered the book before it was even printed and seen. To all 400-plus of you who purchased this publication in advance, may I express my deep gratitude. Likewise those who helped the sales push as they re-tweeted my tweets of self-publicity, who 'liked' my Facebook status or are just sat there reading this book now, I express my appreciation.

And a big, big thanks to my family, who supported me throughout, especially my beautiful young daughter Renia, who still doesn't understand what all the fuss is about when it comes to football. One day, she might. She may eventually even read this book. Who knows?

Scroll of Honour

Shareholders for Albion and the author are greatly indebted to the fans who have supported this project and who have asked that the following be listed for posterity as subscribers:

Paul Eamonn Ager
Moray Allan
Edward Allen
Richard Allen
Vikki Alterman
Franc Andrews
Brian Androlia
Karl Androlia
Axel Andsäter
Sue Aston

Beddgelert Baggie
Peter Alan Baggott
David Bailey
David & Sue Baker
Wes & Rich Ball, & Brad Herbert
Gillian Barker
Paul Barker
Anthony Barnes
Joan Barnsley
Tom Barron
Andrew Bassett
John Bassett
Jeremy Bate
Hugh Batkin
Alex Bawn
Dave Baxendale
Michael Beckett
Ian Beech
Graham Belt
Andrew Benbow
Keith Beresford
Paul Beresford
Alessio Bianco
Jack Bickley
Grant Bird
Luke Birtwistle
Robin Blake
David Bloxham
John Boaler
Greg Bodycote
Stian Bøe
Phil Bowden
Trevor Bowler
Simon Bradbury
Garry Brandrick
Kevin Brandrick
Neil Brandrick
Daniel Brannigan
Jack Simon Branson
Simon John Branson
Bob Brearley
Paul Brettle
Michael Brooke
Kay Brookes
Tracy Brookes
Dave Brown
Phil Brown
Karen Burford
Ian Burkhill
Arthur Burt
Ray and Hannah Butler
Alan Bynion

Ray Caddick
Chris Cadman
Philip Calcutt
Ste Calloway
Carol Carter
Daniel Carter
Jonathan Carter
Rachel Carter
Tony Carter
Martin Cashmore
John Castle
Brian Chappell

Paul Chappell
Martin Chatwin
Terence Checketts
Conrad Chircop
Harry Clapham
Bryn Clark
Neil Clark
Darren Clarke
Nick Clarke
Tony Clarke
Alan Cleverley
Lew Clews
Brian Joseph Cocks
Douglas Roland John Cocks
Stuart Coles
Louise Collieu
Paul Collins
Paul, Phoebe & Noah Cooke
Caroline Coombs
Big Frank Cooper
Mark Cooper
Trevor Cornfield
Dr Clement Cottrill
Mark A. P. Covington
Arthur Henry Cowell
Alan Cox
Liam Cox
Cameron Craig
Sandy Craig Jnr
Gemma Croom
David Cunneen
Sarah Cutler

Chris Daniels
Peter Davenport
Lee Davies
Tony Davies
Andrea Davis
Judith Davis
Mike Davis
Paul Davis
Roger Davis
Tina Dubberley
Tony Dubberley
Trevor Dubberley
John Dunn

Jonathan Eden
Paul Edge
Stefan Edström
Steve Emery
Christopher Ewing

Jon Fearn
H. C. Fellows
Adam Fisher
Anthony Fisher
Tony Fisher
David Fleming
Derek Franks
Andrew 'Boo' Freeborn

Paul Gainham
Chris Gardner
The Gibbard Family
Aron & Gemma Goode
David J. Goodman
Geoffrey S. Goodman
Matthew Grange
Anthony Green
Roger Greenfield
David Grove
Ryan Guest

Graham Hackett
John, Chris & Niamh Hackett
Richard Haddlesey
Andrew Haddleton
David Haddleton
John Haddleton
Clive Haddon
Chris Hale
Warren Hall
Dave Harrell
Judith Harris
Linda Harris
Tim Haskey
Simon James Haynes
Ashley Hayward
William Hayward
Andy Heselgrove
Adam Hess
Glenn Hess

Steve Hewitt
John Hickman
Mark Hill
Miles Hill
Rob Hindley
Bjorn Hjelm
John Holland
Duncan Holman
Ashley Holmes
Stephen Holmes
Stewart Holmes
Michael & Matthew Holton
Adam & Kirsty Holton
Becky Homer
John Homer
Paul Homer
William Alan Hook
Harry Houghton
Ian Hoult
Suzanne Howard
David Howson
Stefan Hubscher
Andrew Hudson
Nigel Hughes
Desmond C. Humphries
Nigel S. Humphries

Leonard James
Neil Jelley
Howard Jennings
John Jennings (Bretforton Baggie)
Rich Jewels
Bryn Johnson
Darrel Johnson
Dave Johnson
Michelle Johnson
Bryn Jones
Dave Jones
David Brian Jones
Ian Jones
Keith Jones
Matthew Christian Jones

Olle Kannö
Adam Kemshall
Don Kendrick
Roger Kendrick
Simon Kendrick
Andrew & Tara Kenrick
Brian Kite
Carlton Kiteley
Peter Knowles

Richard 'Boy' Lakin
Andrew Lambourn
Ian Joe Alex Lane
Dave Langran
Robert Laughran
Richard Laughran
Martin Leather
Jack Lewis
Hans Liljeberg
Paul Lissaman
David Lissimore
David Lones
Andrew Lowe
Graeme Lowe
Ryan Lugg

Naz Malik
Bryan Malsbury
Old Seth Manversmain
Kaitlyn Martin
Patrick Martin
Dave Matthews
Jonathan Mattsson
Marty McCann
Ian McLeod
Thelma McLeod
Tommy McMullan
Andrew McVicar
Mark Meagher
Andrew Miles
John Miller
Robert L. Mills
Colin Millward
John Millward
Paul Millward
John Monkton
Christopher Moore
Helen Moore
June Moore

George Morgan
John Morrall
Barry Morris
Brian Mulcahy
Gwen Mullins
Scott Mullins
Jackson Mulvihill
John Murley
John & Diane Murray
Katie Murray
Roger Murray
Steve Murray

Norman Neal
Roger Neal
David & Daniel Neale
Mike, Tom & Ben Neale
Margaret & Frank Neale,
& Alistair & Hannah McCallum
John Matthew Newton
Chris Nicklin
Mike Nicklin
Steve Nock
Geoff Noon
Henry Noon
Stephen Noon
Steven Nurcombe
Arthur Nye

David Frederick Oakley
Roger Oakley
Martin Oliver

Bob Parsons
Tom Parsons
Gavin Paul
David Payne
Garth Pearce
Steve Pearcey
Stephen J. Pearson
Michael Perkins
Lee, Vera, Adam, Jamie
& Jennifer Perry
Rob Phipps
Derrick Pickin
Laurence Pickin

Theo Pickin
Neale Pitchford
Tony Pratt
Andrew Price
David Price
Justin Price
Matthew Price
Robert Price
Nigel & Chris Pritchard
Mitch Pryce
Brid Pulker

Mick Ratcliffe
Andrew Ravenall
Becci Rayner
Janet Rayner
Alastair & Joanne Reader
Charlie Reynolds
Eddie Reynolds
Hannah Reynolds
Nathan Reynolds
Derek Riley
Roger O. Rimmer
Peregrine Roscorla
Ron Rose
Julian Rowe
John Russell
David A. Rutter

William John Sadler
Daniel Sanders
Richard Sanders
Jonathan Saunders
Michael Saunders
Richard Saunders
Graham Shelswell
Jason Sherwood
Martin Shilvock
Andrew Sidebotham
Laurence Silvester
Graham Simcox
Lakhbir Singh
Philip Skidmore
Ryan Skidmore
Barry Slack
Jonathan, Dominic, Matthew Slim

Mathew Smart
Bill Smith
John 'Smiler' Smith
Len Smith
Mark Smith
Tony, Julia, Ellie, Abby
& Charlie Smith
Geoff Snape
Val Snell
Michael Snell
Ross Snell
Will Spencer
Malcolm Sperring-Toy
Alison J Stacey
Anthony Stanley
Mark Stevens
Richard Stokes
Roger M Stubbs
Lesley Styles
Phil Surridge
Harry Syer

Darrell Taylor
David Taylor
Ian Taylor
John Taylor
Lee Thacker & Dad
Bernard B. Thompson
Christopher David Thornton
David Thorpe
Peter Thursfield
Michael Tomkinson
Robert Tomkinson
Mike Tomlinson
Robert Tomlinson
Ashton Toon
Nicholas Tranter
Paul Tranter
Stephen Tranter
Stephen Paul Tranter
Dick Tregea
Leslie B Trumpeter (in memory of)
Michael Turbutt
Gary Turley
Ben Turner

Paul Viles
Robin A. B. Viner

Keith Walker
Peter Mason Wall
Christiaan Wallett
Nicholas Wallett
Dean Walton
Brenda Want
Jon Want
Jonathan Want
David Ward
Russell Wardle
David J. Watkin
Philip Watkin
Brian Webb
Dougie Webb
James Stanley Webb
Francis Welch
Mark Welch
Michael Welch
Oliver Westbury
Jon Westwood
Jessica Wharton
George Wheatley
Jordan Wheeler
Tony Whittington
Keith Wibberley
Dave & Di Williams
Hugh Williams
Matt Williams
Neil Williams
Stephen Williams
Sam Willis
Ben Wills
Terry Wills
Jon Wiltshire
David Winwood
Jonathan Winwood
Todd Withers
David Wright